International Mediation in Civil Wars

This book evaluates the role of international mediators in bringing civil wars to an end and makes the case for "powerful peacemaking" – using incentives and sanctions – to leverage parties into peace.

As internal violence within countries is a principal threat to international peace in the post-Cold War era, the question of how these wars end has become an urgent research and policy question. This volume explores a critical aspect of peacemaking that has yet to be sufficiently evaluated: the turbulent, difficult, and often bloody period beyond the onset of formal or open negotiations to end civil wars and the clinching of an initially sustainable negotiated settlement. The book argues that the transnational flow of weapons, resources, and ideas means that when civil wars today end, they are more likely to do so at the negotiating table than on the battlefield. It uses bargaining theory to develop an analytical framework to evaluate peace processes – moving from stalemate in wars to negotiated settlement – and it rigorously analyzes the experiences of five cases of negotiated transitions from war and the role of international mediators: South Africa, Liberia, Burundi, Sri Lanka, and Kashmir.

This book will be of much interest to students of conflict management, international security, conflict resolution, international mediation and political violence.

Timothy D. Sisk is Associate Dean and Associate Professor at the Josef Korbel School of International Studies, University of Denver and Director of the Center for Sustainable Development and International Peace, a research and policy development institute at the Graduate School of International Studies, University of Denver.

Series: Security and conflict management

Series Editors: Fen Osler Hampson
Carleton University, Canada
Chester Crocker
Georgetown University, Washington, D.C.
Pamela Aall
United States Institute of Peace, Washington, D.C.

This series will publish the best work in the field of security studies and conflict management. In particular, it will promote leading-edge work that straddles the divides between conflict management and security studies, between academics and practitioners, and between disciplines.

1 **Negotiation and Conflict Management**
I. William Zartman

2 **Conflict Management and African Politics**
Negotiation, mediation, and politics
Edited by Terrence Lyons and Gilbert M. Khadiagala

3 **International Conflict Mediation**
New approaches and findings
Edited by Jacob Bercovitch and Scott Sigmund Gartner

4 **International Mediation in Civil Wars**
Bargaining with bullets
Timothy D. Sisk

International Mediation in Civil Wars

Bargaining with bullets

Timothy D. Sisk

Routledge
Taylor & Francis Group
LONDON AND NEW YORK

First published 2009
by Routledge
2 Park Square, Milton Park, Abingdon, Oxon OX14 4RN

Simultaneously published in the USA and Canada
by Routledge
270 Madison Ave, New York, NY 10016

First issued in paperback 2010

Routledge is an imprint of the Taylor & Francis Group, an informa business

Typeset in Baskerville by Wearset Ltd, Boldon, Tyne and Wear

British Library Cataloguing in Publication Data
A catalogue record for this book is available from the British Library

Library of Congress Cataloging in Publication Data
p. cm. – (Security and conflict management; 4)
1. Conflict management–International cooperation–Case studies.
2. Peace-building–International cooperation–Case studies. I. Title.

JZ5601.S57 2009
341.5'2–dc22
2008026692

ISBN13: 978-0-415-47705-5 (hbk)
ISBN13: 978-0-415-60940-1 (pbk)
ISBN13: 978-0-203-88495-7 (ebk)

In memoriam
Donald S. Rothchild, 1928–2007

Contents

Illustrations

Figures

Tables

Acknowledgments

This book is about the pathways through which societies torn by civil war escape mutually injurious violence through negotiation and the role of international mediators in such peace processes. The project arose in the context of my work on the end of apartheid in South Africa nearly 15 years ago. In 1991, as I was conducting dissertation research on the institutional parameters of a negotiated settlement, it became clear that the initial euphoria around the beginning of peace talks was being replaced by a horrid despair: even as the overall trajectory of the country was toward peace (at least for me, but certainly not to everyone, during that volatile and violent time), violence was actually escalating as faction-fighting surged. Curiously, too, this pattern of heightened violence seemed not to be spontaneous; quite the contrary, the violence seemed to directly track the negotiation process, peaking at moments of stagnation and breakthrough alike.

At the same time, colleagues such as John Darby working in Northern Ireland, and those observing other conflict settings, also began to see patterns of violent incidents associated with peace negotiations; in previous conflicts, too, such as the Paris talks to end the Vietnam War, parties escalated conflict as peace talks approached. Certainly, the advent of the Oslo process in 1993 and the subsequent events in the Middle East (most dramatically and sadly, the assassination of Israeli Nobel Peace Laureate Yitzhak Rabin in 1995) reinforced the belief that heightened political violence is intricately and complexly linked to peace negotiations.

In South Africa, Northern Ireland, and Israel/Palestine, to name just a few situations, it was as if violence was being turned on and off like a water tap, in concert with the bargaining process happening at the peace table. This book is a modest attempt to address a highly complex research question about a recursive relationship: Why and how do parties in civil war negotiations use violence to affect what happens at the table, and how and why does what happens at the table affect the propensity and intensity of violence on the streets? What are the implications, then, for international mediators as they try to work the parties toward a lasting peace agreement?

I owe many words of gratitude for those who have supported the subsequent research on the violence–negotiation nexus from which this book emanates. The project was originally supported by a fellowship from the Norwegian Nobel Institute in 1995; many thanks to Dr. Geir Lundestad, Executive Secretary of the Norwegian Nobel Committee, for his support and encouragement for what he rightly termed an ambitious project, and to Odd Arne Westad, then-director of the Institute's Fellowship Program.

The research was also supported by a generous grant from the Program in Global Security and Sustainability of the John D. and Catherine T. MacArthur Foundation. Research support from the United States Agency for International Development supported work on the Liberia case study, and a grant from the Carnegie Corporation of New York's Program in International Peace and Security has supported research on peacebuilding which is incorporated into this book.

Research assistance on South Africa, Sri Lanka, and Northern Ireland was handily carried out by Jeremy Rabideau, former University of Denver graduate student. On Kashmir, many thanks to colleagues at the United States Institute of Peace, especially David Smock, and Ambassadors Robert B. Oakley, Samuel Lewis, and Harold Saunders with whom I was involved in "track-two" mediation efforts on Kashmir and South Africa, and on the dispute over Nagorno-Karabagh. The United States Institute of Peace Grant Program supported aspects of this project in its support of a related research effort on democratization after civil wars through a grant award together with Anna Jarstad of the Uppsala University, Sweden.

I would also like to thank two anonymous reviewers for their insightful comments on the book for Routledge. And to thank my wife, Andrea Smith Sisk, for shoveling snow during the Colorado blizzards of 2006/2007 as I intensively finalized the research and writing.

The book is dedicated to Professor Donald S. Rothchild, a scholar of the highest class; the sad news of his passing came on the day the manuscript's first draft was finished. For years, about every other month at various meetings together, Don would make a point to ask how this project was coming along and to provide encouragement, advice, and some delicate prodding to urge its completion. While pleased that I could now report to him that the project has come to fruition, it is with deep regret that I will not have the benefit and pleasure of Don's understanding, insights, and critique on the book.

Introduction

Pursuing war, negotiating peace

The principal, immediate challenge to international peace and security for nearly two decades following the crumbling of the Berlin Wall in 1989 has been the scourge of mostly internal or civil wars. In these post-Cold War conflicts, millions have died, suffered injury, displacement, or forced removal, or been plunged into poverty by the economic tailspins that typically accompany civil wars. To add insult to injury, the principal characteristic of these modern civil wars is that they are essentially "unwinnable" struggles. Why? Because modern civil war often cannot be solved by military means alone, particularly when the putatively "weaker" rebel factions have access to valuable natural resources or, by propagating extremist beliefs, are willing and able to mobilize followers to perpetrate mass terrorism.[1] In contrast to a determinative military victory, the most common outcome in contemporary civil wars is that the protagonists will end up, sooner or later, pursuing peace at the negotiation table, together with international mediators, thrashing out the messy terms of a negotiated settlement. For peace in contemporary civil wars, there exists an undeniable need to end wars at the peace table, not on the battlefield.

This book is about complex, multidimensional peace negotiations to end contemporary civil wars at the bargaining table, popularly known as the "peace process," and the role of international mediation in them. The phrase reflects the pragmatic reality that today's peace negotiations are not solved by a single agreement or pact, but instead war termination involves extended or iterative bargaining processes that unfold over time. Moreover, such processes are also "horizontally" complex in that they unfold at various levels: from local-level community conciliation, to elite negotiations among the contending forces, to international official and unofficial mediation, to high-level consideration by the United Nations (UN) Security Council or, increasingly, the International Criminal Court as it pursues the perpetrators of mass atrocity. Whether such extended and multilayered processes are successful is measured not in the paper they produce – cease-fires, settlements, resolutions – but rather by the extent to which violence on the battlefield is substituted, over time, with open-ended bargaining in democratic political institutions.

In this book, I evaluate what I argue is the critical question of twenty-first century peace: When do extended peace talks to end civil war progress sufficiently to secure a comprehensive negotiated settlement? Alternatively, why do peace processes *fail* to progress, leaving the protagonists in war to continue killing in often futile and ultimately self-defeating efforts to end the conflict through outright military victory, even though modern civil wars are essentially unwinnable? This puzzle is at the heart of international mediation to pursue peace in civil wars through negotiations at the peace table.

The challenge facing scholars and practitioners alike is to understand the pathways and terms through which civil war conflicts can come to an end through sustainable negotiated settlements. While there exists excellent seminal scholarship on war termination in general (Pillar 1983), and some very good recent research on the questions of war termination in contemporary civil wars (Darby and MacGinty 2003; Doyle and Sambanis 2006; Fortna 2004a, 2004b; Höglund 2004; Licklider 1993; Mack 2005, 2006; Mason *et al.* 1999; Paris 2004; Zartman 1995b), there is an urgent need for a theoretically consistent analysis of the phases and outcomes of negotiation in contemporary civil wars. This is true despite the fact that the phrase "peace process" long ago entered the mainstream journalistic and policy-maker jargon as a way to describe the complex pursuit of civil war's end through extended and multilayered negotiations.

Peace processes are common in contemporary international relations. Throughout 2008, peace processes unfolded in a number of civil wars and lesser intensity internal conflicts: Azerbaijan, Burundi, Colombia, Côte d'Ivoire, Cyprus, Democratic Republic of Congo, Georgia, Indonesia (Aceh), Iraq, Kashmir, Kosovo, Nepal, the Philippines, Somalia, Spain, Sri Lanka, Sudan (Darfur), Timor-Leste, and Uganda, to name a few.[2] Yet our concepts and tools for analysis are haunted by outmoded and inaccurate concepts and approaches to conflict resolution that fail to recognize the integral nature of political violence as a bargaining tactic. All too often, there is a presumption that international mediation is like other peacemaking (e.g. by mediators in family, organizational, or neighborhood disputes); this presumption is palpably false. Indeed, in conclusion the book argues that international mediators in civil wars must be more clearly assertive – *powerful* – in bringing contemporary civil wars to an end, both for moral reasons (to reduce war's harm) and for interest-based reasons (to provide international peace and security for all).

Bargaining with bullets: the violence–negotiation nexus

It is a common, debilitating misconception that the onset or renewal of negotiation means an end to violence as leaders and publics choose the path of peace over war. On the contrary, in today's peace processes to end civil wars, political violence (and the threat of violence) is a ubiquitous feature of talks: violence is a beyond-the-table tactic used not as an alternative to bargaining, but as an integral element of negotiation. International mediation, or "peacemaking"[3] in UN parlance, far from being neutral, passive, and unbiased, must confront the stark reality of political violence as an inherent element of peace talks, employed by states and rebel forces to affect the process terms of peace negotiations. Consequently, international peacemaking – in order to induce an end to civil wars through negotiation – must act powerfully to confront and manage political violence designed to affect or derail peace negotiations.

Political violence often increases after talks begin precisely because protagonists use violence as a beyond-the-table tactic to affect the nature, pace, and outcome of negotiations. They seek, through violent acts, to communicate strength to maximize bargaining positions, to weaken opponents, to prevent being sidelined, or to sabotage the talks altogether. Violence is perpetrated by those who are official parties to the talks (such as a government's security forces or a rebel faction) and by "spoilers" not at the table (rejectionists such as government-sponsored militias, individual extremists and ideologues, or criminal warlords opposed to ending the conflict through negotiation) (Stedman 1997; Zahar 2003, 2006a, 2006b; Höglund and Zartman 2006; Newman and Richmond 2006). While this book involves an analysis of spoilers in some contexts (e.g. elements of the white right wing in South Africa or possibly the Liberation Tigers of Tamil Eelam (LTTE) in Sri Lanka), it is primarily about violence used by parties at the table and spoiler rejectionists alike. Indeed, there is continuing debate about the utility of the notion of spoilers in any event, because the term itself defines acts of violence from the perspective of those in a peace process vis-à-vis those outside; a more careful conceptualization recognizes that understanding the internal dynamics of parties and questions such as instrumental violence and group loyalty allows for greater nuance in understanding the underlying motives of violence beyond simple notions of "spoiling" the peace (Zahar 2006a). As this book shows, violence may well be perpetrated to affect the question of inclusion or exclusion in peace processes, and to influence the terms of settlement itself.

Whether and how violence affects peace negotiations is a matter of evaluating progress toward settlement and the eventual end of political violence. "Success" as such can only be measured with considerable hindsight, and "success" is so subjective a term as to render it an elusive concept to measure. Thus, the more appropriate problem to explain in peace processes is *progress* through the phases of bargaining (the dependent variable for this study). Progress is defined as continued concession-making and convergence of positions within and across phases; digression is defined as stagnation (without steady concession-making and convergence), reversal, or collapse of the bargaining process.

This book hones in on a critical aspect of peacemaking that is appreciated intuitively but has not been sufficiently evaluated: *the turbulent, difficult, and often bloody period beyond the onset of formal or open negotiations to end civil wars and the clinching of an initially sustainable negotiated settlement.* During this time, war-making (battlefield activities) and other acts of political violence – organized, collective acts of mass harm, perpetrated to affect the political process – often escalate, plunging the society even further into the "untold sorrow" – an eloquent phrase found in the UN Charter – that war brings and making a negotiated settlement to war more elusive. In each of the cases analyzed in this book, violent acts have been integral to protagonists' bargaining strategies. The "success" or failure of a peace process often depends on whether the negotiations can progress in the face of ongoing, even intensified, violence.

Although the primary concern of this book is the period between escalation to violence and negotiated settlement, there is humble recognition that there are equally significant perils in post-agreement implementation and the overall durability of negotiated peace (Hampson 1996; Jarstad and Sisk 2008; Stedman *et al.* 2002; Walter 2002). Indeed, it was after the international community mediated a negotiated settlement to end civil war in Rwanda (the Arusha Accord, August 1993) that genocide unfolded, during the initial period of implementation of the pact's provisions; in Rwanda, political violence after a peace agreement failed killed 800,000 people in 100 days.[4] The implication of the Rwandan experience is that clinching a comprehensive peace settlement is not enough: the perils of violence last well into the post-agreement period where the task shifts from ending violence to preventing its recurrence through post-settlement peacebuilding.[5]

I argue that because violence is such an integral part of bargaining in contemporary peace negotiations, international peacemakers must be better prepared to anticipate, prevent, confront, and eventually supplant violence with lasting bargaining institutions embodied in a putatively democratic state. International peacemakers, in order to end bloody civil wars sooner rather than later, must act with determination, coercion, and incentives blended in well-designed strategies to induce the parties to settle the conflict through negotiation. To guide the bloodied protagonists in civil wars down the long road from war to peace, a more concerted, powerful peacemaking is required. Moreover, powerful peacemaking comes not just from mediators with resources, such as military backing or money (although these help), but from the global credibility and integrity that international mediators bring to civil war negotiations. One of the central themes of this book is that mediation is most effective in civil wars today when it is carried out under the auspices of the UN, and when there is a strong international coalition of member states willing and able to act together to back UN efforts and to use their own power and prestige to leverage civil war protagonists to embrace and implement a negotiated settlement.

The book seeks to contribute to our understanding of peace processes and to international peacemaking through its analysis of the violence–

negotiation nexus. If armed conflicts are about violence, and a peace process is a set of phases or stages to bring an armed conflict to an end, there is a crucial need to critically analyze the means of connection between violence and negotiation as conflicts escalate and (as they inevitably do) de-escalate.[6] The theoretical approach and analytical framework presented in Chapter 2 is premised on the belief that de-escalation patterns in contemporary civil wars, while each having their own contexts and idiosyncrasies, have common elements that can be discerned and analyzed in a more theoretically consistent fashion.

Peace processes sometimes progress to yield "success" in stopping the killing, whereas at other moments they palpably "fail" and the horrors of war continue. In the Israeli–Palestinian context, the clinching of the Oslo Accords in October 1993[7] was heralded as a peacemaking success – winning the protagonists a shared Nobel Peace Prize – even though the Oslo process ultimately failed to bring about a comprehensive settlement to the conflict, being replaced by the still-elusive "Road Map to Peace" (and the more logical alternative in terms of sequencing, the Geneva Accords).[8] From the moment of high hopes with Oslo to the Road Map that led nowhere, the Israeli–Palestinian peace process is a lesson in the perils of failure to progress in peace talks. When progress stalls – either as a result of "defection" by parties at the table or because of crises created by spoiler violence (both occurred in the post-Oslo period[9]) – re-escalating political violence can doom the peace process to stagnation, thereby enhancing insecurities and the likelihood of greater confrontation and killing.

The Israeli–Palestinian case also raises key issues of *sequencing*: namely, whether negotiation of security should indeed come first (stopping the violence is the highest priority) in the absence of broader agreement on a settlement formula (in this case, "land for peace" and a "two-state solution"). Thus, peace processes are puzzling because there is an intricate, complex, multidimensional, and ultimately *recursive* relationship between the violence, or fighting, and the negotiation process, or talking. Sometimes violence tends to reinforce the imperatives of peace, pushing the parties in talks to make progress and eventually settle, whereas in other instances violence causes the parties to lose trust, retract from previous concessions, and often to abandon the peace process for war altogether.

It is often argued that, for negotiations to progress to end civil war, security on the ground – achieved through cease-fire – must come first. This logic, pursued in so many struggles such as in the Israeli–Palestinian conflict or today in war-torn Iraq, is deeply flawed. On the contrary, the research presented here shows that in civil wars, agreement on a political settlement – a "formula" for peace involving power sharing, transitional justice, and in the long term democratization and state (re)building – *precedes* security, not the other way around.

The case for peacemaking with power

The case for powerful, coercive peacemaking in today's brutal, usually intrastate or "civil wars" is based on the norm- and self-interest-based conviction that the international community cannot simply stand by and watch as the horrors of war unfold and the world's carefully constructed norms of humanitarian law – which found their origin in prior brutalities and genocides – are eviscerated.[10] Moreover, internal conflicts are deeply injurious to international peace and security (see Chapter 1), with serious costs to all states in the international system (a fact recognized well before the horrors of 9/11 showed that civil wars offer mobilization opportunities for global criminal and terrorist groups).

Horrid atrocities, some with genocidal violence, in Cambodia, Somalia, Bosnia, Algeria, Angola, Rwanda, and Sierra Leone were all stark symbols of the utter inability of the UN and its member states, however individually powerful, to meet the new forms of the "scourge of war" that the post-Cold War era presented. Attacks on UN peacekeepers, international humanitarian workers, and journalists drastically increased in the 1990s and 2000s. Global numbers of refugees swelled to more than 20 million, and total international humanitarian aid, at $9.2 billion in 2007, accounts for nearly 10 percent of all overseas development aid.[11] The internal wars of the post-Cold War period produced profound negative externalities for the entire world, producing regional or local spillovers and contagions and generating the sources of deep insecurity for all states in the international system.

Kofi Annan, UN Secretary-General during much of the period in which civil wars came to dominate the world body's peace and security agenda, reiterated the imperatives of strong international action to stem civil wars as the 1990s came to a close. He said in the context of discussion on the Kosovo crisis:

> The bloody wars of the last decade [the 1990s] have left us with no illusions about the difficulty of halting internal conflicts – by reason or by force – particularly against the wishes of a sovereign state. But nor have they left us with any illusions about the need to use force when all other means have failed.[12]

This conclusion, for more forceful intervention to bring internal conflicts to an earlier end, is the argument that essentially won Annan and the UN the Nobel Peace Prize in 2001.[13] Annan deserved the prize for this principal critical insight: today's civil wars are brought to an end only when there is deep, sustained, and determined commitment and engagement by the international community, and only when peacemaking is carried out with a coordinated blend of international sanctions and incentives, to include when necessary strong leverage and, in the most offensive instances, strong military force – powerful peacemaking.

In the most extreme instances, where allegations of genocide or the harboring of terrorists galvanizes the will of the international community, the track record of imposing sustainable peace through *diktat* alone is a dubious one. Using overwhelming military force to end civil war is a useful means of conflict suppression (as in the NATO intervention in Kosovo in March 1999, Operation Allied Force[14]), but extended occupation and transitional administration does not automatically or uniformly lead to sustainable peace. Peace cannot be imposed on the protagonists in civil wars, despite overwhelming fire power. Progress toward peace is possible, however, when the international community acts in concert and with power to affect the parties' perceptions of the costs of conflict and the benefits of peaceful settlement, and when international mediators work the process through to the clinching and post-agreement implementation of a negotiated settlement.[15] Kosovo and many other conflicts of the 1990s and 2000s have indeed required a concerted and long-term effort in peacemaking – long, tedious, detailed bargaining facilitated by the international community, often and ideally carried out under the security and policing umbrella of the UN. At a minimum, powerful peacemaking in the Kosovo case has kept the conflict "cold" (i.e. mostly non-violent) while the great powers thrash out (or not) the difficult question of final status or sovereignty for the disputed territory.

Peace processes offer hope but they also raise theoretical and pragmatic concerns. First, because military victories are allegedly more stable than negotiated settlements (a fallacious premise, as shown in Chapter 1), it is better, for all concerned and especially from a national-interest perspective, to let wars burn themselves out (Luttwak 1999). From the other end of the spectrum, from a critical theory perspective, international mediation conducted by dominant powers in the Westphalian international system reinforces global order and interests to the detriment of society's evolution away from rule by power and might; in this view, the international system simply isn't capable of promoting a just peace after civil war (Chandler 2002; Richmond 2002).

Such conclusions – whether from realist or critical voices – are deeply misguided. The guiding principles of international mediation in societies torn by war are clearly liberal and progressive, precisely the approach needed if the promises of international peace are to be realized (Doyle 2004). Liberal orientations are transformative toward common-interest international norms, rooted in a justifiably "just war" interventionist orientation (when resort to force is considered) that provides the best basis for sustainable, peaceful changes in violence-inducing power relationships (Fixdal and Smith 1998). Liberal interventionism, however, can be carried out with imprudent means, and for this reason there has been strong caution about blindly pursuing an intervention-for-peace agenda, especially with regard to post-conflict peacebuilding in which liberal economic reforms and electoral processes may go against conflict-management imperatives (Paris 2004). As well, if not carefully crafted, international peacemaking efforts can smother and overwhelm local initiatives and traditional or indigenous approaches (MacGinty 2008); hence, there is an appropriate call for great local ownership in peacemaking. However, the "local ownership" idea becomes farcical when gross violations of human rights occur, when millions are displaced, and when the parties fail to progress toward peace on their own.

More pragmatically, as well, it is argued that intervention isn't desirable in all situations or that in some situations the process was primarily internal, such as in Northern Ireland or South Africa.[16] It may be true that conflicts with lesser intensity or shorter duration may be less in need of external help in peace processes; at the same time it would be unwise to underestimate the extent to which international mediation did play a role in these cases. In Northern Ireland, the legacies of earlier efforts of mediation and in the indirect application of incentives were both essential antecedents of and elements in the peace process (Bloomfield 1997; Byrne and Ayulo 1998). In South Africa, international mediation was both indirect through economic and cultural sanctions and direct through high-level emissaries and through the deployment of UN observers at a critical turning point in the process.

Finally, there are those who argue that international mediation is desirable, but it simply isn't effective and, indeed, can do more harm than good. These critics are perhaps right to point out the deficiencies and disappointments in peace processes, but they fail to recognize that when internal violence reaches the severity of civil war (as Northern Ireland, for example, technically never did in terms of comparative measures of conflict intensity) the international community – and particularly the UN – has both the moral and common-interest mandate to become involved. My argument is that when war reaches the intensity and common duration of civil wars today, there is little alternative – for the protagonists and those in the international community alike – to the powerful involvement of external parties to provide assertive stewardship in the pursuit of peace from both normative and interest-based perspectives.

As well, the simple reality is that the policy-maker debate (including states once recalcitrant on external engagement to manage internal conflicts, like China) is not a question of whether international mediation occurs, or even whether it should or should not occur, but rather what are the ways in which outside assistance to endogenous peace processes can be made more effective.

This book argues that negotiated settlement in civil wars is indeed aided by international mediation but progress or regression in clinching peace is explained principally by the willingness and ability of the protagonists themselves (particularly, key top-level elites) to escape a mutually hurting conflict trap. However, even when elites are motivated to escape costly civil wars, they cannot clinch and implement settlements alone.

Progress from war to sustainable settlement demands the protagonists be prodded and sometimes threatened by a determined and deeply engaged international community using persuasion, pressure, and – in the direst instances – military power to leverage the parties into settlement and to guarantee its implementation.

International peacemaking must use leverage to aid the process of settlement, but also to provide a *formula* (a solution) for settlement. When the international community's role is minimally process-specific (i.e. through facilitation), or when robust peacemaking is prevented by a powerful state, progress toward peace is often elusive ... wars drag on or recur, reaffirming their unwinnable nature. Because parties in peace negotiations bargain with bullets as well as with words, international peacemaking requires a concomitant need to employ no small amount of coercive power and alluring inducement to get the parties to choose peace over war, negotiation over political violence.

Design: a structured, focused comparison

The design of this book follows the spirit of the comparative case study method: in particular, an approach of structured, focused comparison.[17] Chapter 1 sets out the broader problem of evaluating causes, patterns, and trends in post-Cold War civil wars and war termination. To set the scene, existing approaches to understanding the "root causes" of contemporary wars are evaluated; I argue that efforts to isolate a single, most powerful explanation of the causes of civil wars are elusive – elites, economics, and ethnicity typically converge as root causes in a wide variety of patterns and manifestations. The chapter ends with an often ignored aspect of conflict analysis: how violence *escalates*, usually triggered by crisis, and worsens; sometimes violence intensifies unwittingly and sometimes deliberately, but in either pattern protagonists soon find themselves trapped in an entangling, self-reinforcing grip of fear, insecurity, and enmity. For this reason, many of today's longer-running civil wars are rightly termed "protracted."[18]

Chapter 2 presents a theoretical perspective for understanding peace processes, focusing on the complex relationships between violence and negotiation. It highlights the fact that mediators rarely act as lone rangers, and that international peacemaking today must be evaluated from the perspective of multiparty mediation (coalitions of peacemakers). Among other things, the chapter seeks to debunk the myth that international peacemakers are unbiased, neutral, powerless facilitators; on the contrary, they do (and should, I argue) wield considerable power in the pursuit of peace; and they, too, have various incentive structures to engage or to exit, and have to make decisions on whether or how to wield leverage to move the parties toward settlement. From the perspective of bargaining and strategic choice theory, Chapter 3 presents a framework of analysis that evaluates the changing and varied incentives for violence through the phases of negotiation, highlighting the importance of decisions by key protagonists and the violent incidents that precipitate crises and that lead to turning points away from, or toward, peace agreements.

Using the analytical framework in Chapter 3, five cases of contemporary conflicts are compared in a structured, focused analysis of the escalation of violence and a peace process to manage it – South Africa, Liberia, Burundi, Sri Lanka, and Kashmir (Chapters 4–8). These cases offer telling empirical examples of the violence–negotiation nexus and demonstrate the utility of the analytical framework in explaining the path-dependency of war-to-peace transitions. These cases demonstrate a wide range of possible outcomes to crisis-inducing political violence, from negotiated settlement (in South Africa and Liberia), to gray-zone outcomes (Burundi and Kashmir), to war recurrence (in Sri Lanka).

Under what conditions do international mediators tip the balance in progressing away from escalation and entrapment and toward comprehensive settlement? Chapter 9 presents the principal findings of this research and explores the policy-relevance of these findings. The conclusion asserts that peacemaking with power works: carefully blending incentives and sanctions, international peacemakers – especially those imbued with the credibility and clout of the UN – can effectively alter the choices of disputants to discourage a resort to violence or to insulate peace processes from the violence that accompanies turbulent transitions. Even in the most challenging cases – today's agenda features Iraq, Israel–Palestine, and Afghanistan, for example, which share a common feature of highly fragmented parties to the conflicts – peacemakers have opportunities to leverage the parties into a settlement even while violence continues. Thus, this book concludes with ideas for developing and improving powerful peacemaking strategies to help bring internal conflicts to a negotiated end, offering insights from comparative research to assist peacemakers in slowly but surely moving parties away from violently bargaining their conflicts with bullets to peacefully managing them through newly negotiated political institutions.

1 Untold sorrow

Civil wars and war termination, 1990–2007

By 1992, early in the post-Cold War period, there were more armed conflicts occurring worldwide than for nearly 50 years, and most of the violence unfolded within the boundaries of United Nations (UN) member states. While major, international war turns out not to be wholly obsolete as some have argued[1] – as the US-led invasion of Iraq in 2003, the Ethiopia-Eritrea war of the early 2000s, or the cross-border Israeli–*Hizbollah* conflict of 2006 attest – overall mostly internal or civil wars are the principal present threat to contemporary international peace and security. The post-Cold War civil wars were accompanied by hideous features: attacks on civilians increased dramatically, and the protagonists in warfare were often amorphous "non-state actors" – irregular insurgents, paramilitaries, quasi-criminal gangs, and shadowy factions within state security forces.[2]

Some of the post-Cold War conflicts had antecedents in the mid-twentieth century, such as the tensions in Kashmir which find their origins in the partition of colonial India in 1948, whereas others, such as in the former Yugoslavia, were essentially new wars without immediate antecedents of violence. New challenges to "human security" arose in the context of these wars, such as conflict-induced famine, ethnic cleansing, landmines, blood diamonds, small arms, child soldiers, and "state failure"; these pressing humanitarian issues all crowded their way onto the international agenda as a consequence of these conflagrations.[3]

The popular impression that the post-Cold War era witnessed a dramatic increase in the total frequency of all armed conflicts around the globe is only partially correct; it is true that in the early 1990s new wars escalated dramatically and, in general, that they lasted longer than historically has been the case. However, over time, war terminations have outpaced the escalation of new wars such that the number of armed conflicts over the period actually decreased, and this trend continued into the mid-2000s. Another trend is worth noting. Most civil wars today end at the negotiating table rather than on the battlefield, with critical implications for international efforts to end the scourge of war. While in some conflicts there are clear unilateral victories (as in Rwanda after the genocide there), conflicts that end at the negotiating table have important implications for international responses.

Through negotiation, warring factions are disarmed, power shared, new constitutions drafted, elections held to legitimate newly formed governments (or in some instances to determine the sovereign status of disputed territory), transitional justice is pursued, and relief and reconstruction takes place in situations where rival factions retain power and sometimes military control of territory. This chapter addresses three context-setting questions. First, what do we know about the nature and patterns of war during the post-Cold War period? Second, what are the putative root causes of these wars and why did they escalate? Finally, what are the implications of conflict analysis for peacemaking strategies?

Civil war and international security

Armed conflicts, most of which are internal or "civil wars," pose new and dramatic challenges to realizing the UN Charter's lofty aims to "save succeeding generations from the scourge of war which … has brought untold sorrow to mankind."[4] The post-Cold War era, which lasted roughly from the fall of the Berlin Wall on November 9, 1989 through the middle of the 2000s, saw a sea change in the nature and intensity of contemporary war: wars more internal to states emerged as the principal threat to international peace and security as protracted wars between states (such as the World Wars of the twentieth century) became fewer as a proportion of all instances of war. Particularly in the first half of the 1990s, there was a sharp, unprecedented increase in the frequency, or overall number, of armed conflicts on the globe, and most of them are in fact essentially internal to states (but with transnational linkages and global implications). The trend lasts well into the twenty-first century.

By 2005, wars had decreased by 60 percent from an earlier peak in 1992 to the lowest level of warfare on the globe since the 1950s. The overall pattern of the post-Cold War period is an unambiguous one of progressive war termination: old wars are settled much more rapidly than new wars break out. From 1989 to 2004, some 84 armed conflicts (of 118 for the period) had ended despite the onset of new wars in the early 2000s in places such as Côte d'Ivoire and Sudan (Darfur), and the burgeoning sectarian conflict within Iraq.

According to the 2007 Human Security Brief, which uses the Uppsala Conflict Data Program analysis, there is an undeniable trend in armed conflict, such that "worldwide, non-state conflict numbers have undergone a marked and consistent decline since the data were first collected in 2002. In fact, they decline by a third – from 36 to 24 – between 2002 and 2006" (Mack 2008: 6); the same report argues that the trends show an apparent leveling off of armed conflict, despite a clear downward trend in sub-Saharan Africa.[5] Not since 1970 has the incidence of armed conflict been as low if the measure of conflict is "battle-related deaths." Updated data for between 1989 and 2005 revealed a reinforced trend, such that there were, between these years, 121 armed conflicts in 81 locations, of which 49 reached the threshold of "war." In 2005, there were 31 armed conflicts of which all were primarily intrastate, and five of which reached the intensity of war: Iraq (coded as an internationalized internal conflict), Afghanistan, India (Kashmir), Nepal, and Colombia (Harbom *et al.* 2006).

Although headlines in the mid-2000s led with insurgency-related violence in Iraq following the 2003 invasion, or terrorist bombings in London, Lebanon, or Israel, the principal threats to international and human security continues to be found in mostly internal wars; indeed, in Iraq most deaths are the result of sectarian strife rather than confrontation between insurgents and the occupation forces (www.iraqbodycount.org). While the other issues on the international security agenda, such as weapons of mass destruction and the consequences of the *al-Qaeda* 9/11 attacks in the United States, the Madrid bombings in 2004, or events like the Beslan school hostage-taking and massacre in Russia in 2004, are injurious to international security, the principal form of international violence today – as measured in deaths in political violence – continues to be protracted social strife that is internal to countries over national identity, borders, and religion and the state. By 2007, the number of violent armed conflicts had dwindled to the point where the aftermath of misguided US intervention in Iraq clearly emerged as the most violent setting on earth, with an estimated 60,000 deaths between 2003 and 2006.[6] Whether Iraq is a "civil war," sectarian conflict, "international war," or "occupation" really doesn't matter much to those who suffer today from so many lives lost.

Context: the scourge of war into the twenty-first century

During the Cold War, internal conflicts were often seen as contests between superpowers' proxies in the field (governments, rebel forces allied to the big powers), despite the fact that the actual military forces of the Soviet Union and the United States never met directly on the battlefield. Indeed, the danger of quick escalation to an all-out nuclear exchange worked against direct superpower engagement, as Smoke argued in *War: Controlling Escalation* (1977). Realists, such as Mearsheimer, view the Cold War as a period of remarkable global stability. He argues that given the contemporary sense of chaos, one day the relative security of the bipolar standoff between the United States and the Soviets will be missed.

> The next forty-five years in Europe are not likely to be so violent as the forty-five years before the Cold War, but they are likely to be substantially more violent than the past forty-five years, the era that we may someday look back upon not as the Cold War but as the Long Peace.
>
> (Mearsheimer 1990: 35)[7]

If the Cold War produced an essentially bipolar system of international relations from the 1950s through the 1980s, the dominant theme of post-Cold War international relations in the 1990s and early 2000s has been one of fragmentation and multipolarity. The weakening of the sovereign, national state as the central unit of politics is a consequence of globalization and international economic integration from outside and the appeal of ethnic nationalism from within. Lundestad observed that these schizophrenic centralizing and centrifugal trends characterize the post-Cold War period (Lundestad 1993). For this reason, it is difficult to even give the contemporary era a defining name; its reference point is what has come before: the *post*-Cold War era. Rosenau, describing the period as one of "turbulence" in world affairs, wrote presciently: "Local conflicts and violence are likely to persist, even intensify, since the dynamics of decentralization weaken the control that can be asserted over ethnic and aggrieved groups" (Rosenau 1990: 196).[8]

Local security dynamics, with all of their instabilities and complexities, emerged more openly as the overarching context of superpower rivalry dissipated. Väyrynen summed up the problem of internal conflicts in the post-Cold War era, writing that "With the removal of the global overlay, local and regional conflict dynamics can operate more autonomously and with less restraint" (Väyrynen 1993: 104). For example, Western countries and neighbors alike found it very difficult to influence the course of events in tumultuous Central Africa. In the countries of the Great Lakes region (especially Rwanda, Burundi, and eastern Democratic Republic of Congo (DRC)), intense conflicts raged throughout much of the 1990s without the ability of the international community to significantly affect their trajectory; similarly, today, there is little ability or willingness to stem fighting in conflict settings such as Sri Lanka as sanctions have marginal effects and there is no willingness or ability to field substantial military deployments.

What's in a name? "Political violence," armed conflicts, and "battle-related deaths"

Civil war is but one type of internationalized, internal violence, so it is critical to attempt some definitional precision. Violence in contemporary internal conflicts takes many forms, including spontaneous rioting, coldly calculated terrorism by small but motivated groups, targeted assassination and the use of "hit squads," and massive organized violence such as civil war.[9] There is a fine line, perhaps indistinguishable, between actual violence and related acts, such as intimidation, threats of violence, and systematic damage to property or liberty (Tilly 2003: 26–31). Equally ambiguous in some cases is the distinction between criminal violence and political violence. Thus, the intensity of violence in an internal conflict is invariably difficult to precisely measure; in the case-study chapters that follow, for example, best guesses are given from the ostensibly most reliable sources.

Often, the ability to assess levels of fatality can only be approximated post facto, as has been the case in determining the overall fatality count due to war in Bosnia.[10] Indeed, for the purposes of this study it is clear that the threat of violence is often as important as its actual application in terms of influencing an adversary's behavior, even as our measures allow us to operationalize violence in difficult to measure "battle-related deaths." Terrorism, for example, is not an entity against which war can be waged: instead, it is a type of violence of particular interest, precisely because it is indiscriminate, directed at influencing public opinion, and the purposes of terror may be less distinguishable than a military campaign, for example.[11] Nonetheless, terrorism is typically waged for some strategic purpose, more often than not to undermine accommodation among moderates across lines of conflict (reflected often in the case studies that follow), or to wage "asymmetrical" warfare in the context of internal conflicts (such as Spain or Israel–Palestine, or in the campaign waged against the West by *al-Qaeda*).

There is some concern that the measures used to track "armed conflict" obscure the severity and intensity of today's wars. By considering only *frequency* of conflict, we may be lulled into believing there is an overall downward trend in armed violence when it may be that those conflicts now raging are much more intense. In today's wars, civilians are targeted directly; the historically defined line between military combatants and civilians has been distinctly blurred (Kaldor 1999). One way to assess the human costs of war, beyond fatalities, is to consider the exponential increase in refugees that wars generate. In early 2000, at the height of the global refugee crisis, there were an estimated 21.5 million refugees and internally displaced persons; the vast number of these refugees and displaced were homeless from armed conflicts.[12]

Internal wars, regional and global spillovers

The problem of measuring internal conflicts is exacerbated by the fact that few armed conflicts in the contemporary world are truly "internal." These conflicts and their consequences have become internationalized, both empirically and in the realm of international or collective responses to them.[13] Increasingly, it is clear that putatively internal conflicts have strong transnational linkages in at least two ways: in terms of *diffusion* or spread of conflict and in terms of the *consequences* of internal wars as "global issues" (the global issues theme is taken up in "The impetus for intervention and the challenge of peacemaking," p. 30).

The concern with diffusion of civil war is about the escalation of internal conflict across borders and the tangible linkages that make contemporary borders lines on a map. Lake and Rothchild argue in their analysis of ethnic conflict that:

> Diffusion occurs when ethnic violence in one state increases the probability of conflict in a second. In other words, if conflict in Rwanda incites similar violence directly or indirectly in Burundi, the conflict will have diffused. Escalation occurs when a conflict in one country brings in new, foreign belligerents – whether neighbors or great powers with global reach.
>
> (Lake and Rothchild 1998: 23–24)

Related, there is a burgeoning literature on the "internationalization" of ethnic conflict and the cross-border ties through which many ethnic groups derive critical moral and material support (Wolff 2003). In many instances – such as Afghanistan, Kashmir, Sri Lanka, the former Yugoslavia, the former Soviet Union,[14] Rwanda, and Burundi, to name just a few – conflicts are fueled and complicated by strong identity bonds that link groups across borders. For example, the conflict between Tamil separatists and the government of Sri Lanka is linked to the nearby Indian state of Tamil Nadu, and such seriously complicating attempts to peacefully resolve the civil war in Sri Lanka; likewise global remittance flows to the Tigers are significant (see Chapter 7).

Many armed conflicts thus are "regional conflict complexes," or situations in which "neighboring countries experience internal or interstate conflicts, and with significant links between the conflicts" (Wallensteen and Sollenberg 1998: 623). Conflicts may be linked when ethnic groups reside astride international frontiers, or when military or political alliances yield military and political support across borders. For this reason, the civil war in the DRC in the late 1990s and early 2000s earned the appellation "Africa's First World War." If most "internal conflicts" are part of a regional conflict complex, or clusters of interrelated conflicts, there are important implications for efforts at peacemaking. Solving one problem may mean, in fact, solving several, or the failure to address the regional dynamics of conflict may lead to war recurrence.

Civil wars: the elusive search for causation

Arguments about trends in armed conflict and peacemaking strategies in them beg the tough questions about the underlying or "root" causes of contemporary armed conflict in the first place. Explanations for the prevalence of internal or society war may be found in the structure of the international system, such as the historical legacy of colonial-era borders and dysfunctional states, or globalization-induced growth of socio-economic inequalities;[15] other levels of analysis have also entered into the research on the underlying or root or once-removed causes of such conflicts.[16]

While ethnic enmity, religious intolerance, or hate speech are often manifestations of conflicts, many analysts see the ultimate "causes" of conflict in the deep-rooted economic social structures that give rise to group grievances and challenges to the state.[17] Economic and social divisions are often exacerbated by the state. Grievances that develop in situations of political and social discrimination produce the systematic exclusion of (usually) minorities from political power. Invidious discrimination and social hierarchies along group lines lead to perceptions of relative group superiority or inferiority. Examples of such "grievance" related conflicts include the war in Sri Lanka, the long history of the "Troubles" in Northern Ireland, and the 2005 rioting in French urban areas. Indeed, all of the case studies in this book have at times shown significant patterns of such structured socio-economic inequality.

Why do social conflicts in deeply divided societies erupt into organized violence? A central question in the analysis of a conflict is the underlying causes of deep conflict in a society and the chain of events that precipitate violence. An important distinction is between the *background conditions* of an internal conflict, that is, the "causes" of deep-rooted social tension, and *escalatory dynamics*, the progression of moves and counter moves that lead societal interaction away from cooperation and toward violence. The sections that follow evaluate current strands in the literature about the root causes of conflict. However, if a truly robust theory of causes of violence were to be comprehensively and convincingly elaborated, surely the advocate of such an integrated theory would win the coveted Nobel Peace Prize. Indeed, Zartman argues persuasively that any single factor or exclusive theory of intrastate conflict, such as those that isolate out or emphasize greed (economics) versus grievance (social psychological) determinants, is "profoundly uninteresting"; instead, interactions among these drivers (as described in the case studies in this volume, for example) that show the intersection of "need, creed, and greed" offer the best hope for uncovering causal relationships (Zartman 2005: 257). In evaluating causes of war, context is critical.

Social structure: ethnic relations

Contemporary internal conflicts have markedly different characteristics than conventional international conflicts, which may help explain their protracted nature. Many have either their origins or their manifestations as identity or "ethnic conflicts" and they are deeply rooted in national myth and historical narrative.[18] Brown sums up well the role of historical narrative in ethnic conflicts when he writes that:

> Some [perceptual] explanations of ethnic conflict focus on the false histories that many ethnic groups have of themselves and others.... These stories become part of a group's lore. They tend to be highly selective in their coverage of events and not unbiased in their interpretation of these events. Distorted and exaggerated with time, these histories present one's own group as heroic, while other groups are demonized.

> Grievances are enshrined, and other groups are portrayed as inherently vicious and aggressive.... Incendiary perceptions such as these make conflict hard to avoid and even harder to limit.
>
> (Brown 1993: 6, 8, 11)

Gurr posits that relative deprivation between groups, or "structured inequality," is the most important background condition that gives rise to rebellion and revolution.[19] Patterned inequality and discrimination, usually reinforced by public policy, is argued by some analysts to be *the* greatest predictor of violence in ethnic conflicts, as Gurr reported in the landmark study *Minorities at Risk* (1993). Others concur that a history of patterned, structured, and institutionalized discrimination against minority (or sometimes, as in South Africa or Rwanda, majority) communities, repressive state policies, systematic exclusion from political voice and influence, and competition among groups for "relative group worth" is a powerful underlying cause for violent conflict (Horowitz 1985; MacGinty and du Toit 2007). The interaction between structured ethnic relations and patterned inequality as a deep driver of conflict is documented well by Stewart (2001, 2005), who describes such structures in terms of horizontal inequalities, a theme that resonates in the case studies of South Africa, Burundi, and Sri Lanka evaluated in this book.[20]

Elite predation

A central factor often cited is the role of "ethnic entrepreneurs" – political leaders who articulate beliefs in kinship bonds or common destiny, and who mobilize and organize groups to press group claims. Ethnic entrepreneurs may be perceived as benign "interest aggregators" who serve a critical representative function, or manipulative and exploitative power-seekers who mobilize on ethnic themes for their own individual aggrandizement. The problem of ethnic outbidding in contemporary internal conflicts is pervasive. Political leaders, seeking to capitalize and gain on mass sentiments, outbid moderates by decrying acts of accommodation as a "sell-out" of group interests, citing collective betrayal and humiliation. Manipulation of identity to frame disputes in ethnic terms by political leaders heightens the breadth and depth of inter-group conflict. Ethnic outbidding – and mass responsiveness to "playing the ethnic card" – is an especially acute problem in the contemporary era, precisely because a moderate multiethnic center is often unable to sustain itself against the centrifugal forces unleashed by the heated rhetoric of ethnic chauvinism.[21]

A 1995 Human Rights Watch report, *Playing the Communal Card: Communal Violence and Human Rights*, argues that elite manipulation of ethnic identity, usually by weak and vulnerable ruling elites, is often an underlying cause of deadly ethnic violence. The following excerpt illustrates the conclusions.

> The extensive Human Rights Watch field research ... shows that communal tensions per se are not the immediate cause of many of today's violence and persistent communal conflicts. While communal tensions are obviously a necessary ingredient of an explosive mix, they are not sufficient to unleash widespread violence. Rather, time after time, the proximate cause of violence is governmental exploitation of communal differences...
>
> The governmental role can take several forms. In some cases, discrimination that favors a dominant group, or marginalizes a minority from full participation in the society, creates a climate of mutual suspicion and intolerance, and the illusion that one group "deserves" more rights than another. The resulting differential in status can breed violent resentment on one hand while inciting, or being seen to excuse, more violent forms of repression on the other. In this climate, when private attacks on vulnerable community occur, the government may fail to condemn, let alone prosecute, the offenders. Such attacks may even be carried out by official forces, with similar impunity. If the targeted community protests that is considered further evidence of its posing a threat or being alien to the interests of the state, and can lead to intensified repression. The "communal card" is frequently played, for example, when a government is losing popularity or legitimacy, and finds it convenient to wrap itself in the cloak of ethnic, racial, or religious rhetoric.
>
> (Human Rights Watch 1995: viii)

In both cases where there is an identifiable state, and cases where the state has collapsed, creating the capabilities for organized violence is a problem of collective action (Denardo 1985). Political "entrepreneurs" establish incentives and disincentives for participation in violence or rebellion, offering public goods and imposing sanction for non-participation. Popkin's seminal analysis of the development of rebellion in Vietnam, *The Rational Peasant* (1979; see also Popkin 1988), demonstrates how such political entrepreneurs build solidarity and internal cohesion in organizations for the purpose of violent resistance, articulating ideologies, and linking military action to broader political movements. In explaining elite predation, two predominant theories exist, one emphasizing cultural and constructivist factors such as communication, and the other emphasizing more material, political economy factors such as market incentives and more traditional entrepreneurial skills. For this reason, theories of de-escalation that follow in the next two chapters draw upon this insight of the role of elites in conflict analysis.

Studies of organized violence in internal conflicts have highlighted not only the role of political leaders who articulate grievances and organize and lead conflict organizations and the masses that support them, but particularly the influence of mid-level mobilized elites (e.g. a local party functionary or provincial police or guerilla commander) as critical players in the emergence and sustainability of violence.[22] There are inherent incentives for continual factionalism as some mid- and higher-level leaders seek to derive benefits from splintering and forming their own conflict organizations, either to achieve power and rent or to ensure a place in the post-conflict order. Hartlyn's analysis of Colombia's period of *la Violencia* (from the early 1940s to the early 1960s) reaches a similar conclusion: much of the violence was perpetrated by local and mid-level political leaders to enhance their personal well-being and security (Hartlyn 1993: 40).

Contesting the state

Competition for ownership of the state is another common element in the analysis of civil wars.[23] The relationship between the identity group and the state is a critical predictor of violent conflicts.[24] The expropriation of the symbols, power, and resources of the state to the exclusion of significant components of the population in multiethnic societies is a strong indicator of the likelihood of ethnic violence. In these instances, group membership is an entitlement system of state-sanctioned status and wealth to the exclusion of others. In addition to capture of the state by a group, the weakness of the state also allows for ethnic challenges to succeed, creating in such weak-state environments an opportunity structure for insurgent violence (Fearon and Laitin 2003).

For these reasons, ethnic group grievances are commonly targeted at the state, either for minor changes in the rules of interaction – for example, more equitable resource distribution – or for more drastic change such as "political divorce" through boundary change. Esman asserts that:

> The territorial state has everywhere become the arena in which competing ethnic groups' claims are asserted, contested, and regulated.... Rules established and enforced by the state determine the goals that ethnic communities may legitimately pursue and the strategies and tactics they may employ.... The state, then, is a party to most contemporary ethnic conflicts.
>
> (Esman 1994: 18, 19)

The close fit between causes of conflict analysis and the problem of exclusion of key groups from state power raises a number of questions about how state weakness and ultimately failure are related to the outbreak, duration, and settlement opportunities for war.[25] Among these are:

- From Somalia in the early 1990s to Iraq and Nepal today, what are the implications when the state – which has the "responsibility to protect" – is unable to fulfill its core function of serving as the legitimate source of coercive authority?

- How does state weakness and state failure generate broader concerns for the international community, to include neighboring states directly affected by tangible spillovers and all other countries in the international system?
- When does the weakness or failure of a state make the agenda of the international community?
- When and how should the international community engage to prevent state failure and to facilitate state strengthening or to "build" states after violent conflict has ended?

Although conflicts of interest are omnipresent, and it is often said that conflict is a healthy phenomenon, a constructive social process (Kriesberg 2003), the conflicts which are of concern in this study are those substantive disputes within a state that turn violent and which over time, through mass killing, have gone horribly wrong. In general, violence breaks out when the normal process of politics in a state breaks down; state autonomy and capacity collapse and alternative forms of authority arise. The state loses its monopoly on violence when institutional constraints are unable to contain the dispute; it spills over from the halls of parliament and onto the battlefield and the streets.

Many contemporary internal conflicts also feature disputes over sovereignty, to include two of the five case studies analyzed in this book. Conflict situations in which groups claim exclusive title of territory for control or access are generally perceived to be more intractable than those in which there is a high degree of intermingling and economic interdependence and integration. For territorially based ethnic groups, conflict over territory is usually zero-sum – win or lose everything. The problem of zero-sum perceptions in conflict is especially acute when territory is associated with symbolic or psycho-cultural aspects of group solidarity, a "homeland." Perhaps the pre-eminent example of seemingly irreconcilable claims to territory in the modern world is Jerusalem, in which competing claims are based on deeply rooted beliefs and religious claims despite the reality of multiethnicity in that ancient city. For many groups simultaneously, the territory is sacred and must be possessed. For this reason, internal conflicts with a strong territorial dimension are more likely to lead to the vexing problems of secession, irredentism, or forced migration.

Economic drivers

What is manifested as an ethnic- or identity-driven civil war may have its roots in economic and environmental conditions. The upsurge in superficially communal violence is *not* necessarily a product of the end of the Cold War and the re-emergence of primordial, ancient hatreds, as some have suggested was the case in wars in the former Yugoslavia (Kaplan 1993). Instead, the roots are arguably deeper, in modernization, industrialization, urbanization, or environmental mismanagement. For example, Homer-Dixon argues that deep-seated demographic pressures, environmental degradation, and urbanization are often the hidden causes of violent conflict (Homer-Dixon 1991, 1994). That inter-ethnic conflict does not necessarily lie at the root of all of today's internal conflict is illustrated by a look at two of the most violent instances, Somalia and Algeria. In Somalia, the violence crystallized around subethnic, or clan, divisions. In Algeria, the divisions are intra-religious, between more secular Muslims and those advocating an Islamist point of view that seeks to more closely wed religion and politics. These cases poignantly demonstrate that *within*-group conflict can be as destructively violent as *between*-group strife.

These deep-driver approaches emphasize natural resources, access to "lootable" goods – diamonds, oil, timber – and the role of greedy conflict entrepreneurs. Issues of natural resource management (especially of high-value commodities such as oil), access to employment, the absence of water and food security, lack of affordable, decent housing, or systematic economic discrimination – all have been seen as strong underlying drivers of conflict that have over time erupted into violent conflict.[26] War, in this view, is a way of doing business. Economic dependence on single or especially valuable commodities derived from natural resources can enable armed conflicts and may lengthen their duration. Such commodities produce significant income streams, usually for the state.[27] Because democracy is weak in many states, lack of accountability allows those with access to natural resources to dominate a power base, with the ability to raise and afford to pay for military power by recruiting, arming, and retaining foot soldiers. As Collier and Hoeffler argue, "the incentive for rebellion is the product of the probability of victory and its consequences" (Collier and Hoeffler 1998: 564).

It is increasingly clear that exclusion from natural resource returns can lead to mobilization by those excluded and disaffected. Many internal conflicts, for example in Aceh (Indonesia), Mindanao (the Philippines), Nigeria, and Bolivia, are driven in part by the exclusion of local peoples from access to the extraction of and profit from local natural resources, revenues being controlled by either central government or transnational corporations (Arnson and Zartman 2005; Ballentine and Sherman 2003; Ross 2004). Armed insurgency in Nigeria's oil-producing Delta region that erupted anew in 2005 is an example of such conflicts.

Escalation: triggers, traps, and termination

Causal analysis is only half the picture in evaluating protracted conflicts; equally important is how such imbroglios escalate into mass violence. The turn to violence is related to the incentive structure of a conflict in two important, related respects. First, in rationalist terms, individuals and organizations turn to violence because they expect violence to leverage a critical concession from an opponent (such as control of the state) or to affect the balance of power in ensuing negotiations. Violence is expected to achieve limited and specific aims such as a restructuring of the state, or maximal aims such as to subdue the opponent through decisive defeat. When parties strive for limited aims, as most do, this implies that the conflict will ultimately end with some form of accommodation or compromise (Sederberg 1995). In territorial conflicts, violence is seen as the route to autonomy or secession. In these instances, parties who foment violence expect that they can escalate the conflict beyond the limits of what the opponent (defenders of the rump state) can or is willing to endure.[28]

Second, escalation to violence often occurs in the context of state responses to social movements: when states repress social movements pressing deeply felt grievances, the seeds of violent resistance are sewn. As Mason argues:

> The leap to revolutionary collective action is more conceivable for those already engaged in nonviolent activism because it represents a tactical shift in the form of collective action; their participation in nonviolent reformist social movements means that they have already overcome collective action problems.... All that is required is that the movement's leaders shift strategy to apply that machinery in a program of revolutionary violence.
>
> (Mason 2004: 145)[29]

A useful conceptual tool for identifying the outbreak of violent conflict is to focus on a specific event or series of events that trigger, precipitate, or accelerate the outbreak of violence. Conflict triggers can include provocative acts by political leaders, failed elections, abrupt changes in the regional security environment, or violent upsurges such as riots or spontaneous uprisings (Hewitt 1993). Clearly in many recent internal conflicts, an election event with unanticipated consequences, leading to illegitimate or unstable government, has been the trigger event leading to the outbreak of violence. The ill-fated February 29, 1992 referendum on Bosnian independence from the former Yugoslavia was *the* trigger that ignited the civil war.

Triggers are specific events that instigate the turn to violence. Violence in contemporary internal conflicts takes many forms, including spontaneous rioting, coldly calculated terrorism by small but motivated groups, targeted assassination and the use of "hit squads" and dirty wars, and massive organized violence such as civil war. What differentiates political violence, such as criminal violence, is that it serves a broader strategic purpose. "To its proponents," Hewitt writes, "violence is not an end in itself but a means to achieve some social and political outcomes" (Hewitt 1993: 1). By perpetrators of violence, their activity is perceived as legitimate as a necessary means toward desirable goals.[30]

Organized violence in internal conflicts is often a contest between regimes and their challengers, either as rebellion, revolution, or in secessionist struggles. Although this categorizing describes a wide variety of conflicts, there are several conflicts (particularly in the post-Cold War world) where the state fully collapses, leaving a more anarchic situation in which myriad splinter groups vie for power in a free-for-all (e.g. in Liberia in 1997–2004 and Somalia, ongoing). In these situations, there is no government to oppose; the state has failed. Thus, we need a wider typology of the types of violence, beyond war-making as battlefield engagement, that affect the processes of war termination.

Conflict triggers are the first important turning point in the development of civil war. They mark the initial point of escalation, where lines of division between the regime and challenger crystallize, where initial acts of violence by one side or another are reciprocated, and when the conflict begins to intensify. Escalation may be either *vertical*, indicating an increase in the magnitude or intensity of a dispute (usually measured in terms of deaths or injuries in political violence), or *horizontal*, which is a broadening of the conflict to new groups, states, or communities (Smoke 1979; see also Zartman and Faure 2005).

Social traps, protracted conflicts

Escalation is normally assumed to occur in a step-by-step fashion (an escalation ladder), in which parties deliberately respond to acts of violence by an opponent by responding in kind or upping the ante. Smoke (1979: 168) notes that

> There are thresholds in the process of escalation. Unless one belligerent chooses suddenly to breach all the conflict's limits and launch an all-out attack, the escalation of the war proceeds by steps – unilateral steps taken one after another by one side, or more likely counter-escalating steps taken back and forth by both sides against each other.

Thus, the escalation ladder is a fruitful metaphor, with each rung indicating discrete levels of wider or more intense violence.[31]

On the other hand, escalation can be "creeping" as parties unknowingly intensify the conflict without an explicit intent to take the levels of violence significantly higher. Particularly for political leaders facing pressures of time, working with little information within an inefficient decision-making apparatus, escalation can occur not as a result of a well-considered strategy, but simply as the accumulated consequence of a series of small steps. Surely no one cunningly planned or even expected the creeping animosity that occurred in Northern Ireland's "Troubles" when they began in 1969; a series of protests and government efforts to preserve order and the status quo gradually grew more confrontational.

Attitudes especially hardened after protest turned to violence on "Bloody Sunday" in 1972, where British security forces opened fire on unarmed protestors.

Escalation theorists, particularly those who studied the interaction (i.e. the deterrence regime) between the superpowers during the Cold War, observe that every escalation contest has tacit rules of behavior that serve to limit the pace and upper threshold of a conflict's escalation. Rarely do parties commit all their resources all at once to decisively defeat an opponent. Escalation occurs until parties reach a plateau in which no side to the conflict sees further escalation as yielding greater benefit relative to cost; in fact, further escalation is self-defeating, yielding diminishing returns. Limiting escalation in this fashion is in fact observance of tacit rules of interaction: a certain level of violence can be tolerated, but higher levels of violence won't further the parties' aims. This illustrates that even in a hot, violent internal conflict, parties share common interests in containing violence to within levels that are mutually acceptable. Thus, even before negotiations begin parties are pulled between competing impulses of cooperation (however tacit) *and* confrontation.

Escalation theories also help explain why once deadly violence begins it is so difficult to stop. The violence itself generates new incentives for its perpetuation. There are both psychological and strategic reasons for this. Psychologically, studies have shown that participants in violence become committed to it as a way of life – the "cult of violence" (Taylor 1991, 1988). Strategically, governments have an incentive to show firmness, resolve, and staying power in the face of resistance and terror. Challengers have an interest in demonstrating their power to cause further instability, and for stating demands that – if granted – demonstrate that the turn to violence was warranted. That is, parties become *committed* to their course of action, and as violence intensifies so too does the commitment. Thus the turn to violence creates "social traps," or cycles of violence in which parties find it difficult, if not impossible, to escape.

As further detailed in Chapter 2, commitment is the essence of social traps. Parties which have made investments in fomenting violence, or in defending the state from violence by challengers, incur certain "sunk costs" or irretrievable expenses. In order to justify previous commitment to a course of action, parties find avenues of exit from escalating conflict to be closed. Brockner and Rubin (1985) define *entrapment* as a special kind of escalation, in which there are competing pressures for withdrawal and for remaining in a situation over time. Retreat from violence would cause parties to "lose face," or jeopardize their reputation.

The concept of entrapment (and social traps in general) explains why parties may continue to escalate violent conflict even though it may be apparent, even to the disputants, that this course of action is self-defeating. Certainly, the most violent of contemporary internal conflicts – Israel–Palestine and Sri Lanka – poignantly demonstrate entrapment at work, and indeed each of the case studies analyzed in this book experienced moments of conflict entrapment.

Patterns of war termination

Even "intractable" conflicts don't last forever. As Fearon has shown, civil wars tend to last longer than international wars with an average duration since 1945 of more than ten years (Fearon 2006).[32] Historically, we know that by far the majority of civil wars end in victory of one side over the other. Stedman concluded that only about 15 percent of civil wars between the years 1900–1980 ended at the peace table.[33] Barbara Walter has similarly analyzed war termination through comprehensive analysis and she reports that between 1940 and 1990, only 20 percent of civil wars ended in negotiations (Walter 1997). Fearon finds that since 1945 at least 75 percent of civil wars have ended in military victory; of all civil wars in his dataset, 40 percent of these end in a win for the state (crushing the rebels) and 35 percent for the rebels (who win the state). He argues that usually support from an external patron, or the withdrawal of support by an outside state, tends to account for the ability of one side to definitively defeat the other; in his data, only 17 percent of the cases end in negotiation and the sharing of political power in a comprehensive peace agreement. However, there is a deep fallacy in evaluating war termination in the mid-twentieth century together with war termination in the post-Cold War era.

The broad historical trends in war termination changed dramatically in the post-Cold War era; consequently, their utility in explaining current trends is limited and the policy advice that flows from this conclusion is seriously misguided. In 2000, Wallensteen and Sollenberg first reported that of the 108 conflicts since 1989, 75 had ended by 1998. "Of these," they write

> 21 were ended by peace agreements, whereas 24 ended in victory for one of the sides and 30 had other outcomes (cease-fire agreements or activity below the level for inclusion). Many new peace agreements were signed in the middle and late parts of the period, particularly 1995–96.[34]

The trend of conflicts ending in peace agreements rather than on the battlefield persisted into the 2000s such that by 2006 the Uppsala project reported that 34 percent of the conflicts in the post-Cold War period (1990–2005) as a whole ended in negotiated settlements, double the historical average. Between 2000 and 2005, there were nearly quadruple the number of conflicts ending in negotiation than by military victories (16 to four). Starkly, in the 1990s, more conflicts (41) ended at the negotiating table than on the battlefield or in the streets (23) (Mack 2006,

2008: 35; Harbom *et al.* 2006). The 2007 Human Security Brief directly links the increase in negotiated settlements to more extensive peacemaking, finding that "Both the reduction in the number of victories and the increase in the number of negotiated settlements reflect the sharp increase in peacemaking" (Mack 2008: 35).

The Uppsala war termination findings, reflected in the Human Security Report narrative, are useful but they require further evaluation. First, military victories may prove to be more stable, but in most cases military victories do not necessarily yield political stability; Ethiopia and Afghanistan, for example, teeter on the verge of renewed civil war even after initial military successes by rebel forces or international intervenors. Second, de-escalations without settlement (in the Uppsala terms, "Other") are peculiar to mostly minor and some intermediate armed conflicts and are only found in civil wars (such as Iraq versus the Kurds in the early 1990s) in the most unique of circumstances; the "cold conflicts" of the Caucasus (in Azerbaijan or Georgia, for example) did not reach the levels of escalation found in the major civil wars of the 1990s and 2000s. Finally, the category "peace agreements" is too general: there are at least three major subtypes of negotiated war termination: a cease-fire without settlement, an interim agreement, and a comprehensive peace agreement; the first two are highly unstable and account for the majority of cases in which negotiated agreements collapse (as in Sri Lanka or Sudan/Darfur in 2006). In sum, a more contingent typology of war termination possibilities is presented below.

War termination in the post-Cold War period: a typology

- *Military victory.* One side definitively defeats the other and assumes unilateral control of the government; an example in the post-Cold War era is the 2003 defeat of the rebel movement Khmer Rouge in Cambodia, or the definitive victory by the Ethiopian People's Revolutionary Democratic Front (EPRDF) over the Ethiopian state in 1991. In many instances, negotiation or peace processes often follow military victories in major civil wars, as in Afghanistan's Bonn agreement process in late 2001. However, as the continued conflict in Ethiopia and in Afghanistan illustrates, military victories today are often illusory ends to civil conflict.
- *De-escalation without settlement.* Some conflicts de-escalate to levels below what is captured in the quantitative assessments (25 battle-related deaths in the Uppsala project), even though there is no definitive or clear victor. An example in recent years is the Indian state of Nagaland, where the conflict has subsided; however, only major armed conflict, or war, de-escalated without settlement in the post-Cold War period: the Iraqi fight with Kurdish separatists (Democratic Party of Kurdistan (DPK) and Patriotic Union of Kurdistan (PUK)),

ended by 1993 following enforcement of the UN authorized no-fly zone mentioned later in this chapter.

- *Partial settlement: Cease-fire without settlement.* In many instances, such as in Nagorno-Karabagh in 1992, parties reach a cease-fire but do not include in the agreement the terms of settlement (often left to be subsequently negotiated). Much of the instability associated with peace agreements may well be related to the cease-fire-without-settlement type, which is arguably especially prone to war breakdown and war recurrence (see the Sri Lanka study in Chapter 7).
- *Partial settlement: Interim agreement.* As in the Oslo agreement of 1993 in the Israeli–Palestinian conflict, some conflicts may end with a partial settlement or interim agreement; in some instances, as in the Oslo pact, the talks may fail to progress to comprehensive settlement whereas in others (as in South Africa; see Chapter 4) interim agreements may set the stage for subsequent negotiation of comprehensive settlements.
- *Comprehensive settlement.* Of the major civil wars of the post-Cold War period, nearly half (47 percent according to Mack 2006) of those no longer active have ended in comprehensive peace agreements that both address security concerns and include provisions for resolving the underlying incompatibility (such as over territory or control of the government). An example of a comprehensive civil-war terminating settlement is the UN-brokered 1997 peace agreement in Tajikistan.

Arguments that in today's world the international community should sit by and watch protagonists in civil war fight it out – because military victory is more stable than negotiated settlement – are deeply misguided. Some analysts have suggested that military victories in civil wars lead to more stable outcomes than negotiated settlements.[35] Indeed, there is a substantial set of findings that suggest that over time (at least since 1945) even comprehensive negotiated settlements *are* more prone to war recurrence than military victories (see studies on recurrence by Licklider 1995; Fortna 2003; Suhrke 2007). Negotiated settlements inevitably leave many issues ambiguous or insufficiently addressed, or circumstances change leading to one or more parties being in a position to change their terms; settlements are inherently unstable and create new opportunities for the re-emergence of violence. This logic may well suggest that it may be better to let parties to internal conflicts "fight it out" until one side or another (or, in more realistic terms, one group of factions over other factions) definitively prevails.

The alternative point of view is that military victories are *less* stable, leaving grievances among the vanquished unresolved, only to re-erupt at the first opportunity when future crises emerge.[36] The consensus of the international community, reflected in its principles, policies, and actions, is that negotiated settlements are clearly desirable before wars become long, and that *early* settlement or management of conflicts (as in Macedonia), rather than late attempts to end strife (as in Sri Lanka), are even more desirable. The consensus is reinforced by recent scholarship that affirms, through quantitative and case study analysis, that "negotiated settlements of civil wars may in fact produce just as stable a peace as military victories," especially when the parties arrive at power-sharing agreements (Hartzell and Hodie 2007: 9). As well, Walter finds in her analysis that the principal factors in the successful settlement of civil wars are "mediation, a military stalemate, and non-territorial goals … [featuring] third-party guarantees and power-sharing pacts" (Walter 2002: 161).

In today's wars, even after an initial military victory (as in Kosovo or initially in Afghanistan), a negotiation process is required for a sustainable peace. If a peace settlement is to succeed, both in ending the carnage and in promoting reconciliation, the terms of a new, just, and mutually beneficial post-war order must be established through collaboration and dialogue (Mani 2002). Likewise, reconciliation seems a prerequisite to the successful operation of democracy over time, as democratic processes require essential trust that the rights and interests of those defeated in electoral competition will not be vitiated by the victors; democratic processes can reconcile issues, but democracy does not necessarily reconcile relationships (Bloomfield *et al.* 2003: 11).

Most practitioners and scholars agree that civil wars today need a peace *process*, or step-by-step reciprocal moves to build confidence, resolve gnarly issues such as disarmament, and carefully define the future. In other terms, a peace process is an intricate dance of steps – often choreographed by third-party mediators – among parties in conflict to gradually exchange war for peace. If the "give war a chance" logic is accepted and negotiated settlements are often inherently more unstable than unilateral victories, the issue is not only whether and how negotiated settlements should be pursued, but rather how negotiated settlements can be reached *and* made more durable. The ethical consequences of letting parties fight it out, not to mention the direct and indirect costs of internal conflict imposed on the international community, are simply too great. At least one key to the durability of peace in an internal conflict is the sequence of events that produces a settlement and the terms of agreement that are reached; the degree of cooperation that evolves in the peacemaking phase is closely linked to the capacity of peace agreements to become self-sustaining in the long peacebuilding phase (Rothchild 2002).

Why are wars today "unwinnable" and thus more likely to end in negotiated settlements? Part of the puzzle as well is more extensive international intervention in the Cold War's wake. The greater willingness of international actors to intervene in today's conflicts has the effect of putting all parties to the conflict on a more level playing field. The prevailing policy-maker consensus today is that negotiated solutions are more *desirable*, especially from the perspective of the UN, because definitive defeat of an opponent in ethnic conflict may well lead to genocide or ethnic cleansing (forced migration). International intervention through peacemaking (mediation) or peacekeeping (military intervention) may induce more of a balance of power among competing forces, thereby making negotiation more attractive – because the war is really not winnable – and the pursuit of military victory more costly and less likely (Mason *et al.* 1999).[37]

The impetus for intervention and the challenge of peacemaking

Ironically, one of the initial, precedent-setting conflicts of the post-Cold War era was a more conventional war of international aggression. Iraq's ill-considered invasion of Kuwait in August 1990 set the stage, by April of 1991, for a massive humanitarian catastrophe as Iraqi Kurds were punished for their unsuccessful mutiny against the regime of Saddam Hussein in the wake of Iraq's defeat in the Gulf War. Kurds were perishing at a rate of nearly 1,000 per day after being driven into the barren mountains of the country's north bordering Turkey. The tragedy set the stage for a massive humanitarian response code-named Operation Provide Comfort to assist the Kurds. United Nations Security Council Resolution 688 determined that the humanitarian crisis was a threat to international peace and security, and key member states (the United States, United Kingdom, and France) interpreted the resolution to justify collective military action – i.e. no-fly zones and cross-border deployment of military personnel – to provide emergency relief to the embattled Kurdish population *without* the consent of the government of Iraq. With this precedent, the doctrine of humanitarian intervention emerged as a leitmotif of global politics early in the 1990s, superceded today by the norm of "Responsibility to Protect."[38]

At the same time, the tragedies of Somalia – which collapsed as a state following the fall of long-time dictator Siad Barre in January 1991 – also precipitated humanitarian intervention as did, over time, a succession of new wars in the ensuing months in the former Yugoslavia, especially in Bosnia beginning in 1992. Interventionist impulses were reinforced by peacemaking successes. During this period, too, efforts to terminate the myriad war legacies of Cold War, superpower-proxy rivalry proceeded apace: initial peacemaking successes in Angola, Cambodia, El Salvador,[39] Mozambique, Namibia, and Nicaragua, for instance, further reinforced the interventionist impulses of the international community.

Modern internal conflicts are global problems that require a multilateral response (Sisk 2001). Internal conflicts have direct implications for neighboring states through spillovers such as refugees or the spread of weapons, and indirect implications for the entire international community (such as violation of international norms on crimes against humanity, or through the creation of humanitarian emergencies featuring acute deprivation: food insecurity, lack of water or housing, basic safety).[40]

The evolution of responses to civil wars

As the nature of wars changed after the fall of the Berlin Wall, so, too, the system of international response gradually evolved to cope with the "new wars" by creating new institutions and instruments to stem armed conflict within states. In this context, genocide, ethnic cleansing, and massive refugee flows in the first half of the 1990s pushed the management of internal conflicts to the top of the international agenda, even as the emerging doctrine of vigorous intervention quickly faded in the messy local complexities of local realities such as Somalia's where the mission ran aground in the face of determined resistance by local warlords. These events of the first few years following the end of the Cold War set the stage for the following decade or more: the pre-eminence of internal conflicts as the primary *realized* threat to peace was affirmed (nuclear weapons exchange, while not yet realized in recent years as a threat, surely remains a significant *potential* threat to peace).

United Nations responses to the challenge of post-Cold War conflicts emerged quickly: by 1992, Secretary-General Boutros Boutros-Ghali unveiled *An Agenda for Peace*, spelling out the multiple ways in which UN efforts to pursue peace would need to be expanded – prevention, peacemaking, peace enforcement, peacekeeping, and peacebuilding.[41] Over time, in response to the new challenges of the 1990s, the international community also created other expansive new approaches and mechanisms to include most poignantly the doctrines and practices of preventive action, humanitarian intervention, multiparty peacemaking, new-generation complex, multidimensional peace operations, and new norms and institutions such as the International Criminal Court, that was borne from the negotiation of the Rome Statutes of July 2002, to prosecute perpetrators of war crimes and crimes against humanity.

More than a decade after the *Agenda for Peace* the General Assembly created in late 2005 a standing Peacebuilding Commission, reflecting the realization that transitions from war to stable peace would take decades, not years, and generational change, not simply a change of ruling elites. Likewise, regional institutions, such as the Organization for Security and Cooperation in Europe (OSCE), the African Union (AU), and the Organization of American States, all created new institutions and methods for responding to the challenges of mostly civil wars.[42]

Today, there is no way to tidily distinguish between "international" and "civil" wars (as described below). Still, as UN Secretary-General Boutros Boutros-Ghali wrote in the 1995 Supplement to *An Agenda for Peace*, the principal challenge to international security in the post-Cold War era *is* wars that principally play out within countries, "often of a religious or ethnic character."[43] Not only is such war *the* principal challenge to international security, the global community will continue to intervene in them, affirming Boutros-Ghali's statement in the original 1992 *Agenda for Peace* that:

> The time of absolute and exclusive sovereignty has passed; its theory was never matched by reality. It is the task of leaders of states to understand this, and to find a balance between the needs of good internal governance and the requirements of an ever more interdependent world.
>
> (Boutros-Ghali 1992: 9)

The impetus for international intervention

The advent and expansion of satellite television and Internet communication technologies during the 1990s precipitated a globalized stream of reporting and images from these conflicts. Local atrocities unfolded in full view of an entire world's eyes, and commensurately new demands arose for the international community to "do something" to stop the killing. "Intervention" emerged as the leitmotif of international responses to stem the spillovers and contagions of these wars, taking a place of priority alongside long-standing Cold War-era international security concerns such as the management of nuclear weapons proliferation. The impetus for intervention was driven by both normative considerations such as international humanitarian law and interest considerations to prevent spillover of conflicts to other states (Regan 2000).

In the Balkans, Europe and the United States could not stand idly by while the 1948 UN Convention on Genocide was abrogated in the brutal conflict that unfolded in the former Yugoslavia; although further afield in Rwanda or Darfur (Sudan) it was clear that the international community would not or could not act forcefully to prevent or stop genocide. On September 11, 2001, the devastating terror attacks by *al-Qaeda* in the United States reinforced the fact that contemporary conflicts and "state failures" generate national-interest spillovers (such as the harboring of enemy opponents willing to employ asymmetrical war such as terrorism) and are thus global issues that affect even the most powerful states in the international system. Not surprisingly, the United States responded by intervening militarily in Afghanistan with a multinational war-fighting coalition without an explicit UN authorizing resolution (as NATO had done to stem ethnic cleansing in Kosovo in 1998).

The costs of humanitarian assistance for emergencies are borne by international donors, and it is no surprise that the interventionist impulses to stem internal conflicts have come from these states. In 2003, for example, total assistance for complex humanitarian emergencies (those generated by wars) and natural disaster aid totaled some $9.6 billion. As the Carnegie Commission on Preventing Deadly Conflict points out, "In short, once war has broken out, the costs of violence soar."[44] Economists such as Hoeffler and Reynal-Querol have shown that civil wars exact measurable direct and indirect economic costs on societies that last for many years after the violence has stopped, calling civil war "development in reverse" (Hoeffler and

Reynal-Querol 2003). These economists suggest that civil war reduced gross national product by an average of 2.2 percent annually. In social impact terms, the costs of war are measurable in terms of their effects on human resources (death, injury, crime, and fear), population dislocations, societal networks that moderate social relations, environmental quality, infrastructure damage and resource diversions, and "non-reciprocal resources" transfers such as "brain drain" and capital flight (Marshall 2002: 67–68).

In addition to tangible economic and social costs, the moral basis of international society is undermined when flagrant violations of international standards on human rights occur; Table 1.1 highlights the interest-based and normative dimensions of international intervention. More often than not, the international instruments of human rights are violated in civil wars, including in the most egregious situations the perpetration of crimes against humanity, such as genocide, forced migration or "ethnic cleansing," and other violations of international covenants. According to international covenants such as the 1948 Convention on Genocide, states have an obligation to respond to prevent acts of genocide. In some cases, such as Kosovo or Timor-Leste, intervention has been explicitly justified in reference to global norms on the prevention and halting of genocide and crimes against humanity.[45]

The global consequences of today's wars are such that no single state, acting alone, can possibly muster the external legitimacy, resources, and staying power to intervene for peace on its own. Even the United States, whose record of unilateral intervention in Central American states is long, was compelled to seek UN Security Council mandates for its multilateral mission to promote peace in Haiti. The greater the spillover effects of wars, the likelier regional and global powers will intervene to end them. Wars that affect neighbors and that feature unchecked crimes against humanity require a multilateral response, lest intervention in them become an imbroglio for individual states which often lack sufficient military power to succeed.

Table 1.1 The impetus for intervention: interests and norms

Interest-based considerations

- Diffusion and escalation: security of citizens, allies
- Refugees and internally displaced persons
- Direct costs in terms of overseas humanitarian assistance
- Cost to global security: safe for trade, migration
- Wars and environmental degradation; war as "development in reverse"

Normative considerations

- The 1948 Convention on Genocide
- Violations of the UN Charter on Aggression
- Violations of the Universal Declaration of Human Rights
- Other global and regional norms

At the same time, states intervening in civil wars, guided by national-security interests and acting either alone or in "ad hoc coalitions," face legitimacy challenges that go beyond the already difficult operational challenges faced by the UN. While in some ways the Iraq intervention is wholly different from UN operations, in other ways – such as managing the constitution-making process, holding elections, controlling violence, and in economic reconstruction – there are undeniable parallels. Debates swirl over whether the United States, as a powerful global state, should engage primarily in initial military stabilization using overwhelming force and leave the peacebuilding (or state- or nation-building) elements of operations to the ostensibly more legitimate UN.[46] Even when the legitimacy of initial US action is not questioned, the way in which the United States has engaged in "peacebuilding" in Iraq – in particular managing the political or democratization process and the distribution of economic aid – has come under fire as lacking in legitimacy and deeply flawed in strategy and action.[47] Given the legitimacy deficit of US efforts to engage in peacemaking in Iraq, it was not surprising when in July 2007 the Bush Administration finally turned to the UN to help bring stability to the war-torn country. Ambassador Zalmay Khalilizad acknowledged that the UN "In the role of mediator ... has inherent legitimacy and flexibility to talk to the parties, including elements outside of the political process."[48]

Likewise, Afghanistan is unique in that the post-9/11 intervention that toppled the Taliban regime has been more fully embraced by the UN and militarily is presently controlled by NATO. The nature of intervention in this operation defies generalization from the pattern of other interventions that occurred in the mid-2000s (e.g. Sierra Leone, Timor-Leste, Liberia, the DRC, or Côte d'Ivoire) in that these missions have involved UN engagement following a comprehensive, negotiated peace agreement. Despite the complexity in the evaluation of peacebuilding that Iraq and Afghanistan introduce, there is a concomitant rise in the need for complex, multidimensional interventions by the international community for peacebuilding in the wake of war: either in negotiating and implementing negotiated settlements among the protagonists, or in security stabilization and emergency and long-term economic reconstruction.

This demand for external peace and security assistance was a central feature of the 1990s and its relevance has grown substantially in the twenty-first century. The UN Secretary-General's landmark report in May 2005, *In Larger Freedom*, succinctly states the current demands:

> Roughly half of all countries that emerge from war lapse back into violence within five years. These two points drive home the message: if we are going to prevent conflict we must ensure that peace agreements are implemented in a sustained and sustainable manner. Yet at this very point there is a gaping hole in the United Nations institutional machinery: no part of the United Nations system effectively addresses

the challenge of helping countries with the transition from war to lasting peace.[49]

In the new millennium, more "new" wars have emerged to challenge the ability of the international community to respond: a classic rebels-versus-the-state struggle in Côte d'Ivoire, the genocidal carnage in Darfur, and the spiraling sectarian violence following the US-led intervention of Iraq, together with the persistence of war in long-standing conflicts such as Sri Lanka, Colombia, and Kashmir. Even so, internal wars in the early 2000s were still ending more quickly than new ones were emerging, with the end or diminution of major armed conflict in Angola, Sierra Leone, Liberia, the DRC, and Burundi. This pattern of steady decline in armed conflict offers new hope that, through more powerful peacemaking, the promises of the Charter might be realizable in a distant future in which, progressively, new institutions, approaches, and instruments of the international community could effectively help end ongoing internal wars and, over time, prevent societies and regions from descending into the entrapping abyss of civil war.

Did improvements in peacemaking yield success?

The post-Cold War era should be seen as one of considerable, rapid progress in global responses to dangers posed by civil wars. As *New York Times* columnist Thomas Friedman observes, "Compared with the vast repression and nuclear standoff of the Cold War, the post-Cold War era has been much better for a lot of humanity."[50] The "post-Cold War" era now gives way to a new era – the post post-Cold War world, or simply the century-long challenges of the new twenty-first century. In the coming decades, a critical puzzle appears in understanding the pursuit of peace through extended bargaining aimed at securing a negotiated settlement to stop the killing. If the future of international peace lies primarily in peacemaking in civil wars, we must have a better understanding, empirically, of how such conflicts end, and, normatively, how they can be ended sooner.

In 2005, the inaugural issue of the Human Security Report highlighted the awareness that despite a daily diet of news from wars around the world, overall the frequency of protracted internal conflicts, too, had begun to wane. As Andrew Mack observes, "Most people believe that the number of armed conflicts has risen over the past decade, not that it has declined radically. They are wrong." (Mack 2005: 17). At least one reason for the decline in conflict is the strong intervention by the UN and broader international community to engage in aggressive peacemaking.[51] The teleology of peacemaking has been to encourage parties to armed conflicts to exchange the battlefield for negotiation and to embrace a war-to-democracy transition aimed at channeling conflicts into the "normal" parliamentary and public policy dispute resolution processes of the state.[52]

The international community's track record on peacemaking in recent years is decidedly mixed. Either the cup is half empty or half full; the truth is in the eye of the beholder. Clearly there have been peacemaking failures. Some wars grind on despite repeated attempts by the international community to arrange talks and encourage a settlement, such as in Sri Lanka or Sudan (Darfur). And apparent successes can be illusory. Even when a peace accord is clinched, horrific tragedy can still occur. One of the worst moments in the long history of the "Troubles" in Northern Ireland was the marketplace bombing on Saturday August 15, 1998, which killed 29 civilians in a devastating terror attack; the attack by the hold-out "Real IRA" occurred after the Belfast Agreement had been clinched in April of that year and the pact overwhelmingly approved in a public referendum in May.[53] Nonetheless, it is possible to opine that Northern Ireland has indeed clinched "Peace at Last" (Darby and MacGinty 2000b; Neuheiser and Wolff 2002).

Other peace processes have produced an unsatisfactory, frustrating, and often violent, or "cold," peace. The September 1993 Oslo Accords between Israel and the Palestinian Authority and the bumpy peace process that followed has few starry-eyed champions; yet, even with the upturn in violence in late 2000 – the so-called *Al-Aqsa Intifada* – the parties returned to talks for another attempt at final-status settlement. Similarly, a foundation for peace in post-war Bosnia was laid in the 1995 Dayton Accords, yet reconciliation is halting and ethnic nationalist forces that eschew reconciliation still dominate the post-war landscape (Belloni 2008). The contemporary challenge of peacemaking thus lasts well beyond clinching cease-fires, pursuing interim accords, and negotiating comprehensive settlements; indeed, there is no fine line when "peacemaking" ends and "peacebuilding" (through successful implementation) begins (Cousens 2001a, 2001b).

Turning the clock back to the conflicts ended very early in the post-Cold War era, where wars have now been terminated for over a decade or more – Namibia, Cambodia, El Salvador and Nicaragua, South Africa, and Mozambique, for example – the legacies of conflict are still apparent and the wounds of war have not fully healed. In Burundi, Guatemala, Sierra Leone, Liberia, Angola, Haiti, and Timor-Leste, for example, negotiated settlements have been reached, disarmament and demobilization has advanced considerably, new military and police forces have or are being trained, and crowning elections have been held, but the peace remains very tenuous. Societies are fragile, and serious root causes of conflict remain; the state is weak.

Long-standing conflicts such as the Israeli–Palestinian conflict are also ones in which peacemaking is about seeing through transitions through to a two-state solution, managing ongoing violence and providing security, understanding and mitigating regional spillovers and contagions, and working through difficult issues of "final status" in territorial disputes or power sharing in clearly intrastate conflicts … all without a peace process on track. Côte d'Ivoire is also in such an imbroglio: elections in 2006 were designed to crown the implementation of the peace agreement brokered in 2003 in a process but were subject to delay and threats of violence by the parties while peacekeeping troops are in constant danger from the warring factions. In these and in a myriad of other cases on the UN agenda, there is little alternative for the international community than to be engaged in peacemaking in today's wars, and, over the long term, in indefinite peacebuilding to implement settlements once they are reached.

2 Peace processes as a bargaining problem

For nearly every protracted armed conflict in today's world, there is a concomitant peace process. The phrase normally refers to an actual ongoing sequence of events: negotiations in mutually accepted rules of interaction that parties have accepted as a potential means for potentially resolving their differences through dialogue instead of (or, as this book shows, as a companion to) violence. Peace processes are seen as *potentially* resolving differences non-violently because these negotiations often occur while the battles on the ground continue to be waged. As noted in the Introduction, a formal definition of a peace process is: a series of step-by-step, reciprocal, and self-reinforcing actions that are taken to steadily move a conflict away from violence toward regularized, consensual non-violent rules of interaction.[1]

The onset of a peace *process* implies that the parties mutually accept that ultimate resolution of an armed conflict either through military victory or through an immediate simple, comprehensive formula of agreement is unlikely. There are too many players, too many issues, and too much accumulated animosity for quick, easy, imposed, or one-off solutions. Peace processes are analyzed through many different theoretical prisms and approaches, each contributing islands of insight but none of which fully captures the phenomenon. The framework that guides this book seeks to unify these fragments of theory by weaving together concepts and approaches from the burgeoning work on ethnic conflict and its management; negotiation and related game-theory literature; international war termination studies; the literature on terrorism, political violence, and revolution; newly popular ideas within the conflict-management and -resolution genre, such as conflict transformation; traditional international security concerns such as deterrence theory, diplomacy, and international organizations; and the literature on more practical policy issues such as preventive diplomacy.

The central premise underlying this study is that a generalized analytical framework for the analysis of peace processes in contemporary civil wars is attainable and urgent. Even though each internal conflict is highly unique and embedded in its own local and regional contexts, there are common elements across peace processes that can be discerned and presented in a more comprehensive and integrative fashion. In this chapter and in Chapter 3 I present a theoretically consistent approach to understanding peace processes as complex, multiple-level bargaining problems.

Peace processes as a bargaining problem

Iterated bargaining is the essence of peace processes. Peace processes entail a continuing series of straightforward bilateral negotiations, such as those between the African National Congress (ANC) and the South African state in 1989, or an interlinked series of talks such as the highly complex Middle East peace process which in the mid-1990s comprised four bilateral tracks and separate multilateral talks. Often, the "process" may be an incipient or even imagined one, existing only as a policy brief on a desk at the United Nations (UN) or in the sketched proposal of some other would-be conciliator, such as a non-governmental organization (NGO). Peace processes can drag on for decades, such as was the case for so many years in southern Sudan which after countless rounds of fruitless discussions eventually progressed to settlement in 2005 after 21 years of war. In the discourse on contemporary internal conflicts, there is no lack of talk about getting peace processes going, a peace process in crisis, justifications for terminating or sustaining them, their relative success and failure, and in some more skeptical circles, their very utility.

Peace processes have all the general characteristics of any bargaining problem: parties can potentially minimize their costs and increase their benefits by adopting an accommodative strategy; mutual interaction is required to produce an agreement; and many opportunities for a mutually beneficial outcome exist depending on the strategy and tactics adopted during the course of negotiation (Bacharach and Lawler 1981; Pillar 1983: 37; Raiffa 1982: 11–20). As a bargaining situation, peace processes involve both a "process" dimension and an "outcome" dimension. The process dimension relates to the when, where, and how of negotiations. The outcome dimension relates to what and why. The two dimensions of bargaining are inherently linked in a path-dependency: the process by which parties reach agreement fundamentally affects the nature of the outcome and the outcome preferences of the parties affects the positions they take on the process dimension of talks.

Moreover, peace processes are multidimensional in that the process of moving away from violence to accepted, non-violent, and regularized interaction is comprised of many facets: elites who engage in formulating official, authoritative positions on behalf of states or rebel movements, or even claim to represent an entire ethnic group; the press, who report on these official talks; the rank-and-file soldier or paramilitary combatant who fires the shot or launches the artillery attack; mediators (or more accurately in contemporary conflicts, a group of mediators) such as states and international organizations such as the UN, regional organizations, or subregional organizations; the informal conciliators, often NGOs seeking to build bridges across deep divides at the unofficial level among academics, clergy, journalists, and civic leaders; and mass publics, which can be mobilized for violence or demobilized for peace and whose consent for peace is often sought in electoral processes. Indeed, peace processes occur at myriad levels simultaneously. For this reason, it is equally important to conceive of peace processes in terms of coalition politics. Building a coalition for peace, as will be seen, is a matter of building not only linkages between moderates across groups in conflict, but also internal coalitions within groups willing to accommodate with opponents.

The framework for analyzing peace processes presented here is based on two related premises.

- The first premise is that there is a "life cycle" of conflict escalation and de-escalation (Kriesberg and Thorson 1991; Kriesberg 2003: 23), or identifiable points when violent hostilities emerge, intensify and spread, and then retract and end.
- The second premise is that the life cycle of a conflict can be fruitfully studied in a linear fashion, by analyzing the chronology of events between the initiation of violent conflict and its resolution (Lund 1996: 38–39).

There is no presumption of teleology or pre-determination in the onset, perpetuation, and eventual diminution of conflict; the "life cycle" approach is simply a device. As this book shows, it is possible to regress in peace processes, to leapfrog phases, or for a conflict to diminish without either victory or comprehensive settlement.

Violence as tacit negotiation

As a bargaining problem, peace processes in internal conflicts involve both tacit and explicit negotiation. Activities *at* the table and *beyond* the table are necessarily linked; the actual talk is only part of the interaction. Holl notes that classically in war "The intensity or duration of combat may be excessive [in civil wars] because belligerents value the shape of the settlement more than the costs of disagreement" (Holl 1993: 277). The extent to which parties in conflict can affect one another is a function of the level of their interdependency: the more dependent parties are upon one another, the greater their respective bargaining power (Bacharach and Lawler 1981). Brams writes that:

> Negotiations [are] exchanges between parties designed to reconcile their differences and produce a settlement. These exchanges may take different forms, from coolly discussing the terms of a contract

> to blatantly threatening an adversary with some untoward action – and by taking that action if the threat is ignored. Thus, negotiations include exchanges of deeds and words, because the former as much as the latter may signal the possible terms of a settlement.
>
> (Brams 1990: xiv)

The onset of formal (open) negotiations dramatically alters the incentive structure for violence. Parties that choose to negotiate have an explicit incentive to de-escalate violence against other parties that are at the table. Political violence and the threat of violence clearly affect the scope, pace, and agenda of talks during the tenuous phase of conflict de-escalation: violence is used as a "threat move" on the bargaining table. Moreover, ongoing political violence is often integrally linked to the process of negotiation.[2] What happens beyond the table – continuing military engagements, terrorist bombings, assassinations and hit squads, deadly riots, security force atrocities, and faction-fighting – is related to what happens at the table.[3] As Schelling argues:

> There seems to be a widespread belief that "negotiation" or "bargaining" is essentially a verbal activity, even a formal one, and that there is no negotiation unless the parties are in direct verbal contact, even face to face.... The actual talk, especially the formal talk, is only part of this, often a small part, and since talk is cheap it is often deeds and display that matter most. Wars, strikes, tantrums, and tailgating can be "bargaining" as much as talk can be.
>
> (Schelling 1966: 136)[4]

While not all instances of violence may be calculated and strategic – the pathology of fear drives much action – acts of organized violence are clearly strategic in their objectives.

Thus, a central question in any nascent or real peace process is under what conditions political violence serves to prompt parties in conflict into entering and sustaining formal talks on achieving a stable peace and under what conditions violence undermines moderation. Answering this question can help determine under what conditions conflicts are tractable, amenable to management through negotiation and international mediation, and when they are not. Key questions are whether elites purposefully manipulate and organize violence, whether it emanates from a more spontaneous, mass dissatisfaction with peace efforts, or whether mid-level elites (local party bosses, ground-level militia or military commanders, party-aligned warlords, etc.) who resist demobilization for conflict are primarily responsible for fanning the flames.

A critical issue is whether elites can deliver their organizations and the constituencies upon which they depend, and what it means for elites to demobilize their combatants and communities after so many years of mobilization for conflict. That is, it is easier to understand how elites can mobilize organizations and constituencies *for* violence than to understand how they can demobilize them when the moment for peace arrives. These are the principal questions.

- Under what conditions does crisis-inducing political violence prompt disputants to retract from talks, and under what conditions does it prompt disputants to continue talking as the way to stem the underlying causes of violence?
- What actions can third-party mediators take to turn crisis-inducing events into potential stimuli for quicker or continued progress in talks, as opposed to the derailment of the peace process?

I argue that the most important variable is the expected culpability of mid-level elites in fomenting political violence to affect the negotiations, as well as the relevant strengths of moderates versus hard-liners *within* each group, faction, or party.[5] Intra-group and intra-organizational differences – along a hard line–moderate continuum – deserve greater analytical priority in understanding the propensity toward violence during negotiations than inter-group and even inter-organizational animosity. A vignette from Kosovo, where the context was efforts by the UN Special Representative of the Secretary-General Bernard Kouchner to convince the Kosovar independence leader to return to the capital Pristina from exile, illustrates the point; the story is told by Jack Covey, former deputy to Kouchner:

> It took months to understand what Rugova's fears were. Only later did UNMIK [United Nations Interim Administration in Kosovo] learn that shortly after the NATO bombing campaign ended, five of Rugova's bodyguards had been apprehended and tortured by Kosovo Liberation Army (KLA) operatives under the command of Daut Haradinaj. One had escaped, but the other four had been executed. As it turned out, averting a civil war between those rival ethnic Albanian factions would be one of UNMIK's dominant preoccupations.
>
> (Covey 2004: 99)

Violence can hinder or spur progress toward peace in negotiation processes. Höglund has shown convincingly that

> high-profile incidents of violence can have a powerful impact on the dynamics of a negotiation process, since they affect two important aspects that decision makers take into consideration when deciding about the fate of the peace negotiations: the uncertainties of the consequences of a peace agreement as well as the fears of continued armed conflict.
>
> (Höglund 2004: 3–4).

Conceptualizing a "peace process"

Barring complete victory or defeat, peace processes in contemporary internal conflicts entail the de-escalation of violence through a series of phases or stages of bargaining or negotiation, which can be overlapping and mutually reinforcing.[6] This essentially chronological approach to bargaining serves as a descriptive tool for any specific peace process and as a diagnostic tool for its analysis. (The phases approach may equally serve a prescriptive purpose in situations where a peace process is perceived as possible by conflict resolvers, but has not yet begun.) As a process model, the phases approach describes the step-by-step transformation of a situation of violent conflict into more regularized peaceful relations, capturing the common issues and dynamics at various stages of the negotiation process that occur across a wide variety of cases. It can also help specify under what conditions parties progress from one step to the next, or fail to do so by sustaining a stalemate or by terminating the bargaining relationship.

Critical in any process model of conflict termination is the actual sequencing of events that lead to a negotiated settlement, which may contain important implications for the outcome. Does a cease-fire occur before substantive talks on the underlying dispute, or do parties discuss the core issues in the absence of an armistice? Is a military victory more likely to lead to a secessionist outcome than a negotiated settlement? A robust analytical framework should in fact be able to accommodate various sequences of conflict termination, and it should help illuminate how and why some peace processes are sequenced in a certain way in one instance and differently in another, and how and why various outcomes occur.

Moreover, such a process model should lengthen the understanding of what is meant by a peace process by looking back at the origins of the conflict and the pattern of escalation. Even the question of the "onset" of talks deserves a broadened time horizon, looking into the process of prenegotiation through which parties informally consult before taking the risks of going public in open, formal talks.[7] Equally, the framework should account for the latter stages of bargaining, well after the ink is dry on a formal settlement and into the peacebuilding phase to include the critical issues of sustainability of negotiated settlements (although this phase is beyond the principal scope of this book). If a negotiated settlement is not durable, is it a settlement after all?

Progress, not "success"

Conceiving of peace process in terms of phases or stages can also help capture the ebb and flow of the negotiation process and allow for comparison of different critical events and issues across cases. The essential premise of a phases approach is that during the course of negotiations, parties move incrementally – they make *progress* – toward a settlement, staking positions, making concessions, linking issues, formulating agreements, and structuring the implementation process.[8] The settlement, which culminates but does not end the bargaining process, represents the convergence point of the parties' positions. In protracted, violent conflicts it is no surprise that single, comprehensive agreements are not possible.

Parties in violent conflicts need sustained and detailed negotiation processes to work through the various stages of reconciling their differences in order to feel that the outcome of talks – inevitably less than their first preference outcomes – is fair, the best possible solution from their vantage point, and sufficiently strong to protect their vital interests. Finally, a sequential process of give and take can, over time, allow parties to discover a just outcome to their disputes that may not have been evident from the outset of talks. Table 2.1 offers some of the principal conceptual frameworks used to dissect and describe peace processes.

Progress in de-escalating conflicts is evident when parties move through the various phases of a negotiating process. The movement from one stage to another marks a turning point in relations, either toward greater cooperation or, equally plausible, toward confrontation and escalation (Druckman 1986, 2001). When parties transform their relationship from one characterized by a zero-sum perception of the conflict – where one side's gain is another's loss – to a positive-sum perception where mutual gains are possible, they progress across thresholds or transition points that link phases of the negotiation process. That is, the phases of peace processes are linked by identifiable events or turning points which indicate the movement between phases. Because not all peace processes yield peace, it is clear that such turning points can be in the direction toward violence as well as away from it. Licklider writes that

> rather than a single pattern whereby civil violence is ended, it seems more useful to conceive of the termination of civil violence as a set of

Table 2.1 Negotiation in peace processes: who and how

Participants

- Extremists versus moderates
- Within-group dynamics
- Cross-party coalitions
- Bargaining power: symmetry and asymmetry

Tracks

- Secret versus participatory (the latter as a "public" peace process)
- Track-two or "multi-track" diplomacy
- Summits
- Roundtables
- Sub-group
- Venues: neutrality and symbolism
- Decision rules

> processes at which there are critical choice points.... Selection at these points form alternative strategies of conflict termination
> (Licklider 1993: 18).

The concept of turning points or, in Licklider's terms "critical choice points," is essential to the framework presented here. At each discrete threshold in a peace process, disputants face fundamental choices: they can terminate the bargaining relationship, allow for a prolonged impasse to develop, or make the concessions and moves that allow the process to progress to the next phase of resolution.[9] At any given turning point in a peace process, both greater conflict and enhanced cooperation are possible options – the conflict de-escalates only if two or more parties view enhanced cooperation as a better proposition than conflict. The discrete choice or turning points in a conflict situation are key events in a negotiating process that precipitate and indicate movement to the next stage. Invariably, they significantly influence the scope, pace, or agenda of talks. In the case studies in this book, it is shown that turning points are marked by crises that are often precipitated by escalating political violence.

Turning points can be *facilitating events* (those that spur progress) or *interferences* (those that inhibit progress by perpetuating impasse or creating crises). To illustrate, parties in dispute often rely on high-level summitry as a means of breaking an impasse or furthering progress in talks. Summits between or among pre-eminent leaders (often with a mediator present) can result in breakthroughs, facilitating progress in talks and moving them to a subsequent phase, or they can fail to reach accord, resulting in impasse or even setbacks along the way. In both cases, they are critical turning points that define the subsequent phase of the negotiation process. When summits succeed (as have high-level meetings between the president of Pakistan and the prime minister of India over Kashmir; see Chapter 8) they are heralded, yet when they fail (as Sri Lanka talks in Geneva have done; see Chapter 7), there is a palpable sense of setback.

The relationship between turning points and crises is especially important. Crises are events that create such unacceptability with the status quo that they force the disputants to make choices about how to react: crises can either be events exogenous to the peace process (such as a change in the regional environment or in the international system), or internal to it (such as a spasm of violence).[10] It is widely appreciated that crises are critical events in a negotiating process because they often force decisions on parties to either escalate the conflict, cooperate further, or simply to sustain the negotiation process through the storm.

Bargaining with bullets: violence as a beyond-the-table tactic

Because this book is especially concerned with a specific type of crisis in the course of a peace process – instances of political violence – it is important to more fully elaborate on its use as a beyond-the-table tactic. Violence, it is argued, is a tacit bargaining tool used not only by spoilers, but by parties to the negotiation as well. Violence is the main type of punitive tactic, or sanction, in a bargaining relationship in internal conflicts.[11] Equally important to analyze are threats to employ violence and related tactics such as a form of bluff in negotiation.[12] As a punitive tactic, violence is often fomented in response to the inherent incentive structure of the bargaining processes. Darby offers a typology of various types of spoilers, drawing on the work of Stedman, Zartman, and Höglund, and his own research that is useful to the analysis; he describes "dealers" who are prepared to negotiate, "zealots" who fight to the bitter end, "opportunists" whose use of violence is instrumental to other ends (e.g. economic capture), and "mavericks," who perpetrate violence for some personal gain (Darby 2001, 2006b: 146). This typology relates well to Stedman's original conception of spoilers as consisting of three types: total, limited, and greedy (Stedman 1997).

Spoiler violence that is total – derived from pathology of personality or ideological fervor – is in some way instrumentally perpetrated. Richmond observes that spoiler violence is best evaluated in terms of the "devious objectives" of the parties, or the "views, perspectives, and objectives of the parties" vis-à-vis the peace process; such perspectives and views often involve the "continuation of the dispute while avoiding both the costs and concessions of warfare" (Richmond 2006: 72). Although the framework presented here does not assert that all violence is "rational," I claim that parties to, and opponents of, ongoing peace processes regularly and often pursue violence as an aspect of tacit bargaining.[13] Some violence, particularly in ethnic conflict situations, *is* pathological (Rothchild and Groth 1995) and defies explanation in terms of rational-behavior concepts of strategies or incentives. However, in many contemporary conflicts violence is clearly used to further a specific objective related to the pace, structure, agenda, or outcome of a negotiation process. Waterman writes that:

> Occasional, small-scale violence may be accidental, but large-scale and organized violence is a matter of choice.... It is a strategic or even tactical option deliberately taken in the context of a specific set of incentives, a product of cost–benefit analysis.
>
> (Waterman 1993: 299)

While current approaches to negotiations in internal conflicts focus primarily on the *explicit* aspects of the bargaining relationship, this framework seeks to broaden the analysis to include a range of *tacit* behaviors, including violence, that are different sides of the same coin. Seeking to influence an adversary at the table, or on the streets, are both parts of bargaining; the principal difference is the method of communication. Upsurges in violence, either by those engaged in and committed to the negotiation process or by rejectionist parties, are invariably critical turning points in a peace process. Moreover, these crises often occur just prior to, during, or just after other critical turning points that mark the movement of negotiations across phases of the negotiation process. By forcing parties to make critical strategic choices about whether to continue with or abandon a negotiation process, upsurges in violence can often precipitate turning points. For parties engaged in a negotiation, crises may be functional if they reinforce the essential commitment to a negotiated outcome.

Crises are also important for mediators, who may manipulate the parties' perceptions of the situation and their reaction to turn them from moments of peril to opportunities for breakthrough. One of the most important arguments in the literature on negotiation process, which will be tested in this study, is that those factors leading to violence, or tending away from violence, have their interaction *during* phases rather than exactly at the moments of transition. The turning points that signal progress toward a settlement have their antecedents in the previous phase (Druckman 1986).

The phases approach is adopted for this framework of analysis because it highlights a central fact: as a peace process moves from initial escalation through various stages to a settlement and eventually its implementation, the incentive structure for violence by parties engaged in the negotiation and rejectionists changes dramatically. As the peace process unfolds, new information and opportunities arise for parties to influence the structure and direction of the talks and, consequentially, their outcome. The changing incentive structure of the conflict is more fully highlighted in Chapter 3, where the general characteristics of the various phases are outlined and propositions regarding the incentives and disincentives for violence for different types of parties to a conflict are posited. The essential point is that conceiving of a peace process as a series of phases linked by turning points allows for a fruitful analysis of the strategic choices by parties about when to fight, when to talk, when to threaten and bluff, what type of arguments to make to justify their actions, when to concede, and, ultimately, when to settle.[14]

International peacemaking: strategy and power

This framework purposefully adopts an approach to peace processes that suggests conflicts and their termination are the consequences of well-considered strategies by parties. Much like the deterrence relationship between the superpowers during the Cold War, protagonists to wars today formulate strategies to influence the behavior of their adversaries based on clear expectations of the counter-strategy the opponent will employ. In essence, they adopt strategies to advance their aims, and the choice to talk or to fight is one such decision.

Strategic choices by parties on whether to talk or whether to fight, whether to engage the mediator or to pursue an over-the-shoulder strategy or a beyond-the-table tactic – and indeed whether a party might choose both actions simultaneously – are in part a response to the *overall* incentive structure generated by relationships at multiple levels. At different stages of a peace process, either parties to, or opponents of (rejectionists), a peace process may systematically foment violence, or threaten it, as a means of achieving their objectives, depending on their expectations of how violence may serve their aims in various arenas. Any understanding of the violence–negotiation nexus in contemporary internal conflicts must systematically account for decisions taken at these multiple levels of interaction.

Contributions of strategic choice

Before describing the various phases of a peace process in detail, it is important to describe the structure of relationships among parties in conflict and with mediators. Theories of strategic interaction, derived from game theory, offer a useful tool for analyzing the relationships among parties in contemporary internal conflicts. Game theory contributes to the development of a robust framework of analysis of the problems and prospects for international peace in two important respects.[15] First, game-theoretic approaches are useful in analyzing the strategies of conflict and negotiation employed by parties: the decisions disputants make as they pursue the maximization of their expected utilities, for example whether they view the payoff matrix, or outcome possibilities, of the bargaining problem as zero-sum or positive-sum.[16]

Second, game theory can help identify the generic pathways for the discovery of integrative solutions (identification of dovetailing or shared interests by disputants) in the course of the bargaining process. For example, game theory contributes to mediation strategies through the finding that one can encourage moderation and deter "defection" in bargaining relationships by not allowing a player to gain from a defection strategy, even if it imposes additional costs to cooperators to prevent a defector's gain. The framework of analysis for this study borrows the concept of "nested games" to analyze the relationships among parties (including mediators) and the structure of decision-making as the course of a peace process unfolds.[17] The framework only borrows concepts because the purpose is not to develop a fully integrated game-theoretic model, but only to use deductively derived findings for the purpose of identifying general principles that can be evaluated in the case studies that follow. Such an approach allows the abstract and sometimes incomprehensible (except to the experts) conclusions of game theory to be put to use in developing more coherent theories subject to empirical validation (Ostrom 1991).

Specifically, the framework presented here follows Putnam's (1988) analysis of multilateral negotiations in the international arena (specifically the Bonn summit conference of 1978 on G-7 economic cooperation) as a "two-level game." Putnam developed the approach to describe the reciprocal influences of domestic politics on bargaining in the international arena, and vice versa. Putnam shows how negotiators play two games simultaneously: one with their bargaining partners in the international arena, and a domestic game to build and sustain supportive coalitions for the positions taken in the larger game.

Putnam's analysis, which he developed to demonstrate the linkages between domestic policy and international relations in trade negotiation, can be extended to the study of the bargaining relationships in contemporary peace processes by highlighting the important linkages between within-group bargaining and between-group relations, and vice versa. Putnam's finding that "the unusual complexity of this two-level game is that moves that are rational for a player at one board ... may be impolitic for that player at the other board" (Putnam 1988: 434) contains enormous implications for the study of peace processes in contemporary internal conflicts by focusing the analysis on the decision-making structure of critical elites and the relationships between these elites and their organizations and constituencies (often ethnic groups) upon which they rely for support. As is argued below, the role of external mediators adds further complexity to the relationships, extending a two-level model into a more complex, multiple-level approach.

Several of Putnam's findings can be directly applied to the structure of relationships and decision-making in contemporary peace processes.

- Agreements between negotiators are possible only after negotiators have forged sustainable domestic coalitions.
- Parties may voluntarily defect, or terminate the bargaining relationship, or involuntarily defect (meaning that negotiators may make agreements that can't be delivered upon, or failed ratification).
- The possibility of package deals or "synergistic linkages" opens up myriad opportunities for negotiators to affect what happens in various arenas.
- Inter-party negotiators are involved both in a competitive relationship and in a cooperative relationship (in defending the decision to and outcomes of negotiation), thus they may play "over the shoulder" of their respective negotiating partners, seeking to affect the other sides' domestic considerations; negotiators' relationships are both *collusive* and *competitive*.
- The outcomes of bargaining are contingent on both the *intra-party* and *inter-party* dynamics: neither a purely intra-party nor a purely inter-party analysis can account for the nature and terms of the settlement.[18]

The focus on internal bargaining is critical to the framework for analysis presented here. There are considerable differences among analysts of bargaining and negotiation as to whether internal cohesion within a party or within a group in conflict (such as an ethnic group) is more likely to lead to between-group accommodation than deep factional differences that may allow moderates to form coalitions along conflict lines. The argument for cohesion is that well-integrated parties with a clear line of decision-making responsibility and deference to a single leadership can "deliver" at the table. The argument against cohesion is that the absence of within-group splits militates against the forging of coalitions across lines of conflict; certainly in Burundi (see Chapter 6), a split among the dominant Hutu group facilitated the forging of cross-group coalitions. Cohesive groups take hard lines, this argument suggests, portending the problem of irreconcilable differences. In any event, as Denardo (1985: 263) writes: "A coherent explanation of a radical movement's political activity requires a detailed appraisal of both its internal and external environment"; the same can be said of governments.

Peacemaking as a multiple-level game

This multilayered approach to decision-making holds great promise for explaining the possibility of accommodation through the formation of coalitions both within and across conflict lines that affect progress in inter-party negotiations (such as a coalition of moderates, for example). In addition, it can fruitfully describe the phenomenon of "perverse" alliances or coalitions: for example, rejectionist parties that seek the defeat or even elimination of each other's group find themselves on the same side of the fence as they implicitly coalesce to reject accommodation by their more moderate brethren; extremists way well forge a "perverse coalition" of rejectionists. Simply stated, seeing peace processes as multilevel interactions accounts for the inevitable insider and "over-the-shoulder" behavior of those engaged in a peace process as they seek to simultaneously influence not just their adversaries, their own organization and mass support base, *and* those of their opponents.

Moreover, because international mediators are often multivocal and incoherent, as described below, the complexity of interaction can only be explained through an appreciation of the multiple-level dynamics at play. Mediators enter the peace process not just as single-entity conciliators, but they also bring their own interests and domestic considerations to the dispute. Touval and Zartman write that "Mediators are no less motivated by self-interest than by humanitarian impulses … the mediator is a player in the plot of relations surrounding a conflict, and has some interest in the outcome (else it would not mediate)" (Touval and Zartman 1989: 8). Mediators, through inducements (offering benefits or imposing costs, or carrots and sticks), can affect the choices made in both the intra-party and inter-party arenas; within parties, the approach is often to bolster moderates and isolate extremists. In effect, they, too, bargain within disputing parties, inducing them to work toward a settlement.[19] While international mediators are ostensibly neutral (Gibson *et al.* 1996), in reality such neutrality is usually elusive.

Likewise, the notion of a single, authoritative mediator is useful in some settings (such as domestic or legal disputes), but "the mediator" concept does not translate well to international contexts in terms of a unitary actor as well. In most settings, there are many mediators and often a coalition of mediators that works together to bring parties in conflict to a settlement. Consider, for example, the five-member Contact Group approach to mediation in the Bosnian conflict, or the Quartet in the Middle East. The UN, regional organizations, great or regional powers, NGOs, and even eminent individuals have all been involved in mediation in different conflict settings. The simple point is that just like inter- and intra-party negotiations are a matter of coalition-building, so too mediators in contemporary conflicts are coalitions of mediators. This additional complexity argues further for a nested games approach in which the decisions of mediators – sometimes acting in concert, other times acting at cross-purposes – can be accounted for.

The multiplication of mediators is less a matter of choice and more a fact of life. In virtually every conflict setting, the UN and its various suborganizations, regional organizations, key states, regional leaders, humanitarian NGOs, and monitors such as human rights organizations are all engaged; sometimes they act more or less in concert, but at other times they may act at cross-purposes. Sometimes they are all engaged together, and sometimes sequentially. Multiparty mediation refers to simultaneous, sequential (passing the baton), and uncoordinated or composite mediation efforts (Crocker *et al.* 1999: 666). Too many mediators using too many scripts can make matters worse and when mediators fail to coordinate well it can prolong violence. As Crocker *et al.* observe:

> In multiparty mediation, a certain degree of policy convergence is usually desirable, especially when mediation is being undertaken by a coalition or on behalf of a composite body such as the United Nations or OSCE [Organization for Security and Cooperation in Europe]. When broader policy objectives diverge, the result is likely to be confusion and a lack of coordination in negotiating efforts.
>
> (Crocker *et al.* 1999: 687)

One of the most interesting, and challenging, aspects of the new mediation pattern is the problem of coordination, maximization and pooling of leverage, and consensus on the basic purposes and aims. In addition to the inherent problems posed by many cooks in the intervention kitchen – and the possibility that wily protagonists in conflict settings can play one party off against the other (as the Sudanese have deftly done) – there are certain opportunities created as well. As Ould-Abdallah demonstrates in his book *Burundi on the Brink, 1993–1995: A UN Special Envoy Reflects on Preventive*

Diplomacy (2000), the inherently limited leverage available to a UN special envoy can augment leverage through close coordination with local, diplomatic, and NGO communities.

That is, multiparty coalitions allow mediators to "borrow leverage" (or pool resources) from one another to expand the credibility and effectiveness of international action, creating a wider array of opportunities for skillfully blending incentives and sanctions to induce the parties in conflict to de-escalate the conflict. Probably the most effective approach of a Contact Group is to coordinate diplomatic communication and messages and to send clear signals of the international community's expectations for specific action as any peace process unfolds (see Chapter 8).

Multiparty mediation: effective elements

Coordination and legitimacy by the Special Representative of the Secretary-General

Involvement in and coordination of the mediation effort by the UN Special Representative of the Secretary-General (SRSG) lends a necessary credibility and coherence to the initiative.[20] The most important relationship is between the SRSG and the authoritative representatives of key states who can wield the most leverage vis-à-vis the parties. This may include states within the mediation coalition (or Contact Group), but may also involve key patron states for parties to the conflict. Clear leadership may also signal to the parties that a Contact Group remains united and efforts to divide the group will be futile (this was not the case in the Contact Group that proved unable to successfully mediate an end to the Bosnian civil war.) Also, SRSG leadership may allow for the comparative advantages of each member of the Contact Group to be utilized most effectively; SRSG coordinators proved critical to successful mediation in the Mozambique (Aldo Ajello) and Salvadoran (Alvaro de Soto) peace processes.

Close coordination with regional organizations

Similarly, the practice of double-hatting UN and regional organization SRSGs has proven valuable in many conflicts, such as Haiti. As the African Union Peace and Security Council takes shape, the diplomatic, observation, and monitoring capacities of the organization should be evaluated for the role they could play in ending civil wars.

Regular forums for information sharing

The SRSG or other "lead actor" coordinating the mediation coalition should create a regular forum for interaction with official actors (international organizations and states) and a regular forum for interaction with non-state actors (donors, international and local NGOs). The purpose of such forums is primarily for information gathering and sharing, and for coordination of implementation; they have also proven critical in Afghanistan, Burundi, Sierra Leone, and Somalia as mechanisms for coordinating diplomatic, observer, or military peacekeeping initiatives with the efforts of humanitarian relief organizations (particularly the UN High Commissioner for Refugees and international NGOs). Likewise, the mechanism of a "group of friends" of the peace process has also proven effective to coordinate aid and to orchestrate the use of leverage.[21]

A powerful state to play "heavy"

One state, usually an especially interested regional state or a global power with significant influence in the region, should sustain the focus and provide the communications, diplomatic consistency, intelligence, and finance to make the mediation effort effective. This lead-state actor should also be willing to provide strongly structured incentives and sanctions against the parties, particularly states (e.g. leveraging the government). Such a state may also eventually be needed to serve as a guarantor of the accord or as a lead state in an international stabilization force (e.g. the United States in conjunction with NATO in Bosnia). Crocker has described the role of this lead state as the one who must bear "laserlike strategic focus and intensity" required of a core mediator (Crocker 1999: 241).

Staying power

Contact Group-type mediation succeeds best when the parties are able to signal to the parties that they remain ready to engage as long as necessary to see the process through. Weaker parties, especially, may fear that the international community has a short attention span and that once they have committed to a settlement they may be especially vulnerable to defection by the other side as soon as a Contact Group or UN peacekeeping force has folded its tent and departed. Contact Group approaches seem especially well suited to changing the underlying regional subsystems that allow internal conflicts to be sustained. The multiparty mediation approach can lead to major redefinition of hostile relations among states in a region.[22]

Needed: mediators with power

International leverage for ending civil wars derives from the parties' own dependence on an exit to a costly struggle together with the mediators' ability to creatively develop a formula for settlement. Once the international community has reached consensus on a formula for conflict management, it must be prepared to craft a package of incentives and sanctions to induce the parties to accept the settlement plan. In some cases, the international community must be prepared to deploy military force (the ultimate form of leverage) to enforce the terms of settlement it deems suitable to ending the war. In these exceptional cases, a "coalition of the willing" may be called upon to threaten and eventually deploy military force to induce the parties to settle – in effect, as NATO did in Bosnia in August 1995, to "bomb the parties to the table."[23]

Multiparty mediation through a Contact Group mechanism faces special challenges of coordination and resolve: because sufficient leverage must be found through collective action, it may prove more challenging to muster consensus on the tough measures that need to be taken and the sharing of financial and troop-commitment burdens. In situations like Sierra Leone, with its gruesome atrocities highlighted on the world stage, key states did not decide that a strong peace enforcement operation was necessary until after the ragtag insurgents embarrassingly held hostage some 400 UN peacekeepers in May 2000. Force is the most extreme form of leverage, and is used only in concert with a broad range of both non-coercive and coercive measures (George 1993, 1994).

Mediator leverage: non-coercive and coercive measures[24]

Non-coercive (rewards)

- *Purchase.* The use of side-payments (material or symbolic) directly to the parties in conflict to induce them to modify their demands. Examples include the use of significant aid packages to states (such as Cyprus) in the post-conflict environment, or direct promises of financial and material rewards. Perhaps the most dramatic example of the latter is the Italian payments to the Mozambique National Resistance, RENAMO, and especially to leader Alfonso Dhlakama to sign a ceasefire and eventually to forego violence during the election.[25]
- *Insurance.* Guaranteeing non-defection by the other parties (if the recipient grants concessions), mediators can induce weaker parties to accept vulnerabilities in the post-accord environment. The British, for example, used insurance approaches during the Lancaster House negotiations to induce the white minority regime of Ian Smith to accept majority rule; insurance proved sufficient to prevent initial war recurrence, but over time the Mugabe regime defected on the spirit (but not legal terms) of the agreements to protect the property of many white Zimbabweans. Insurance may include promises of the deployment of a UN peacekeeping force – although parties in today's conflicts realize that Chapter VI peacekeeping operations do not usually provide enduring guarantees against defection by their opponents.[26]
- *Legitimation (conferring legitimacy).* Recognition and validation of a group or faction's cause is a source of leverage in the mediator's toolbox

that is often underappreciated. This may also involve affirmation that a group – for example an ethnic political party – serves as the valid representative of those it purports to represent. When, for example, the UN General Assembly adopted a resolution in 1975 declaring the African National Congress to be the authentic representative of South Africa's disenfranchised majority, it augmented domestic political power with international status. At times, international mediators have used contingent recognition to leverage parties into peace, such as in 1992 when the United States suggested it would recognize the government of Angola if UNITA's Jonas Savimbi did not participate in the elections in good faith.

Coercive (threat or punishment)

- *Pressures.* Diplomatic pressures are routine moves and take any number of forms, including persuasion, mass media appeals, withdrawing recognition, or public shaming (e.g. in human rights reports). For pressure to leverage parties into peace agreements, one of the strongest tools is the threat to withdraw or disengage once the parties have become dependent on the international community. In negotiations over a settlement in Sudan in 2003/2004, the United States used multiple pressures against the Khartoum regime. These included signaling Sudan that it would be the next target of the war on terrorism and strong congressional action that imposed sanctions if the regime did not negotiate with the insurgent Sudanese People's Liberation Movement (SPLM).[27]
- *Sanctions.* Punitive measures imposed to reflect explicit disapproval of a particular regime or movement imposed as a way to induce change in policy or behavior by the target. Sanctions regimes have been used in any number of cases, including Liberia, but the purpose is usually related to a specific harmful action (e.g. weapons proliferation, human rights abuses) and not directly tied to the onset of peace talks. An exception is the Comprehensive Anti-Apartheid Act of 1986 which explicitly called on the South African regime to negotiate, and included escalating sanctions if it did not and easing of sanctions if good-faith talks began. With the increasing use of sanctions by the international community in peace-process contexts – including indictment before the International Criminal Court (ICC) – the debate on sanctions has intensified, including disagreement about their appropriateness as an intermediate step between pressure and force, their effectiveness, unintended consequences, and the conditions under which they should be imposed, withdrawn, or lifted (or, in the case of ICC indictments, simply not pursued). I argue that these measures – including ICC engagement, smart sanctions, and lists of designated terrorist organizations, are promising new instruments that if evenly

applied in a measured fashion introduce forms of incentives for parties to, first, behave according to the international humanitarian law during war and, second, to negotiate an end to conflict as a way to escape the punitive force of international law (as has been the case in Uganda following the indictment of Lord's Resistance Army (LRA) top-five leaders; moreover, the indictments have created intra-party splits in the LRA, which may lead to separation of hard-liners and moderates in peace negotiations).

- *Military force.* The ultimate coercive incentive. With the advent of peace enforcement in the UN's civil war lexicon beginning with Boutros Boutros-Ghali's 1992 *Agenda for Peace*,[28] military force has been systematically employed as a means of multilateral intervention to coerce the parties into a cease-fire and to provide security for a broader peace process. Today, coercive intervention under Chapter VII of the Charter seems routine: starting with Somalia, and most recently in East Timor (now Timor-Leste) and Sierra Leone, the Security Council has repeatedly authorized member state "coalitions of the willing" to undertake peace enforcement in civil wars.

The typology of leverage presented here is not exhaustive, and it does not address what is perhaps the most difficult, case-by-case policy challenge in international mediation of civil wars: how to contextually mix or blend the incentives and sanctions to move the parties toward peace. This is the subject of the conclusion (Chapter 9).

3 Peace through negotiation

Escaping untold sorrow

A phases approach to conflict escalation and de-escalation assumes only that the emergence of violent conflict and its eventual termination have a beginning and, eventually, an end. But there is no deterministic teleology implied. Certainly not all conflicts work their way through the various phases outlined here to arrive at a sustainable negotiated settlement; no case will fully comply with such a neat pattern of de-escalation. Indeed, the data presented in Chapter 1 suggest that historically only a small minority of internal conflicts once-and-for-all terminate in negotiated settlements. At any given phase of the conflict, it is equally possible that parties will choose an "exit" strategy of their own, either withdrawing from the conflict altogether, going back to violent conflict and escalation, or simply resuming a stalemate that may be more comfortable than the inherent uncertainty of further talks.

There should be no assumption that the phases of negotiation are wholly discrete: that the issues that arise in the substantive formal negotiation phase, for example, are not the subject of hot dispute during prenegotiation; or, for example, that escalation to a mutually hurting stalemate must last a decade rather than a few days. I argue, however, that as peace processes progress through the various stages presented here, the incentives and disincentives for violence change dramatically for various parties to a conflict; when violence occurs, it creates crisis and imposes choices on the disputants and mediators alike. The onset of talks, like any transition process, opens up a host of new uncertainties for political actors who are unsure how the negotiations will affect their vital interests and their objectives. The uncertainties and vicissitudes of a peace process fundamentally change the cost–benefit calculus of those at the table as well as those opposed to negotiation. This uncertainty explains why, in some instances, levels of political violence can actually *increase* after the onset of talks among the principal disputants in an internal conflict. This insight provides a gateway into a framework for analysis for peace processes that sees the unfolding of events as a complicated bargaining process.

From escalation to stalemate

When governments are unable to defeat challengers, and challengers are unable to decisively topple governments, a mutually hurting stalemate develops. Neither party can ultimately prevail through force nor force the opponent to capitulate. In Zartman's terms, a mutually hurting stalemate exists "where the countervailing power of each side, though insufficient to make the other side lose, prevents it from winning" (Zartman 1993: 24). Indeed, in the vast majority of contemporary internal conflicts, parties are not able to muster the material resources, political will, and international support to decisively defeat an opponent. And, as mentioned in Chapter 1, in ethnic conflicts decisive defeat of an adversary is clouded with ambiguity, for while a state may defeat an insurgency force, it cannot realistically expect to eradicate an entire ethnic group. The turning point that marks the end of a conflict's escalation is when the intensity of violence reaches a plateau in which the conflict does not ebb, but neither does it continue to intensify.

The "comfort" of war

Stalemates in internal conflicts can indeed be a comfortable plateau for groups in conflict, having escalated their strife to a point where although they are unable to defeat an adversary, they too will not be defeated. Wagner (1993: 260) identifies two reasons why protracted stalemate may be a better choice for disputants than the inherently risky strategy of seeking to escape a stalemate through entering negotiation. Both reasons are related to the parties' *expectations* about the future course of the conflict. First, parties may expect the military balance to turn soon in their favor and maybe then they can decisively defeat an opponent (see also Wagner 2000). Alternatively, they may expect that even though a negotiated settlement may be inevitable at some point in the future, they have the military upper hand and with prolonged fighting the adversary may settle for less than what is presently demanded. When any side in a conflict harbors such expectations, the stalemate is perpetuated.

Indeed, a fluctuating stalemate in which one party or another appears ascendant is a polarizing condition, perpetuating conflict and not leading to avenues for resolution. As time drags on, more resources are poured into defeat of the opponent, the rhetoric of war is taken to new heights, and the conflict is gradually accepted as a necessary fact of life. Governments begin to view internal conflicts as a fixed cost, and the "true belief" motivation of insurgents limits options for de-escalation. The costs of stalemate are seen as fixed investments, and no benefits could accrue from accommodation – in part based on the belief that the adversary is not ready to accommodate. Kalyvas' analysis of civil wars historically demonstrates that once polarization occurs and violent interactions begin, there is a certain self-sustaining quality that emerges as an endogenous character of mutual victimization, and internal logic for the perpetuation of violence evolves (Kalyvas 2003).

In most situations, stalemate leads to less conciliatory political leaders and becomes a self-reinforcing trap from which the parties are unable to escape. Weak leaders of states in conflict have clear reasons to protect the war cause in order to rally the public and protect their own incumbencies and justify the loss of life and military campaigns. Insurgent leaders use government violence to legitimize organized resistance and to mobilize disadvantaged groups in the cause. The incentive structure for each leads to the management and perhaps manipulation of the stalemate, but certainly not its resolution.

The arrival at a "mutually hurting" stalemate suggests that parties have reached the point where further escalation is self-defeating, and indeed further pursuit of the conflict imposes greater costs than benefits. In theory, all parties could potentially gain from cooperation but (similar to the prisoners' dilemma game) their immediate incentives mitigate against such cooperation. Moreover, the role of external parties in contemporary internal conflicts often reinforces conditions of stalemate, by providing cross-border resources to parties (such as support by neighboring regimes of insurgents), by enhancing their legitimacy, or by simply participating in the open international arms market. The Liberia imbroglio (Chapter 5) has been a case in point.

Even would-be conciliators in conflict situations can unintentionally perpetuate stalemates; in many contemporary conflicts, the international community encourages parties engaged in a military confrontation to adopt confidence- and security-building measures (CBMs) to help contain escalation, such as military-to-military hotlines or early warning systems of military action, but in doing so provide incentives for parties to continue their antagonistic relationship with the knowledge that the opponent is unlikely to decisively escalate the conflict. For example, the deployment of peacekeeping troops in Cyprus may well have prevented eventual resolution of that dispute; the use of CBMs in the Kashmir conflict is outlined in Chapter 8.

A constellation of expectations

As is evident from the foregoing analysis, the mutually hurting stalemate leaves little scope for the discovery of a mutually beneficial solution; the incentive structure of stalemate mitigates against the risky trade-offs and compromises that are necessary to move toward the onset of negotiation among bitter adversaries. The condition to turn a stalemate into a pathway for a negotiated settlement is a demanding one; as Wagner (1993: 235) writes, "A negotiated settlement … requires that all parties to the conflict prefer the terms of the settlement to the expected outcome both of further fighting *and* of further bargaining."

The characteristic of the mutually hurting stalemate that facilitates at least half of the above-stated condition (expected outcomes of further fighting) is the common perception among parties in conflict of a rough balance of power between (or among) them. An essential premise is that negotiations progress best under conditions of relative symmetry, in which the parties have the capacity of veto over each other's ultimate goals (Zartman and Rubin 2000a). A balance of power stems from not only the military capabilities of both sides, but also their legitimacy both within the state and internationally. Indeed, there are various "components" of power for parties in internal conflicts (Blalock 1989; Druckman and Green 1986). Bacharach and Lawler (1981: 41–79) offer an extended argument that identifies bargaining power as containing both objective and subjective components, and suggest that a balance of power emerges as a function of the tactics and ability of the parties to manipulate resources such as information. The greater the degree of interdependency among parties, the more likely the parties will reach parity in their bargaining power, opening the door for fruitful negotiations.

Thus, there is an important distinction between an actual military balance of power and the parties' *perceptions* of a relative symmetry of power (Zartman 2000). Indeed, in many internal conflicts different parties wield different types of power in their own spheres; the government may control the trappings of state, enjoy international recognition, and may control a much more capable military, but the insurgents control key territory and may possess the hearts and minds of critical publics such as minority groups. Parties in internal conflicts may control such different spheres of power, roughly equal in the balance. Moreover, states may have an existence and other interests independent of the conflict, with limited resources and interest to devote to decisively winning an armed struggle. On the other hand, insurgents may devote their all to the conflict; their very survival depends upon it. In sum, the government may enjoy an asymmetry of military power, whereas the insurgents may enjoy an asymmetry of commitment, or what George termed an "asymmetry of motivation" (George 1994). The cost–benefit calculations of further fighting may be markedly different for different parties depending on their level of devotion to the conflict (Zartman and Rubin 2000b).

Thus, *perceptions* of power parity are essential to the existence of a mutually hurting stalemate. For all sides simultaneously, an expectation must exist that future escalation of the conflict will not decisively defeat the opponent nor will further commitment of resources fundamentally affect the eventual outcome should a negotiated settlement be reached. Only when there are *convergent expectations* about the consequences of further fighting – that it really won't make a significant difference – does a mutually hurting stalemate ensue. Zartman writes that a mutually hurting stalemate

> is based on the notion that when the parties find themselves locked in a conflict from which they cannot escalate to victory and this deadlock

> is painful to them both (although not necessarily in equal degree or for the same reasons), they seek an alternative policy or "Way Out."
> (Zartman 2008: 22; see also Zartman 1985, 2000)

Prenegotiation

The mutually hurting stalemate is a necessary structural condition for the onset of a negotiation process in internal conflicts, but it is certainly not a sufficient one. In different internal conflicts, a mutually hurting stalemate may "objectively" exist with remarkably different levels of political violence. The condition is resistant to measurement in terms of actual levels of deaths in political violence as a proportion of a population, or by measuring the time in which disputants are engaged in a conflict without the real prospect of decisive escalation.[1] The question "When does a mutually hurting stalemate hurt *enough* to turn intransigence into opportunities for accommodation?" is a one measured only in terms of the perceptions of the parties. They must commonly share a sense of urgency to bring the stalemate to an end through decisive de-escalation.

When parties do realize the condition of a mutually hurting stalemate, and appreciate its implications for their own entrapment in a violent conflict, the dispute is argued to be "ripe" for the onset of exploratory talks among the parties, or prenegotiation.[2] The turning point from stalemate to ripeness begins with the emergence of a small core of moderates across conflict lines willing to engage in meaningful and potentially binding discussions about the onset of formal negotiations – or "talks about talks." Prenegotiation precedes formal negotiation among the parties precisely because it is exploratory talk, "feeling out" the position of the other side, assessing whether the other party is willing to engage in concession-making and reciprocity, and determining its capability to deliver at the bargaining table.[3]

Because they are exploratory, prenegotiation talks are often held in secret, and often include important but unofficial opinion-leaders in conflict settings who are close to, but not official representatives of, government or other parties in conflict – "track-two diplomacy."[4] Prenegotiation is entertained because of the low exit costs for disputants; if they fail, no face is lost because the talks were unofficial and exploratory, and indeed were really not talks at all. Prenegotiation is a learning experience. Stein (1989: 257) writes that "Without an analysis of the process of getting to the table, we cannot explain the shape of the table, who gets there and who doesn't, what is on the table, and equally important, what is kept off."

Ripeness: a matter of intuition or measurement?

Prenegotiation becomes possible when a conflict reaches a stage of ripeness. But when is a moment ripe, and to whom? The ripeness concept, much debated in the conflict management and negotiation literature, is defined as the moment when the perceptions of all parties converge on the belief that negotiation, reciprocal compromise (*requitement*), and the arrival at a mutually beneficial settlement will yield greater dividends than continued conflict. Ripe moments are generally considered as moments of convergent expectations by all parties. Zartman writes that:

> Whereas "ripeness" has generally been discussed as a symmetrical property preparatory to resolution, the characteristic asymmetry of internal conflict suggests that it be examined in terms of one side alone. Rather than looking for a ripe moment in the attributes of the conflict, a search for the ripe moment in the position of one side alone can give some clue as to how that party can act to bring the other to conciliation. If either side follows up a successful escalation with conciliatory terms, the conditions can be created for … a move to conciliation on the other.
>
> (Zartman 1993: 20)

The initial act of conciliation is a critical one. It is invariably a high-risk strategy, as the opposing party may seize upon a sign of conciliation as weakness and, rather than responding with a reciprocal act of conciliation, may "defect" or escalate in order to take advantage of the perception of weakness. Only when parties reciprocate one another's conciliatory moves, generating trust that further conciliation will generate a positive response, can there be movement away from confrontation to cooperation.[5]

Following Zartman, a ripe conflict has two dimensions. Most important is the intensity dimension, or vertical dimension, and its two components of deadlock and deadline. *Deadlock* refers to the existence of a mutually hurting stalemate under conditions of a perception of a rough balance of power: parties are unable to achieve their aims unilaterally, resolve the problem independently, or to score a unilateral military victory. *Deadline* refers to the perception of an impending worse outcome, or a new crisis or catastrophe, if action is not taken to alter the status quo. Second is the alternatives dimension, or horizontal dimension, of ripeness. Alternative "tracks" or policy options, except for negotiation, are closed; that is, parties have no better option than to engage the opponent(s) in face-to-face talks. The essence of a ripe conflict is that the major (i.e. the most powerful) parties in a conflict have strong incentives to avoid the status quo, and the alternative of further escalation of violence is blocked.

There are several conditions that lead to ripe moments. It is widely appreciated that a significant leadership change can induce ripeness, as new leaders fail to carry all of the "sunk costs" or depth of commitment of their predecessors. Leadership change through elections, succession, or even violent overthrows of conflict group leaders can lead to the ripe moment. In ethnic conflicts, profound splits in the community on issues of moderation and conciliation, versus "standing pat," can open avenues for new coalitions to emerge (Huntington 1981). In many situations, *splits* among the dominant community and its political elites are a precondition to conflict management through negotiation.

A second conflict condition that ripens a conflict is when the previously disadvantaged party is ascendant and the more advantaged party is descendent. That is, when the party with the militarily upper hand begins to slip and the underdog gains ground, the point at which the parties reach a relative parity is the moment when a conflict is ripe for prenegotiation. Such a moment may be fleeting and very brief, for there are powerful incentives for both parties not to enter negotiations: formerly more powerful parties may expect to regain their strength and strike a better bargain later, and ascendant parties hope to gain further power before negotiating even if they can't win outright in the long run. Identifying the exact equilibrium point of symmetrical power among disputants is at best a difficult enterprise.

The ebb and flow of violence is a critical factor in the creation of a ripe moment. Is a conflict ripe when the level of violence is expected to go higher, when it reaches an apex, or when it begins to decline? Are there possibilities for conflicts to be ripe "early," without a low threshold of violence (as in Macedonia in the clinching of the 2001 Lake Ohrid agreement), or "late" and even "very late," that is after very significant levels of violence? The mutually hurting stalemate notion implies that the moment is ripe when levels of political violence flatten out, or reach a plateau, but may sharply escalate if action to de-escalate is not taken.

The perceptual changes necessary to turn stalemate into ripeness can occur following a dramatic upsurge in violence, for example a planned or unplanned escalation, often some dramatic event such as a costly but indecisive battle or incident of mass terror. The crisis may have entailed significant mutual loss but did not move the conflict toward resolution. Moreover, parties may alter their perceptions about the costs of continued violent confrontation and the potential benefits of negotiation when they anticipate an impending crisis, which will also impose considerable costs without tangible gain. Much depends on the parties' *expectations* of future violence, and the costs (and possible benefits) that such expectations will yield. As the case studies in this book vividly illustrate, a military stalemate must be accompanied by the ability to imagine a secure exit through negotiation in order for a condition of ripeness to exist; in this way, Zartman's original formulation of the concept is sustained.

Can mediators "induce" ripeness?

The entry and behavior of mediators is critical in turning potentially ripe moments into unambiguously ripe moments. While some mediators, particularly international organizations such as the United Nations (UN), are permanently "on call" in a conflict, other mediators (such as states) must carefully time their entry and actions to help ripen a conflict. Even states or other mediators may intervene prior to ripeness to get a process of exploratory talks open and to be "in position" when conditions change on the ground. A mediator's decisive entry into a conflict, and the means and method of its intervention, is contingent upon a keen sense of timing. Invariably, a mediator's initial action to intervene is premised on the expectation that the parties' positions are flexible and that continuation of the conflict is inimical to the mediator's interests (Touval and Zartman 1989).

Mediators may intervene with different objectives at different stages of a conflict. A mediator's objectives at an early point in a conflict's escalation are to keep a dispute non-military or to prevent outbreak of violence. At higher levels of escalation, mediators may seek to contain violence, terminate it, or prevent its recurrence. Invariably, mediator interventions are fraught with ethical and normative considerations, for entry, or the absence of it, significantly affects the balance of power and perceptions of the parties. For example, is the suppression of mass violence by a state a legitimate policing action, or illegitimate repression of a minority group? Is engaging a particular disputant conferring legitimacy on that party as a player that must be accommodated at the bargaining table?

As described in Chapter 2, mediators intervene by offering formulas for potential settlement or for procedural disputes, and bring with them a range of inducements (carrots and sticks). Mediators play a critical role in transforming a conflict from one of stalemate to a mutually hurting stalemate that is ripe for resolution. Touval and Zartman (1989: 13) write that

> the mediator may even need to reinforce a stalemate, using its own resources to add negative arguments and inducements to keep the parties from trying to resolve the situation unilaterally. The stalemate must be seen by both parties as unbreakable, except in the direction of a bilateral agreement reached with the help of the mediator.

Mediators are widely seen as impartial actors, but rarely is this the case. Indeed, mediators do not need impartiality; they simply need to have sufficient leverage with all sides to move them toward a settlement. All sides, for some reason or another, engage the mediator because they seek to improve or maintain their relationship with it. Mediators use this leverage to alter the protagonists' perceptions in order to "induce" a ripe moment. One example of such action is the role of the United Kingdom in convincing bordering states to pressure Zimbabwe's rebels led by Robert Mugabe by conditioning the acceptance of the Lancaster House settlement terms or face the removal of his military bases on their territory: this tipped Mugabe's expectations from one of believing he would win the war to one in which he might well lose.[6]

The essential point is that a mediator's entry into a conflict and its collective actions significantly affect the incentive structure of the conflict. Mediation changes the cost and benefit calculations of disputants through the use of inducements, threatening to withdraw benefits, applying sanctions, conferring legitimacy, and offering side-payments. As indicated above, parties bargain tacitly and explicitly not only among themselves but also with the mediator. This is particularly true in the case of collective mediation, where several mediators are working together toward resolution, sometimes in concert and sometimes at cross-purposes. Parties may have special relationships with a member of the mediator coalition, or may seek to play the interests of one mediator against the other. In many cases, mediators may seek to create crises in order to precipitate a ripe moment. This may occur by setting deadlines or otherwise confronting the disputants with the need to make serious strategic choices toward conciliation or confrontation (an important feature, for example, of the mediation effort led by George Mitchell in Northern Ireland).

Mediators undertake important tasks in the prenegotiation phase, underscoring the purpose of the parties' need to engage in exploratory or preparatory talks before "going public." Mediators are critical in each of the seven functions that characterize the prenegotiation phase: helping keep risks low by keeping talks informal and exploratory; helping parties analyze the relative costs and benefits of agreement to negotiations versus the status quo; establishing a pattern of reciprocity and trust among the parties that conciliatory moves will not be exploited for unilateral gain; helping parties build an internal support base for conciliation by offering support and, potentially, tangible side-payments; setting the agenda for talks and determining the parameters of the range of possible outcomes; identifying the participants at formal talks, not only those to be included but the equally important task of excluding certain players; and building bridges or coalitions across conflict divides (Stein 1989).

The Holy Grail: a formula for settlement

The role of mediators in developing formulas for resolution in prenegotiation talks is particularly important, and it is often an underappreciated or even ignored element of international intervention in civil wars. Formulas are broad principles framed to narrow the parameters of a conflict's outcome; a formula defines an overarching concept that frames the parameters of the solution and defines the terms of trade or establishes a principle under which the conflict can be cooperatively managed. In economists' terms, it defines the contract zone. In order for parties to accept a formula, often but not always proposed by a mediator, it must be seen as just and satisfactory; cover all major issues; incorporate all sides' demands; and contain a basic vision of post-conflict arrangements. A formula is not a settlement, but rather a statement of the scope of the conflict's outcomes and the general procedures to get the parties to settlement: a formula is an agreement on certain basic conceptual issues that need to be resolved before the bargaining on details can begin in earnest (Druckman 1986), for example a general declaration of principles or framework agreement.

The extent of specificity of the formula will vary widely precisely because while substantive agreement at the prenegotiation phase may be desirable, it may not always be possible. In some cases, where outcome preferences are widely diverse but where parties are sufficiently desperate to begin talks and move away from violence, procedural agreement may be less fruitful but nonetheless all that is available. Successful prenegotiation moves the parties into the beginnings of a nascent negotiation process in which they begin to evaluate the potential for mutually beneficial outcomes and identify the range of possible settlements that will serve mutual interests. For this reason, it is often called the first step in the "diagnostic" phase of negotiations (Zartman and Berman 1982). It is important to note that parties need not agree on the final shape of a settlement at the prenegotiation phase; they must simply agree on two broad principles and a general set of procedures. Saunders (1985) aptly describes the three tasks of the prenegotiation phase: "defining the problem," "developing a commitment to negotiation on the part of the parties," and "arranging the negotiations."

Although in most situations it is difficult to pinpoint precisely when the prenegotiation phase begins (in part because the very first contacts are normally the closest of guarded secrets), there is wide agreement that the phase ends with an agreement on a formal declaration of principles, a public commitment to negotiate in good faith, and, more often than not, a declaration of cease-fire. These agreements, which are usually explicit but not invariably so, form the basic framework to guide the ensuing protracted negotiations. These agreements are perhaps the most critical of all turning points in the negotiation process, where parties openly signal intent to move from an openly confrontational stance to a cooperative, problem-solving stance. Parties in conflict do not cease being adversaries, but they do embrace each other as implicit partners in de-escalating the conflict.

Negotiating security

The movement from prenegotiation to open, formal negotiation is signaled by the parties' "going public" with their intent to replace fighting with talking. Announcement to the public that a party is negotiating with a bitter adversary is a major turning point in the de-escalation process.[7] This turning point signals, more than any other, that political leaders are willing to accept the inevitable risks and costs associated with direct negotiations – such as charges from immoderate rejectionist parties of appeasement, betrayal, or capitulation – in pursuit of the still-unrealized benefits of a negotiated settlement. Going public, or the public acknowledgment that a regime or insurgent group will together seek a negotiated settlement, radically transforms the landscape of a conflict and significantly alters the incentive structure for violence. The move is especially risky for governments, who open themselves up for charges of negotiating with terrorists, in effect "rewarding" violence.[8]

The onset of open negotiation unleashes a new, uncertain interregnum. The status quo of violent conflict without end is transformed into a situation in which the old order is likely to be changed, yet the parameters of the post-negotiated settlement order have not been established. The period after the immediate onset of negotiations raises many questions about the period of transition and the opportunities and dangers it may pose and for how long, but also about the terms of a settlement and the many problems that are as yet unresolved. Parties with the capacity for violence, such as security forces and insurgent paramilitaries, are especially uncertain about their fate. How will we as tools of war, they ask, fare in an environment in which political leaders have pledged peace? Precisely because not just the security forces, but all segments of society, are deeply uncertain about their futures after the onset of formal negotiations in internal conflicts, the preliminary negotiation period is a highly unsettled and turbulent period.

From enemies to Nobel Laureates?

The preliminary formal negotiation phase is also marked by the changing dynamics of coalition-making; in a short period of time, as in South Africa, Israel–Palestine, and Northern Ireland in the mid-1990s, former adversaries may find themselves as co-Laureates as the Norwegian Nobel Committee bestows prizes not just for making peace, but in their own symbolic way to push peace processes along. Erstwhile enemies on the battlefield, such as a government and insurgent group, find themselves in an implicit coalition defending the choice for negotiation, re-orienting their rhetoric toward moderation and compromise, and articulating the benefits of negotiation and the costs of continued violent conflict. At the same time, they remain adversaries in the negotiation, with widely divergent aims and hopes for the ensuing talks. Importantly, the relationships among parties at the table are marked by both cooperation (as partners in talks) *and* competition. Perhaps the most contentious issue, often at the heart of these early negotiations, is the release of prisoners jailed for the perpetration of violence during the war (Darby 2001: 67–68).

New coalitions also emerge as rejectionists on the flanks of the emerging moderates decry negotiation and seek to outbid the moderate parties for public support. Political leaders who enter negotiations generally expect that they have a sufficiently cohesive coalition to support the onset of talks and that they can sustain that support throughout the negotiation process – they hope to "carry" their constituencies with them, and even to potentially benefit politically by bringing the conflict to an end. On the other hand, political leaders may not enjoy sufficient deference from within their own organizations or within their own constituencies; entering into negotiations with erstwhile adversaries may lead to deep fissures and enhance factionalism within parties and within supportive segments of society.

That parties begin to initially cooperate – through the dynamics of concession-making – does not mean that they fully cooperate, of course. Although the incentives for violence diminish, until the negotiation reaches a point of no return, incentives to use violence to affect what happens at the table continue to exist. Indeed, the military tool for influencing an opponent is often a more direct and effective instrument than behavior at the table; violence is a means of imposing significant "disagreement costs" on the opponent (Pillar 1983: 160–164). The purposes of violence against an opponent with whom one may be negotiating include weakening the opponent, denying an opponent's objective, demonstrating commitment or determination, altering the opponent's bargaining position, directly affecting the shape of a settlement, or to hasten or delay conclusion of a settlement. All of these behaviors are seen in the following case studies.

Equally important is the threat of violence – a tactic that "attempts to attain the benefits of cost manipulation without suffering actual losses of life or resources in the process" (Pillar 1983: 183). In sum, as negotiations proceed, the balance of power among adversaries can change for many reasons, and parties to negotiation may foment violence in order to affect perceptions of the balance of power. In such instances, negotiating while fighting is analogous to simply opening another "front" in which to wage the war, using different instruments to pursue the same objective. Certainly this particular pattern is seen in the case of Sri Lanka, detailed in Chapter 7.

In the second type of sequencing, parties reach prior agreements to limit or suspend violence before beginning formal talks; they pledge to forego violence while negotiating. Parties to a dispute use the cessation of violence as a critical confidence-building measure before they begin to bargain in earnest on the underlying issues in the dispute that affect their vital interests. The sequencing of events in a peace process holds enormous consequences not only for the procedural dimension of negotiations, but for the outcome dimension as well. Touval writes that:

> Sequencing … has consequences. Warring parties are more likely to settle when the continuing confrontation hurts badly and produces grave risks. A cease-fire, ending the bloodshed, is likely to ease the pain and reduce the risks. It will create a tolerable stalemate, a situation that disputants might find preferable to the alternative of granting the concessions necessary for a compromise settlement.
>
> (Touval 1996: mimeo)

That there are two basic paths to preliminary formal negotiation demonstrates the difficulty of assessing whether the parties come to the table because a conflict is truly ripe, or simply as a tactical response to international pressures; it is never easy to assess the true intent of belligerents. The problem of tactical cease-fires is a well-known one, with many an example of cease-fires that do not hold. For this reason, the sequencing of issues in formal preliminary negotiation varies significantly across cases.[9] For the purpose of analysis, this framework assumes a common sequencing – cessation of overt hostilities prior to preliminary formal negotiation. It is believed that this sequence corresponds to the experience of most peace processes in contemporary internal conflicts, in part because the cessation of killing is the mediator's pre-eminent goal. However, the findings of this research suggest that this sequential logic is flawed, and that prior agreement on the fundamentals of settlement terms is essential to realizing security in the long run.

Intent: the primacy of security pacts

In many cases, a critical question is whether being at the table is a tactical move by parties – subduing the opponent through other means – or is a genuine search for a mutually beneficial solution. The test is whether the parties progress and reach preliminary agreements on the cessation of violence, or whether the negotiation process fails to progress. During preliminary formal negotiation, the parties do not yet engage in the underlying substantive differences of their conflict, but rather focus on the security dimensions of the conflict that pose a threat to their vital interests and on the preconditions to substantive talks that one party or another establishes. The focus on security issues is understandable, for parties need certain guarantees that while the negotiation process moves forward, other parties will not use the interregnum to gather strength and wage the conflict more intensely in the future.

Security issues include the implementation of the procedures of cease-fire, release of political prisoners or hostages, demobilization or redeployment of troops, the implementation of security guarantees (such as the deployment of external observers/monitors and often UN peacekeeping troops), measures for police and security force reform, etc. The parties' emphasis on security guarantees is the hallmark of the phase. Movement within the phase occurs when parties reach interim procedural agreements, or "pacts." Pacts, which are common to democratization as well as peacemaking processes, are mutual security agreements in which parties forswear the use of violence to achieve their aims in exchange for protection under agreed-upon rules of the political game (O'Donnell *et al.* 1986, pt. IV: 37–39).

Pact-making during the preliminary negotiation phase establishes important rules of interaction that help define the incentive structure for violence and peace once the open bargaining process is under way. Such rules of interaction can be formal or informal, that is reflected in written agreements or in observable patterns. For example, does the structure of talks (bilateral or multilateral) lend itself to the eventual inclusion of some rejectionist parties? Do negotiations proceed secretly or in public, or a mix of both? Do the parties reach agreement at the highest levels first, or do negotiators bicker until impasse and then request intervention by higher authorities? How visual or public is the role of the mediator and to what extent and in what manner do mediators employ inducements? The extent to which the negotiations are structured to be amenable to influence from beyond the process will influence the incentives and disincentives for violence. If the negotiations are structured so that parties *expect* events in the street to affect events at the table, the incentives for violence are heightened. Conversely, if the process is insulated from external pressures, there are fewer incentives for violence.

The preliminary formal negotiation phase, which deals with detailed and often technical security issues, is a phase in which the parties further establish confidence (or trust) as well as test the general viability of the underlying principles agreed to during the prenegotiation phase. The extent political leaders can maintain and even expand their own support base, while demobilizing their publics away from violence, is a critical element in the sustainability of talks. The preliminary formal negotiation period is one in which both moderates and rejectionists alike explore the depth of public support for negotiation as an alternative to violence.

The preliminary negotiation phase also establishes the pattern of concession-making, which in a successful negotiation will be characterized by reciprocal moves and more-or-less equal commitment to taking steps that move the process forward. Disputants may trade away some of their bargaining chips while reserving some for later rounds of talks. During this initial period of interregnum, parties can determine the other sides' flexibility and general bargaining behavior and begin to create some sense of predictability in the process of bargaining. In sum, a difficult but successful tussle over security issues in a negotiation process helps set the stage for subsequent good-faith bargaining when it comes to tackling the (equally and perhaps more) difficult, substantive issues that lie at the heart of the dispute. Still, security without agreement on a formula is unlikely to last except in those cases – such as Kosovo – where peace is "imposed" by external actors.

Negotiating settlement

As the talks move from security issues to substantive issues, such as the division of territory or the nature, form, and structure of the state, it is a signal that parties have entered the phase of negotiation in which the actual terms of a settlement are being thrashed out. Parties in internal conflicts face essentially two choices for the settlement of underlying disputes: separation, or secession, and sharing, or creating the structures for living together (Sisk 1996; Roeder and Rothchild 2005). Likewise, in recent peace accords, there is increasing attention to the economic dimensions of peacemaking and the inclusion of specific language in settlements to address the thorny issues of land, natural resource management, and economic distribution in the post-agreement period (Wennmann 2008). The purpose of a substantive settlement is to reconstitute "normal" politics in a society and to create new, mutually beneficial rules of the political game for distribution of public goods. Ultimately, parties in a negotiation process to resolve deep-seated conflict arrive at institutional solutions: rules and procedures through which to arbitrate their differences peacefully in parliament rather than violently on the street.

Settlements in internal conflicts reflect the convergence point of the parties' preferences over new rule structures, or institutions, for the state once arms have been laid down. Waterman (1993: 292) argues that "civil wars are conflicts over political order," and settlements in them entail the "re-creation of the conditions for a viable, common political order." Importantly, settlements do not end conflict: they are simply agreements to continue bargaining under consensually defined rules of interaction. Not surprisingly, settlements in internal conflicts often take the form of new constitutions or significant packages of amendments to existing constitutions. In the course of formal substantive negotiations, parties formulate their positions based on their expectations of how the structure of the new institutions will serve their interests; they exercise "analytical imagination" about the costs and benefits of alternative institutions, such as the structure of federalism or the choice of an electoral system.[10] Therefore, settlement does not end conflict, even though the term implies some sense of finality: instead these agreements are at best *promises* to end violence by creating new rules of the game to which all parties at the table can agree to peacefully *manage* conflict.

Settlements in internal conflicts can be either interim or final (or comprehensive). In interim settlements, parties are able to arrive at some basis for reconstituting normal politics but cannot agree on, or prefer to defer, highly sensitive or unresolved issues. Interim settlements are usually partial agreements, whereas final settlements purport to be comprehensive in scope. All settlements seek to formalize patterns of interaction and in this respect they seek to establish new incentive structures in their own right, resolving some of the uncertainty about the new rules of the game that characterizes earlier phases of the peace process. In many cases, they are package proposals that resolve multiple issues simultaneously by linking them.

A negotiated settlement reflects the mutually beneficial convergence point (or "Pareto-optimal equilibrium") among the parties' positions in the talks. However, as such, they are "second best solutions for all sides since each would obviously prefer to win."[11] The settlement freezes in time the balance of power among the parties, which may have shifted dramatically during the preceding phases of a peace process. Even though parties may have entered negotiation because of a perception of relative parity in power, subsequent events may have strengthened or weakened one side or another. This change in fortunes may well be reflected in the terms of a settlement. The settlement reflects the new constellation of forces and codifies and institutionalizes the relative bargaining power of the disputants. Settlements are attractive for all parties when they contain the likelihood of greater benefits for parties than they would achieve by abrogating negotiations and returning to the battlefield. Successful settlements are a formula of positive-sum gain for all parties.

Although this view of settlements suggests that it is primarily the interests and power of the disputants that frames the terms of a settlement in an internal conflict, international mediators and others external to the conflict also clearly influence (either on the basis of principle or interest) not only the process of conflict resolution, but also the outcome. By insisting on the territorial integrity of a state, such as in Bosnia or Chechnya, for example, the international community tends to induce parties in the direction of sharing, and may even seek to dictate the terms under which groups live together. Although it is often said that mediators have a process bias, it is equally essential to understand how they affect the terms of settlements in internal conflicts. The September 1995 Agreed Basic Principles for Bosnia (the Dayton Agreement) is a case in point: the terms of the accord were formulated by the mediator (the five-nation Contact Group, led by the United States), not by the parties to the dispute independently.

Partition refers to the creation of an entirely new state that enjoys full sovereignty and international recognition. As noted above, secession remains a strong taboo in the international system. Some question the prevailing policies of the international community that systematically works to keep troubled states together. Kaufman writes that:

> Stable resolutions of ethnic civil wars are possible, but only when the opposing groups are demographically separated into defensible enclaves. Separation reduces both incentives and opportunity for further combat, and largely eliminates both reasons and chances for ethnic cleansing of civilians. While ethnic fighting can be stopped by other means, such as peace enforcers by international forces or by a conquering empire, such peaces last only as long as the enforcers remain. This means to save lives threatened by genocide, the international community must abandon attempts to save war-torn multiethnic states.
>
> (Kaufman 1996: 137)

Others adamantly disagree with the Kaufman thesis, citing the need to defend the principle of tolerant, multiethnic diversity and the importance of not rewarding disputants with territorial ambitions who may have committed war crimes; these are the principal reasons why the international community insisted upon the maintenance of Bosnia's territorial integrity at the Dayton talks, for example (Burg 1995).

In all other wars today, partition – despite being sometimes advocated by secessionist forces – is simply unlikely and improbable. The bias against partition by all the major world powers, and particularly the five Permanent Members of the UN Security Council – remains incredibly strong. The stark consequence of this basic reality of the international system is clear: in most civil wars, the terms of settlement will involve living together and some kind of agreement to share political power. I argue that the debate over partition is misguided: even after civil war that results in the proverbial two-state solution (e.g. the Israeli–Palestinian dispute or Kosovo, for example) antagonists are destined to coexist together.

The aim of power sharing in peace agreements is clearly conflict management, not conflict resolution. Their terms are critical for the viability of post-settlement implementation and of the possibilities for sustainable peace: as Rothchild observed,

> In some cases, the very incentives required to reassure weaker parties and gain commitment to a bargain in the initial period can cause political instability later on, if rigid power-sharing institutions come into conflict with the need to concentrate power at the political center in a unitary state structure.
>
> (Rothchild 2002: 135)

This fact makes power-sharing solutions problematic in that they need flexibility over time, yet disputants require hard-and-fast guarantees to settle.

Finally, many of the more celebrated settlements in recent years have featured "democratization as conflict resolution," explicitly marrying the goals of conflict amelioration with the introduction of competitive, multiparty politics. These features of power sharing are illustrated well by the three "strands" in the Northern Ireland peace process that led to the 1998 Belfast Agreement combined with "complementarity" that linked official talks with unofficial, community-based initiatives (Bloomfield 1997).[12] With linked issues and complex decision-making rules, this accord has created a power-sharing system, which seeks to provide incentives for bargaining in several arenas on a wide range of issues.

Many suggest that it is the genius of the Belfast Agreement that all parties could defend the agreement as containing the elements of what they had fought for all along. Moderate Republicans could claim that the agreement represents the first step toward accession to Ireland; moderate

Loyalists could claim that the agreement preserves British sovereignty.[13] These elements of power sharing help us understand the key components of such agreements. In sum:

- Negotiated settlements that create power-sharing institutions create political institutions that are broadly inclusive of all major mobilized groups in society, and decisions are made through negotiating, issue trading, and the search for consensus or near-consensus decision-making.
- The key elements of power-sharing institutions are: (i) inclusion of all major mobilized actors; (ii) influence in decision-making, not just representation in governing institutions; (iii) moderation, and the search for common ground; and (iv) ongoing bargaining or negotiation within the new rules of the game that the peace agreement has established.

A long-standing misconception of power-sharing institutions is that they are all of a specific type, which for many years has been called "consociationalism" (Lijphart 1977, 2004). The elements of this approach to power sharing are well known: grand coalitions, proportional representation, cultural autonomy or federalism, and the mutual veto. Yet this prototype of power sharing is but one of what is in fact a very broad range of political options for settling ethnic conflicts, the gist of which can be exceptionally different in terms of aims, structures, and effects on promoting inter-group moderation and compromise. What are the principal options for sharing power?[14]

For many conflicts today, such as Azerbaijan (Karabagh), Sudan, or Sri Lanka, autonomy is often seen as a reasonable way to balance the claims of states for territorial integrity and the claims of rebel forces for secession. Autonomy is not a term on which there is a consensus definition, as the tortuous negotiation of autonomy issues in South Africa, Sri Lanka, and Kashmir attest.[15] Nonetheless, Ghai's definition is the most useful:

> Autonomy is a device to allow an ethnic group or other groups claiming a distinct identity to exercise direct control over important affairs of concern to them while allowing the larger entity to exercise those powers which are the common interests of both sections.
>
> (Ghai 2000: 484)

Among the forms of autonomy are symmetrical federalism in which all units enjoy similar powers, and asymmetrical federalism that might provide enhanced powers to a particular region (Coakley 1993).

Probably the most appealing candidate for autonomy as a solution is the Kosovo imbroglio. United Nations and Organization for Security and

Cooperation in Europe proposals for the solution of the Kosovo problem are an example of potential autonomy solutions in ethnic conflicts in which territory and ethnicity largely overlap. United Nations Security Council Resolution 1244, of June 10, 1999, clearly defines the mandate of the UN Interim Administration Mission in Kosovo (UNMIK) as promoting autonomy and self-government within the limits of territorial integrity for Yugoslavia. The resolution authorizes UNMIK to

> establish an international civil presence in Kosovo in order to provide an interim administration for Kosovo under which the people of Kosovo can enjoy substantial autonomy within the Federal Republic of Yugoslavia, and which will provide transitional administration while establishing and overseeing the development of provisional democratic self-governing institutions to ensure conditions for a peaceful and normal life for all inhabitants of Kosovo.

Yet as the continuing tensions and as yet unresolved status of Kosovo demonstrates, the idea of autonomy as a solution is more common than its actual acceptance by the parties in conflict. Autonomy is a difficult option for power sharing precisely because it fails to satisfy the preferences of neither states, which fear a "slippery slope" toward disintegration, nor secessionist groups, which demand nothing less than full sovereignty and state-hood. While autonomy must remain on the table as an option, it has in practice seen little success as a means of resolving the issues on the table in settlement negotiations. For this reason, among others, Kosovo's independence seems likely.

Another possible option is a looser form of autonomy, not always explicitly territorial, or consociationalism (Lijphart 2004). The option is in essence a *group building-block approach* that relies on accommodation by ethnic group leaders at the political center and guarantees for group autonomy and minority rights; in essence, this approach is "consociational" in that it encourages collaborative decision-making by parties in conflict. The key institutions are: federalism and the devolution of power to ethnic groups in territory that they control; minority vetoes on issues of particular importance to them; grand coalition cabinets in a parliamentary framework, and proportionality in all spheres of public life (e.g. budgeting and civil service appointments).

Like Bosnia, Lebanon has a political system in which representation and autonomy for the country's main religious groups is guaranteed in the constitution. Systems of communal representation have been attempted in many settings over the years, as described by Lijphart, an advocate of this approach, in his seminal book *Democracy in Plural Societies* (1977). Some criticize an approach that structures the political system around ethnic identities, arguing that mechanisms such as communal representation "reify" and help harden ethnic differences, and that the use of the mutual veto will lead to gridlock in decision-making. Certainly, Nigeria's proliferation of federal states after independence and into the Third Republic is a classic example of the use of further division to address the problems of territorially distinct ethnic blocs.

In contrast, the integrative approach eschews ethnic groups as the building blocks of a common society and purposefully seeks to integrate society along the lines of division. In South Africa's 1993 interim constitution, for example, ethnic group representation was explicitly rejected in favor of institutions and policies that deliberately promote social integration across group lines. Election laws (in combination with the delimitation of provincial boundaries) have had the effect of encouraging political parties to put up candidate slates – if they want to maximize the votes they get – that reflect South Africa's highly diverse society. And the federal provinces were created so as not to overlap with ethnic group boundaries (South Africa's groups are more widely dispersed in any event). Reilly's analysis demonstrates how the key to such integrative approaches (or "centripetalism," because it tries to engineer a center-oriented spin to political dynamics) is the electoral system; its strongest possible effect is to engender the development of multiethnic political parties (Reilly 2003).

The integrative approach seeks to build multiethnic political coalitions (again, usually political parties), to create incentives for political leaders to be moderate on divisive ethnic themes, and to enhance minority influence in majority decision-making (Horowitz 1985). The elements of an integrative approach include electoral systems that encourage pre-election pacts across ethnic lines, non-ethnic federalism that diffuses points of power, and public policies that promote political allegiances that transcend groups. Some suggest that integrative power sharing is superior in theory, in that it seeks to foster ethnic accommodation by promoting cross-cutting interests. Others, however, argue that the use of incentives to promote conciliation will run aground when faced with deep-seated enmities that underlie ethnic disputes and that are hardened during the course of a brutal civil war.

Although this typology presents two conceptually distinct approaches, it is clear power-sharing options can be pieced together in a number of ways. Power sharing can also include measures to divide power, and can have many manifestations (Roeder and Rothchild 2005). Like any menu, levers of democratic influence can be combined to suit individual tastes. In deciding which power-sharing institutions and practices might work, there is no substitute for intimate knowledge of any given country.[16]

Nearing settlement: incentives to kill

Importantly, the formal substantive phase of a peace process – especially as this phase nears an end and a settlement emerges on the horizon – affects the incentives for violence. Once settlements are reached, a significant turning point occurs. For parties to a conflict, the incentives for violence fall away all together. The further employment of violence becomes illegitimate; disputes are not to be resolved in the streets, but rather within the newly created institutions envisaged by the accord. For rejectionists, however, there may be one last opportunity to reverse the pattern of accommodation: prevent the terms of the accord from being implemented.

Implementing settlements, building peace

Clearly, as all the cases of settlements in peace processes demonstrate, reaching an agreement is not the end of the process; violence can erupt with a vengeance even after moderates have agreed to a comprehensive settlement. The implementation phase of peace processes can be just as volatile, just as violence-ridden, as early phases of the process; as Darby notes, "Peace processes are the consequence of violence, and violence seriously affects their direction.... It continues to determine their outcome even after a peace accord has been reached" (Darby 2006c: 8). MacGinty shows how societies "inherit" violent interactions from previous periods and that "the blithe acceptance of a peace process or peace accord 'as a good thing' is not enough, particularly when the quality of peace experience by inhabitants in the war-affected area is poor" (MacGinty 2006: 115). Successful implementation requires translating the terms of agreement on paper to real institutions and practices that re-orient politics from the street to the parliament. Usually, however, implementation of settlements in internal conflicts does not occur in a vacuum. Earlier interim agreements or security pacts have been put into place, leaving behind them both lessons from the past and structures for cooperation.

Much of the ink that has been spilled on internal conflicts in the post-Cold War era deals with the complexities of implementation of peace agreements and the ingredients for "successful" international intervention at the implementation stage (e.g. Namibia, El Salvador, Nicaragua, Cambodia, Mozambique, South Africa, and Haiti) as opposed to failure (Rwanda, Angola in 1992).[17] Issues such as demobilization, removal of foreign troops, de-mining, resettlement of refugees and displaced persons, economic reconstruction and development, and new elections are but a few of the myriad aspects of peace accord implementation.

Nearly all settlements in contemporary internal conflicts envisage elections as *the* turning point that unambiguously signals the advent of the post-conflict era (Kumar 1999; Reilly 2003). Elections serve many purposes, but clearly one of them is to legitimize the terms of the accord through popular participation. Increasingly, the international community becomes engaged in elections in internal conflict situations, such that the mediator or international organizations such as the UN become participants in guaranteeing the terms of the accord. Although elections are by no means the only aspect of implementation, because election events usually culminate a peace process they are critical choice points in terms of the incentives and disincentives for violence.

War-to-democracy transitions

At the end of the day, beyond a transitional process, a peace process is in the long run a matter of democratization and development. The link to democratization is evident in the view that over time the only form of governance consistent with international law is democracy and its essential feature of the protection of human rights. More practically, democratization is seen as a way to strategically engage parties in negotiations on a mutually acceptable settlement. Kofi Annan succinctly described the connection between democracy and peace in 2001.

> At the center of virtually every conflict is the State and its power – who controls it and how it is used. No conflict can be resolved without answering those questions, and nowadays the answers almost always have to be democratic ones, at least in form.... Democracy is practiced in many ways, and none of them is perfect. But at its best it provides a means for managing and resolving disputes peacefully, in an atmosphere of mutual trust.[18]

Yet building peace through democratization also raises dilemmas. Arguably, democratization and trust-building may not easily go hand-in-hand, as electoral processes induce social conflict (as parties and individuals vie for power) and indeed elections may be the catalyst for new violence. Baker captures the inherent tensions in international action in peacebuilding strategies, stemming from the counter-vailing pressures within the international community (and, conceivably, within individuals such as policy-makers who are internally weighing alternative approaches to war termination):

> Conflict managers tend to concentrate on short-term solutions that address the precipitous events that sparked the conflict; above all, they seek a swift and expedient end to the violence. Democratizers tend to concentrate on the longer-term solutions that address the root causes of the conflict; they search for enduring democratic stability. The former see peace as a precondition to democracy; the latter see democracy as a precondition for peace.
>
> (Baker 1996: 568)

A critical issue is whether the process of elections contains incentives for rejectionists of peace settlement to participate in the process, even campaigning against the accord itself. Whether rejectionist parties choose to fight accommodation from within the new system (as the Pan-Africanist

Congress did in South Africa), or whether they boycott it and seek its demise from without (as the Khmer Rouge did in Cambodia), is in part a matter of the terms under which the election will be held. Thus, the electoral system is a key incentive structure that affects the propensity for rejectionists to foment violence. If a rejectionist party believes it can win a few seats in the new parliament, rather than being completely excluded from the new system, this incentive may be enough to widen the base of the peace process and bring in those with the capacity to "spoil."

The perceived free and fair nature of elections is a final turning point that must be crossed. Elections can be triggers for conflict, as mentioned above, even with the acceptance of a comprehensive peace agreement. Angola's failed 1992 election, in which the loser of the election's first round of balloting (Jonas Savimbi's UNITA party) returned to the battlefield rather than accepting the inevitable loss at the polls, stands as a constant reminder from contemporary experience of the critical importance of implementation. In this case, the UN peacekeeping force was wholly inadequate for the task, and the UN overseers of the peace process implicitly allowed the parties to contest the election before security agreements – particularly the demobilization and containment of the government and UNITA's militaries – had been completed.

Settlements in internal conflicts contain the inherent problems of enforceability and compliance. When the election is over and the UN peacekeepers leave, there is no external party to further guarantee the accord. For this reason, Wagner writes that

> one of the disadvantages of a negotiated settlement is that, because no combatant is able to disarm its adversaries, a settlement requires that all the adversaries retain some semblance of their organizational identities after the war, even if they are disarmed. While such an agreement may facilitate the ending of one civil war, it may also facilitate the outbreak of the next.
>
> (Wagner 1993: 261)

When a peace process "ends" is as ambiguous a question of when it begins. As Miall *et al.* observe, longer-term transformation of protracted conflict must take place on a number of dimensions: context transformation, of the social environment; structural transformation, in the nature of conflict embedded in relationships among the protagonists (such as dominant and weaker parties); actor transformation, in which elite and public attitudes and behavior change; issue transformation, of the way in which the dispute is fundamentally framed; and personal and group transformation, in which moderation prevails over extremism (Miall *et al.* 1999: 156–157). Social and actor transformation after a bitter and often protracted conflict is necessarily a complex and long-term objective. Protracted conflicts likewise leave economic and environmental catastrophes in their wake, legacies of enmity that require years and even decades of purposeful socio-economic development to address.

At the end of the day, it is utterly unrealistic to expect that the underlying root causes of conflict will be definitively resolved at the end of a peace process; perhaps a more sober goal is the management, not resolution, of difference. Nevertheless, when talks overtake war, violent encounters fall away as new conflict management processes are consolidated and, ideally, with time the incentives for achieving political aims peacefully emerge predominant and habitual. Whether a peace process will ultimately prove to be durable is a question of whether the initial commitment to accommodation reflected in a settlement can be broadened and deepened over time.

Appendix to Chapter 3

Peace processes: questions for analysis

This appendix provides a brief analytical framework for the comparison of five post-Cold War conflicts (Chapters 4–8) that saw various stages of progress in the negotiation or implementation of settlements (including regression from cease-fire and negotiation back into conflict, as in Sri Lanka). The purpose of the structured, focused comparison methodology is, as George writes, to "formulate the idiosyncratic aspects of the explanation for each case in terms of general variables" (George 1979).[19] In implementing the methodology, the procedure is to identify a series of distinct questions that can be systematically applied to each case related to the key variables identified.

The structured, focused comparison method cannot definitively test the hypotheses presented in this analytical framework, but it can serve to refine them and improve our understanding of the central research question. Nor can the study definitively address the overarching question about the long-term durability of the negotiated settlements, even though it purports to shed some light on that question by assessing the critical path through which negotiated settlements are reached. Toward that end, if the comparative analysis of the violence–negotiation nexus leads, like other broader theories of negotiation, to "predictability in the process of bargaining" (Bacharach and Lawler 1981: 3), it may also lead to predictability in successful responses to minimize the deleterious effects of violence on the peace process.

The conflict and its context

- What is the context for the conflict in terms of its historical development?
- What underlying or core issues are at stake or are disputed?
- What is the structure of the conflict, essentially bilateral or multilateral?

- What role (benign, malevolent, or both) have external parties played in the development of the conflict?
- What is the regional context in which the conflict plays out, that is are there transnational ties across ethnic groups or similar relationships?
- Is the conflict new strife or the re-eruption of old enmities?

Conflict escalation

- What is the nature of escalatory dynamics?
- What discernible trigger events have occurred?
- What is the ebb and flow of political violence, as measured in terms of deaths in political violence as a proportion of the population?
- What are the military capabilities of the parties and other aspects of bargaining power?
- To what extent does a mutually hurting stalemate objectively exist?
- Do the parties perceive a mutually hurting stalemate?
- What turning point or critical event(s) marked the progression from conflict escalation to a mutually hurting stalemate?

Prenegotiation and ripeness

- Did previous talks occur, and if so what lessons did the parties draw from them (i.e. did they succeed or collapse)?
- What set of factors brought the parties to the table?
- What was the role of third-party mediators in bringing the parties to the table, and how intrusive was mediator intervention? If mediation was intrusive, what mix of inducement was applied?
- What was the nature of the agreement, explicit or implicit, that culminated the prenegotiation phases?
- In what ways does the pattern of violence during the prenegotiation phase relate to negotiation-related events?
- What event marked the transition from prenegotiation to preliminary formal negotiation?

Preliminary formal negotiation

- How did the parties deal with the sequencing of talks and with the linkage dilemma (no talks without cease-fire; no cease-fire without talks)?
- What was the agenda of the preliminary formal negotiations?
- Did violence by the negotiating parties continue after the preliminary formal talks began?
- Did rejectionist parties foment violence to derail the talks, and if so to what effect? What was the nature and type of rejectionist violence? What was the effect of rejectionist violence on the progress of talks?

- How was violence related to negotiation events?
- When did peaks and valleys in the negotiation process occur? How were they related to critical turning points in terms of timing? How does political violence affect the talks in the preliminary formal negotiation phase? What structures, if any, were put into effect for joint management of the problem of ongoing violence?
- What event marked the turning point from preliminary to substantive formal negotiation?

Substantive formal negotiation

- Were the general parameters of the settlement fully defined at the outset of negotiation?
- What was the pattern of interim settlements and their implementation?
- To what extent, and in what manner, can specific upsurges of violence be directly related to finalization of the settlement?
- To what extent, and in what manner, did the nature and structure of the violence affect the terms of the settlement?

Implementation

- Did violence by the negotiating parties continue after the conclusion of a settlement?
- Did rejectionist violence, if any, continue into the implementation period?
- How did the negotiating parties, as well as mediators, deal with violence during the implementation phase?
- To what extent, and in what manner, can specific instances of violence be directly related to implementation events such as elections?
- What has been the overall pattern of violence in the time since implementation of the settlement?

4 South Africa

Negotiating democracy after apartheid

South Africa's conflict is not always considered, properly, a "civil war." Because the resistance to apartheid was primarily a loosely organized, nearly spontaneous rebellion, scholars have generally not seen the conflict in classic government versus rebel terms, although clearly the African National Congress (ANC, a political party, or more accurately a social movement) and its military wing *Umkhonto we Sizwe* (MK) were a classic African national liberation force; but the forces of MK and the government of South Africa never engaged in large, epic battles, at least not directly on South African soil. Nonetheless, with levels of fatality in political violence that tally at least to 24,000 from 1984 to 1998 (du Toit 2001: 34), the conflict deserves analysis from the perspective of war termination through a peace process. This is especially true given what some have described as a "miracle," the successful reaching of comprehensive negotiated settlement in an essentially endogenous, or internal, peace process with considerable international intervention but very little direct, substantive mediation.[1]

From 1948 to 1994, particularly, South Africa was ruled by white nationalists who implemented policies of systematic racial segregation known as *apartheid* (separateness), depriving the black majority of dignity, citizenship, living wages, and access to land. Apartheid sparked an internal revolt from the disenfranchised black majority, embodied in the anti-apartheid struggle of the ANC which rebelliously opposed the white minority state with non-racial nationalism and socialism. The regime responded with a period of repression and a regional policy of destabilizing its neighbors. South Africa in the 1970s and 1980s was a bellicose regional hegemon – an aggressive power that fomented civil war and political strife in Angola, Botswana, Mozambique, Zambia, Zimbabwe, and Mozambique in order to keep its own internal opposition at bay. Apartheid's pernicious policies of racial segregation and regional conflict left deep social wounds throughout southern Africa that contribute to today's social chasms along class, race, and ethnic lines.

Resistance to the cruel polices of apartheid, the legally entrenched form of racial segregation that was implemented by South Africa's while minority government (National Party, NP), stimulated a wide anti-apartheid centralist revolt led mostly by the ANC. Between 1948 and late 1989, exacerbated by the Cold War, the conflict was characterized by a cycle of revolt and repression, with escalating levels of state violence and anti-apartheid resistance and counter-violence (Lodge 1983). Significant events in this spiraling cycle of revolt and resistance occurred in 1960, 1976, and 1984–1988.

By 1989 the country was approaching, in parts, "ungovernability," with predictions of an unbridled civil war along racial lines. Remarkably, a confluence of events yielded a moment ripe for the onset of settlement talks in mid to late 1989: isolated and gripped with the notion that they must "adapt or die," white minority leaders began to secretly negotiate with representatives of the black majority the dismantling of apartheid and the introduction of a new, non-racial democracy.[2] During 1990–1994 the country witnessed a remarkable social catharsis in which the principles of tolerance, negotiation, diversity, and democracy prevailed throughout four years of tumultuous talks. It was this culture of negotiation and bargaining over a common future that led to the Nobel Peace Prizes for the last white minority president, F.W. de Klerk, and the ANC's Nelson Mandela, who was once the state's most notorious political prisoner yet became the country's first president in celebrated "liberation" elections in April 1994.

Political violence was an endemic feature of the transitional period. Some 14,000 lost their lives in political violence between 1990 and 1994. There were several crisis-inducing events that threatened the talks beginning in June 1990, just after the Groote Schuur pact. Faction-fighting between the Inkatha Freedom Party (IFP) and ANC – mostly the youth wings – was extensive, especially in greater Johannesburg and the KwaZulu-Natal region. Significant events were the June 1992 Boipatong massacre, which prompted Mandela to withdraw from talks (along with a lack of progress in multiparty constitutional negotiations). The failure of state security forces to prevent the killing implicated both the IFP and the NP in the incident. Later in 1992, after a bloody shootout in the town of Bisho, for which the blame was laid at the feet of the ANC leadership, the parties returned to the table and made an implicit agreement to negotiate despite (or even because of) the violence.

The April 1993 assassination of ANC and South African Communist Party leader Chris Hani by a white right-wing gunman failed to derail the talks despite widespread public protests. Efforts by white right-wingers to disrupt talks in June 1993 (they drove an armored vehicle through the plate glass window of the hotel where talks were being held) failed to prevent the Interim Constitution from being sealed that month. Significantly, a white right-wing bombing campaign and an eleventh hour ANC-IFP shootout in downtown Johannesburg (the Shell House massacre) in the early months of 1994 failed to prevent the celebrated elections in April that brought Mandela to power and ended apartheid.

Violence clearly stalled the progress of the South African talks. Terrorist bombings and mass murders, faction-fighting, assassination of mid-level political leaders, rioting and mayhem, all accompanied South Africa's transition. Prior to the Boipatong incident, violence had the effect of inhibiting progress in talks. Mandela's refutation of the talks after Boipatong is probably the best affirmation of this instinctive response. After Boipatong, with a nearly 3,000-strong United Nations observer mission deployed (UNOMSA, the United Nations Observer Mission in South Africa), political violence failed to derail an agreement.

The ANC, particularly, changed its view and recognized that much of the violence was aimed at derailing the peace process. Particularly after the Bisho massacre in 1993, the ANC resolved that upsurges in violence would not stall the long march to freedom. The ANC's changed position was summed up by key negotiator Kader Asmal who explained that the party had concluded that failure to clinch a comprehensive transitional pact would "hold the country hostage to violence and violent men."[3] Thus, a settlement was clinched in June 1993 despite the ongoing strife on the street, a pact that was successfully implemented into 1994 and followed by a comprehensive constitutional settlement in 1996.

The "turbulent transition"

South Africa's history is a story of conflict from its very start, spurred by European settlement territorial conquest, frontier expansion, and nineteenth century global imperialism that generated internal competition between white settlers and the black African population over land and resources such as water.[4] Formal South African history is dated to the arrival of the Dutch East India Company in 1652 (although there were indigenous groups living there prior to the arrival of the Dutch); external rule from the metropole eventually transferred to the British in the late eighteenth century (1797). Conflict between the original Dutch-derived settlers, known as "Afrikaners" (or as "Boers," a term that later became perjorative), and British imperial rulers was heightened over differences about slavery and the exploitation of the country's rich mineral wealth. War between settlers and indigenous tribes and between Afrikaners and the British Empire in the Boer Wars of 1899–1902 occurred with frequency in South Africa's past. Afrikaner settlers, known as *Voortrekkers*, defeated a Zulu army at the Battle of Blood River in 1838.

South Africa was established as an independent state in 1910, following Afrikaner defeat in the Boer Wars. The Union featured a political system that created a parliamentary democracy for the minority whites but that excluded majority black South Africans from exercising voting rights. Discrimination against black South Africans grew in the 1910–1945 period, with the enactment of laws that led to dispossession of land, denial of workers' rights, and the creation of reserves in which blacks were to exercise self-determination. During this period, the country also experienced extensive labor strife, especially on the gold and diamond mines that were at the heart of the rapid urbanization that became Africa's most industrialized city, Johannesburg.

Driving much conflict over the years have been policies of racial segregation, pernicious practices that European settlers employed from South Africa's very beginning in the mid-seventeenth century and that changed but flourished under apartheid in the twentieth century. Segregation was accompanied by acute economic deprivation, which created long-standing, historically entrenched overlaps between race and class or what has become known in South Africa and other similarly patterned societies as "horizontal inequalities." Within the white minority, differences between English- and Afrikaans-speakers (Afrikaans is a derivation of Dutch) led to the creation of a strong Afrikaner nationalism and a drive for language, employment, and labor rights for this relatively deprived segment of the white population.[5]

South Africa: untangling root causes

From 1948 to 1990, South Africa was gripped by a bloody period of revolt, reform, and repression. In whites-only elections in 1948 a virulently nationalist Afrikaner party (the NP) won the elections and began to expand and more systematically implement policies of racial segregation. *Apartheid* – an extensive system of social segregation along putative race and ethnic lines, defined and enforced by the state – was implemented over a period of 40 years (1948–1988) in an eventually futile attempt to prevent a rapidly modernizing South Africa from becoming a multiethnic society in which the majority black population would necessarily win the right to vote. Apartheid was more than just a plethora of bigoted laws and policies; justification for its excesses was deeply rooted in a religiously rooted, ethno-nationalist ideology created by ideologically driven political elites to politically mobilize Afrikaners beginning in the 1920s.[6]

The myriad injuries inflicted by apartheid precipitated a revolutionary backlash. In response to black exclusion and racial segregation, an African nationalist armed opposition arose to first reform and later to defeat the white minority regime through a revolution of national liberation. The ANC was formed in 1912, making it one of the oldest surviving political organizations in Africa. Defiance and non-violent civil disobedience in the 1950s – particularly over the pass laws – gave way to armed struggle in 1960. The ANC, which led the anti-apartheid movement, emulated the ideology and strategies of other liberationist movements in Africa, and it forged an enduring alliance with the South African Communist Party and other opponents of the regime. During the Cold War, the ANC received support from the Soviet Union although it was always a mostly African nationalist organization that was wary of the full embrace of extreme communist ideology. Likewise, virulent black racial nationalism was also disavowed by the ANC; from the 1950s, especially, the ANC has been devoted to a "nonracial" ideology in response to the imposed racial and ethnic divisions of apartheid. Over time, the ANC has included many white, Asian, and "Coloured" moderates.[7]

Resistance to apartheid cruelty stimulated a wide anti-apartheid revolutionary struggle led mostly by the ANC. The ANC pursued non-violent struggle until 1960 when its fight against apartheid turned revolutionary; the ANC allied itself with the South African Communist Party and eventually with the powerful internal trade unions (COSATU, the Congress of South African Trade Unions). Nelson Mandela, leader of the ANC, was sentenced to prison for sabotage in 1964 and imprisoned for 27 years. From 1948 to late 1989, internally the conflict was characterized by a cycle of revolt and repression, exacerbated by the Cold War (South Africa was seen by the West as a pillar against communism), with escalating levels of state violence and anti-apartheid resistance. Anti-apartheid resistance featured strikes and other non-violent tactics and counter-regime violence in the armed struggle launched in 1960. Externally, the South African government regionalized the war through interventions in Angola, Botswana, Mozambique, and Zambia.[8]

Deep-rooted causes of apartheid

- Natural resource competition, related to exploitation of newfound gold, diamonds, and other precious minerals at the height of the industrial revolution (1877).
- Labor competition in newly urbanized settings such as Johannesburg in the 1890s–1940s, with downwardly mobile white workers seeking protection from upwardly mobile black labor.
- The growth of "wild" racial capitalism, with massive fortunes accumulated from the country's rich ores, fueled by wretched working conditions on the mines.
- Anglo-Afrikaner tensions following the Boer Wars, creating sharp internal differences within the white minority and setting the stage for the evolution of anti-imperial Afrikaner nationalism and demands for self-determination.
- Afrikaner chauvinism and *baaskap* (domination) after World War II, with the effort of this minority within a minority to create a separate state and national identity for white South Africans.

Escalatory dynamics: a cycle of revolt and repression

Significant upsurges of rebellion occurred in 1960 (Sharpeville), 1976 (Soweto), and in the broad-based popular uprising of 1984–1989. Feeble and ill-considered reforms that made minor changes to apartheid but left the system basically intact generated new frustrations over white minority rule. From 1984 to 1989, resistance against apartheid grew domestically and internationally; much of the pressure that mounted on the South African state was economic, forcing the governing elite to consider new strategies to protect basic economic stability (such as coping with international financial sanctions) (Price 1991). The trade unions under the banner of COSATU grew more assertive in defiance of apartheid and in pressing for wage increases and social services.[9] The South Africa Council of Churches and many other local and national civil society groups defied authorities in massive protests; young militants made the townships "ungovernable." An internal umbrella coalition called the United Democratic Front (UDF), allied ideologically with the exiled ANC elite, emerged internally to directly challenge the apartheid regime's control of the townships. The international community began to impose ever-escalating sanctions, beginning with an arms boycott in 1977. The popular uprising reflected a still-prevalent political culture in South Africa around destabilizing "mass action."

Violence in South Africa sharply escalated in the late 1980s. In the critical KwaZulu-Natal homeland, putative home of the country's largest ethnic group, the ANC was challenged by the breakaway IFP, a Zulu nationalist movement led by traditional leader Chief Mangosuthu Buthelezi. Many viewed the IFP as a puppet of the regime, with its attacks on the ANC abetted by the apartheid police. Between 1984 and 1990, an estimated 5,500 died in political violence in South Africa in struggles between the anti-apartheid resistance and the police and in ANC-IFP faction-fighting in KwaZulu-Natal that seriously escalated in 1988 and spread to the Johannesburg urban megalopolis. Violence took many forms: attacks against the apartheid state and its institutions and symbols, faction-fighting between the ANC and IFP over local turf (often emanating from single-sex workers' hostels or dormitories), and systematic elimination of rival leaders through assassinations.[10]

By the late 1980s, it appeared to even the most informed observers that South Africa was heading for all-out racial war coupled with Zulu-Xhosa faction-fighting among the black population (the Xhosa are the second largest black ethnic group and are prominent in the ANC). Many view the origins of the KwaZulu-Natal violence in terms of mobilization and counter-mobilization by the ANC and IFP in anticipation of rapid political change (Human Rights Watch 1991: 18–19).[11] Despite having a control of the formal reins of power, a repressive police state, the largest army in Africa, and six nuclear weapons, the apartheid government could not control the streets. The effect of revolutionary violence, as du Toit convincingly argues, is that it significantly weakened ties between the state and society, leaving a feeble, illegitimate structure for governance; this fundamental weakness and illegitimacy of the state also accounts considerably for the inability of either the state or the opposition factions to limit violence encounters during the transition period, directly inhibiting the search for a formula to end apartheid by mutual agreement (du Toit 2001). It was in this context that rogue elements of the police forces committed the worst atrocities, among them the infamous Trust Feeds massacre of December 1999, when 11 people (including women and children) were killed at a funeral in KwaZulu by so-called "special constables" led by police officer Brian Mitchell who had facilitated the attack,[12] Mitchell later tearfully apologized before the Truth and Reconciliation Commission (TRC) on these events in an unforgettable moment of gripping drama.

Evaluating ripeness in South Africa

A confluence of events, including the end of the Cold War, yielded a moment "ripe" for the turn to negotiation in 1989. Peace talks began formally in February 1990, following an extensive period of prenegotiation (1986–1990) in which politicians, businessmen, and civil society leaders began to meet privately and explore solutions to the violence and to South Africa's deep social problems of race and inequality. Among the causes of apartheid's collapse were the inability of the white minority government to sustain the economy in a globalizing world; foreign sanctions and diplomatic incentives for change; and the inability of the state's security apparatus to contain insurrection. Giliomee has evaluated the decision-making process of President de Klerk in pursuing a peace process with the ANC: in sum, he made a calculated political choice to talk given the external international environment, pressures mounting from within the left and right flanks of white politics, and pinching economic sanctions, together with a tactical decision to gain leverage in negotiation by acting early to initiate talks rather than waiting until less favorable developments demanded it (Giliomee 2003: 636–637).

Most important in the initial days of South African transition was a period of prenegotiation, which began as early as 1986 but grew in frequency and culminated in meetings between ANC president (then prisoner) Nelson Mandela and apartheid-era president P.W. Botha in July of 1989. In these and myriad other meetings, described well now in several books (see Waldmeir 1997; Sisk 1995: 67–74; du Toit 2001: 53–55), important agreements were reached on the structure and sequencing of the South African talks. Du Toit reports that there were some 44 meetings between Mandela and government justice minister Kobie Coetsee at the Victor Verster prison in the late 1980s, culminating in the famous president and prisoner summit of July 5, 1989, during which Mandela was brought from the prison for direct talks with then-president P.W. Botha. Significantly, following Botha's resignation (partially for health reasons) shortly thereafter, de Klerk continued the prenegotiation and met with Mandela for a landmark set of talks on December 21, 1989.

These agreements had important ramifications for constitution-making. Among the principles on which the parties agreed were:

- The "New South Africa" would feature full enfranchisement of all citizens; the ANC agreed to address the concerns of the white majority, and agreed to drop its claims to nationalize key industries or to immediately expropriate land.
- The post-apartheid constitution would be democratic and would take into account the country's diversity.
- There would be a cessation of violence premised on an interim period of negotiation on release of prisoners and return of exiles; this would be followed by a period of substantive negotiation on a new constitution.

Transitional violence: 1990–1994, "turning the tap"

South Africa witnessed a dramatic historical turn in the transition from apartheid to democracy that unfolded in the early 1990s, after decades of escalating tensions and violence. The "New South Africa" came into being because of three major factors: a sense of shared and common destiny, a high degree of inter-group economic interdependence, and the abject failure of grand apartheid's attempts to territorialize and reify race and ethnicity.

Initially, the talks that began in 1990 were bilateral – between the NP and ANC led by F.W. de Klerk and Nelson Mandela, respectively – but they eventually became multilateral, broadening to include parties to the right of the NP (notably, the white right-wing Freedom Front) and ANC (notably, the Zulu-nationalist IFP), small African nationalist parties on the radical left such as the Pan-Africanist Congress (PAC), and small, moderate, bridge-building parties such as the Democratic Party (DP). Former homeland governments also participated in the multiparty talks, making them eventually (and especially at the time of the April 1994 elections that ended apartheid) widely inclusive of all the major political forces.

Preliminary pact-making

Perhaps the most important interim negotiated agreement was the first, known as the Groote Schuur "minute" of May 1990.[13] This first accord linked commitment to renunciation of the ANC's armed struggle with normalization of political freedoms, the return of exiles, the release of political prisoners, and the eventual move to full enfranchisement and elections. The pact defined "nonracial democracy" in a united South Africa as the ultimate outcome of the talks. Subsequent pacts were reached in 1990, 1991, 1992, and 1993.[14]

In 1992 and 1993, the growing inclusivity of the process was apparent, including some of the parties of the right and the left of the political spectrum. All along, the process of negotiation was smoothed by small, moderate, bridge-building parties such as the DP. Former homeland governments also participated in the multiparty talks, making the peace process eventually (and especially at the time of the April 1994 elections that ended apartheid), widely inclusive of all the major political forces in the country. This broad inclusion is pointed to as a key element in the success of the transitional negotiations. Within white politics, de Klerk made a strategically wise move to test opinion with a referendum on the peace process, which garnered 62 percent of the vote; this allowed the internal game of white politics to be settled sufficiently for the government to be able to concede in the negotiation arena.

The transition was turbulent and bloody, and spikes in violence were often closely related to – occurring just before or immediately after – transition pacts. In the first three months following the onset of formal NP–ANC talks, violence escalated rapidly; some 951 people died in the strife from June to August of 1990, for example.[15] The epicenters of the violence were in KwaZulu-Natal, where the IFP and the ANC battled for control of the province. Much of the strife was centered on IFP-loyal migrant workers' hostels, which came into conflict with those in neighboring, informal township settlements that supported the ANC. While there were some ethnic overtones (Zulu-Xhosa), the violence was more party-political than ethnic, as illustrated by the within-group struggles among the Zulu in KwaZulu-Natal. Both parties organized self-defense units, which engaged in running battles with each other and with the police. The police were widely accused – and it was later proven – to be acting as a "third force" stoking the enmity by arming and aiding the IFP; this pattern of state support for factional violence had antecedents in the apartheid era, when the government created vigilantes.[16]

Indeed, political violence threatened the talks from the very beginning; in March 1990, a month after Mandela's release from prison, the South African Police opened fire on a group of UDF supporters in Sebokeng, south of Johannesburg, killing 12 and wounding 281 (Human Rights Watch 1991: 23). The ANC canceled its initial round of talks with the government, which resumed only again in April, and in secret.

Political violence: a "turbulent transition"

White right-wing militias and political parties, elements of the South African Police and intelligence services, elements and often the leadership of the IFP, all openly rejected these agreements and fomented violence to bring them down.[17] Similarly, for much of the negotiations outbidders on the ANC's left such as the PAC rejected the talks and members of its armed wing continued to wage an armed struggle. Controversy continues over whether then-president F.W. de Klerk and his senior cabinet officers sought to derail the accord by stoking political violence by clandestine security forces and *agents provocateurs*. Despite the reporting of a myriad of human rights organizations on the violence, and an investigation by the Truth and Reconcilation Commission (TRC), there is no direct evidence that President de Klerk manipulated, directed, or condoned the role of the security forces in stoking political violence.[18] Indeed, the TRC found that there was no coherent entity behind the allegations of a "Third Force," although there was sufficient evidence on individuals and groups within the state that had come forward to confess the perpetration of political violence during the transitional period. Figure 4.1 provides the most illustrative example of the spikes and valleys in political violence, as measured by fatalities over the years of the South African transition. Its peaks were associated with key turning points in the negotiation process. Table 4.1 provides aggregate annual data on fatalities in the most violent years of the transition from apartheid to democracy.

Violence-induced crises: three key turning points in the South African transition

- *The Boipatong massacre, June 17, 1992; Bisho, September 7, 1992.* These two events had exactly opposite effects. After the Boipatong incident in which hostel dwellers from the IFP-allied Kwa Madala hostel attacked and killed 49 ANC supporters in the Boipatong township (near Vanderbiljpark), the ANC called off talks, violence escalated, and the direct talks were suspended. The ANC widely believed that the police had facilitated, escorted, or enabled the attack, although subsequent investigation revealed police incompetence as the primary

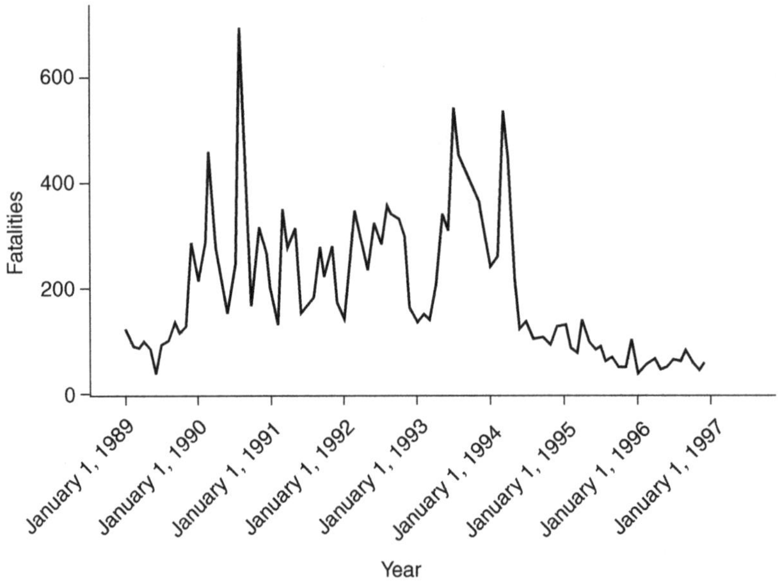

Figure 4.1 Political violence in South Africa's "turbulent transition" (source: South African Survey (1997), as reported in Guelke 2000: 241).

Table 4.1 Transitional violence in South Africa, 1990–1996 (number of deaths attributed to political violence)

Year	*KwaZulu-Natal*	*Entire South Africa*
1990	1,811	3,699
1991	1,057	2,706
1992	1,427	3,347
1993	1,489	3,794
1994	1,464	2,476
1995	905	1,044
1996	536	1,057
Total	8,689	15,123

Source: Adapted from du Toit (2001). Based on data compiled by the South Africa Institute of Race Relations. Data for 1995–1996 from *Human Rights Review*, as reported by Guelke (2000: 241).

form of complicity.[19] The perception of culpability for the Boipatong attack, however, clearly rested with the government.

In the Bisho incident, on the other hand, the ANC was seen as culpable in an ill-fated march on the capital of the government-allied Ciskei homeland in which ANC leaders made crucial tactical mistakes that ended up costing 29 lives.[20] The talks resumed and quickly progressed on a wide range of previously intractable issues.

- *The assassination of Chris Hani, April 10, 1993.* Following the murder of South African Communist Party chief Hani by a conspiratorial group involving a prominent former Conservative Party MP Clive Darby-Lewis and the gunman, Janusz Walus, South Africa teetered on the brink of civil war. The two men believed that the killing would instigate a crisis that would end the transition from apartheid. Indeed, following the assassination millions marched in the major cities, precipitating street-level chaos and costing dozens of lives.

The April 1993 assassination failed to derail the talks despite widespread public protests following his death; although Hani had previously called for "people's war," prior to his killing he emerged as a critical voice for moderation, talks, and peace.[21] Efforts by white right-wingers to disrupt talks on an interim constitution in June 1993 failed to prevent the Interim Constitution from being sealed that month. Significantly, a white right-wing bombing campaign and an eleventh hour ANC-IFP shootout in downtown Johannesburg (the Shell House massacre) in the early months of 1994 failed to prevent the celebrated elections in April that brought Mandela to power and ended apartheid. The ANC leadership, particularly, changed its view and recognized that much of the violence was aimed at derailing its pursuit of power. Thus, a settlement was clinched in June 1993 despite the ongoing strife on the street and implemented as from 1994 despite the constant threat of social meltdown.

The assassination was the most significant of many crises that occurred during the transition. Its significance was marked by the reaction it invoked: rather than derailing the peace process, the murder had the effect of stiffening the resolve of elites to see through the peace process to comprehensive settlement. Following the assassination, which occurred on Easter Sunday on the driveway of Hani's suburban Johannesburg home, Mandela flew from his ancestral home in the Eastern Cape to the scene to calm a nation on the brink of a violent confrontation; he spoke on SABC national television:

> We are a nation deeply wounded by callous, uncaring men who plot such heinous crimes with impunity. The cries of our nation are heard from old men who bury their sons and daughters, wives who weep for their husbands, communities who endlessly bury young and old, infants and pregnant women. This killing must stop.
>
> Chris Hani championed the cause of peace, trudging to every corner of South Africa calling for a spirit of tolerance among all our people. We are a nation in mourning. Our pain and anger is real. Yet we must not permit ourselves to be provoked by those who seek to deny us the very freedom Chris Hani gave his life for. Let us respond with dignity and in a disciplined fashion.[22]

- *The Shell House incident, March 28, 1994.* Pitched battles between ANC and IFP supporters broke out in the streets of Johannesburg a month before the transitional elections in April 1994. In this incident, culpability clearly lay with the IFP, which had organized the event to demonstrate bargaining power in anticipation of the electoral process revealing relatively low levels of support in society. Eleven IFP supporters demonstrating in support of the political demands of the Zulu King (Zwelithini) were killed by an ANC security guard (reportedly, with a history of ill discipline) as a crowd of supporters had begun to surge toward Shell House (the ANC's party headquarters in Johannesburg), apparently in an effort to occupy the building.[23] Following this incident, the IFP (an erstwhile spoiler) was brought into the talks through a process of negotiations eventually brought to fruition by an international mediator (see below); in the bargain, the IFP's concession to contest the election was matched by assurances by the ANC on the status of the Zulu King, rights and roles for traditional leaders, and a role in the power-sharing government for party leader Mangosuthu Buthelezi.

Toward settlement

The most important feature of the interim agreement was the agreement by the ANC on a period of interim, essentially consociational, power sharing. Why did the ANC, clearly garnering the support of a majority of the electorate, agree to a period of interim power sharing? The basic rationale for ANC acquiescence to power sharing – demanded by the incumbent NP regime – is outlined in the controversial 1992 ANC discussion document authored by former Communist Party leader Joe Slovo, "Strategic Perspectives."[24] In order to prevent a counter-revolutionary threat to the new political order emanating from the bureaucracy and security forces, sharing power with the outgoing white minority regime (and implicitly political foes like the IFP) was a self-interested, "strategic" necessity for the ANC. But these concessions would be limited by a sunset clause that would allow formal power sharing to expire after five years.

Key elements of the 1993 Interim Constitution

- *The GNU.* A Government of National Unity (GNU) would govern for up to five years, which would include all major parties on the South African scene. Each party winning more than 5 percent of the vote would be entitled to a proportionate number of seats in the 27-person cabinet. Decision-making in the cabinet would not be based on majority rule, but instead decisions would be taken in a "consensus-seeking spirit" without formal–legal constraints.
- *Constitutional Assembly.* Based on the outcome of the 1994 elections, a new 400-member National Assembly and province-derived Senate would sit jointly in a Constitutional Assembly to craft a new, permanent national charter. The decision rule for approval of the new charter was 2/3rds, although the pact included a complicated deadlock-breaking mechanism.
- *Electoral principles.* The parties agreed to a proportional representation list system (amended in February 1994 to include national and regional ballots), full adult franchise, and the creation of an Independent Electoral Commission to oversee the vote slated for April 1994.
- *Regionalism.* Nine provinces would be allowed to adopt their own constitutions "consistent with the constitutional principles and national constitution" and these would be certifiable by the Constitutional Court. The powers and functions of local governments are enumerated. Provision is made for the establishment of traditional authorities and of provincial houses of traditional leaders.
- *Security.* The constitution provides for the integration of the South African National Defense Force with the armed wings of the liberation forces and the creation of the South African Police Services.
- *Constitutional principles.* The Interim Constitution contained a series of 32 constitutional principles that delimited the parameters of the final constitution, particularly on the powers of the regions. These principles were the most important substantive aspects of agreement that guided subsequent constitution-making.

- *Economics.* Private property rights are guaranteed, but expropriation (especially land) is possible under certain rules and with compensation of fair market value. Trade union rights are assured, but the Interim Constitution also included an employer "lock-out" clause.
- *Judicial review.* A Constitutional Court – appointed by the president – would be established to have wide original jurisdiction to determine the constitutionality of any statute, regulation, or administrative procedure. The court was empowered to certify the final constitution as in conformity with the constitutional principles.

The "strategic perspectives" pragmatism was backed up by political foresight and finesse, manifested by the ANC concessions of early 1994 to the Freedom Front and the IFP – potential spoilers of the pact – that brought these parties into the GNU at the eleventh hour and averted a bloody showdown at the moment of regime change following the liberation elections of April 1994. The establishment of a clear time frame proved salutary in the South African case. By firmly setting a non-negotiable deadline for elections, the ANC created what is known as a "departing train" scenario. If the potential spoilers had not jumped aboard at the last minute, the elections train would leave the station and leave these parties in the political wilderness. This time frame – a key plank of the Record of Understanding – revealed that clear benchmarks in time for progress can help induce progress in reaching constitutional agreements (as deadlines did later in South Africa with the negotiation of the final constitution, and as they have in Northern Ireland's Good Friday agreement).

Informal power-sharing institutions, 1990–1994

- Working groups on political offenses and political prisoners, established by the Groote Schuur minute (pact) of May 1990.
- Armed Action Working Committee, established by the Pretoria minute of August 1990 and later a Liaison Committee created by the D.F. Malan minute of February 1991; ANC/IFP liaison committees on political violence established in bilateral talks to address the East Rand/KwaZulu–Natal conflicts. The creation of the Conference for a Democratic South Africa (CODESA I) in December 1991 and its five working groups, which collapsed in May 1992 at the CODESA II conference.
- National, regional, and local-level peace committees enabled by the National Peace Accord of December 1992.
- The reliance of *bosberaad* (or bush meeting) conferences as deadlock-breaking sessions, in which the details of the transition were thrashed out in ANC–NP bilateral negotiations.

- The Multiparty Negotiating Process, April 1 through July 1993, in which the interim pact was negotiated; the most important decision-making structure was the Negotiating Council.
- The establishment of the Transitional Executive Council, or multiparty cabinet committee, to oversee the government during the election campaign and establish multiparty control over broadcasting, finance, and the security forces.

Managing spoilers, July 1993–April 1994

A significant share of the violence, particularly the high-profile, crisis-inducing events that directly affected the negotiation process, was perpetrated by right-wing spoilers. White right-wing militias and political parties; rogue elements of the South African Police and intelligence services; and members of the IFP, often in collusion with that party's local leadership, all openly rejected the NP–ANC agreements and fomented violence to bring down the peace process. Similarly, for much of the negotiations, outbidders (extremists) on the ANC's left, such as the PAC, rejected the talks, and members of its armed wing continued to wage a feeble armed struggle. Occasionally, PAC cadres carried out attacks as well, mostly notably the July 25, 1993 attack by PAC loyalists at the St. James Church in Cape Town, killing 11 and wounding 50; in TRC testimony, it was affirmed that this attack was authorized at the highest levels of the PAC's military wing (APLA, the Azanian People's Liberation Army). Three of the four perpetrators of the attack were granted amnesty by the TRC.[25] Attacks by APLA, primarily on civilian targets, accounted for a small but symbolically important set in unsuccessful attempts to derail the peace process train.

Clearly, the IFP was culpable in much of the violence as it perpetrated "facts on the ground" in an ultimately somewhat futile attempt to demonstrate power in the negotiations. Indeed, there is evidence from the TRC that ANC–NP agreements on an election in the June 1993 settlement created incentives for the IFP to foment violence to prevent the election going ahead (on the terms that had been agreed to without them and without the white right-wing parties); the TRC reported that "With the IFP's chief negotiator threatening a civil war if the elections went ahead without the IFP, deaths from political violence in July and August 1993 soared to 605 and 705 respectively, compared to 267 in June 1993" (Truth and Reconciliation Commission 1998: 584). Likewise, in many cases it was difficult to differentiate between violence that had both a criminal and a political component: Mary de Haas observed that "much violence which appears criminal also serves important political ends, such as that of the amaSinyora gang which terrorized sections of KwaMashu in Durban for several years, during the late 1980s and early 1990s" (de Haas 1994: 227).[26] Nonetheless, she concludes that:

> There is ... correspondence between escalating conflict [in 1993] and what is happening [in talks] at the World Trade Centre. Whilst great caution must be exercised in positing causal relationships between unreliable death statistics and what is happening in the broader society, there is no denying the coincidence between the sudden intensification of violence [near Johannesburg], which was so clearly orchestrated, and the breakthroughs in negotiations, particularly given the war talk by the conservative forces...
>
> (de Haas 1994: 244)

Efforts by 3,000 armed white right-wingers to disrupt talks in June 1993 failed to prevent the Interim Constitution from being sealed that month. White right-wing attacks were spectacular, such as a major bombing campaign in early 1994, but in the end failed to have a major effect on the progress of talks.[27] In the end, armed resistance to change by the right wing ended on the streets of Mmbatho, Bophuthatswana in March 1994, when an extremist off-shoot organization (the *Afrikaner Weerstandsbeweging*, or AWB) were killed in a failed attempt to seize the homeland in cooperation with the apartheid-era puppet leader, Lucas Mangope. Following the rout, from which photographs of the bodies of two dead AWB paramilitary men were carried in the major papers around the world, the political leader of the right wing, General Constand Viljoen, agreed to the entry of the Freedom Alliance into the political process.[28] Viljoen had previously had a significant number of negotiations with Mandela on Afrikaner cultural rights in a post-apartheid South Africa.

Overall, however, the violence on the streets forced the ruling party to make key concessions in the negotiations, as the IFP–ANC violence caused the state to concede more to the ANC in talks, particularly over control and reform of the police, the timing of elections, and over the extent and nature of power sharing. As Adrian Guelke explains:

> First, the violence projected an image of instability that threatened investment and hence economic growth, particularly because the location of the main arenas of conflict, the townships on the East Rand, lay at the heart of South Africa's manufacturing industry. Second, the violence also threatened to reverse the progress the government had made toward the normalization of relations with the outside world as the result of the liberalization of the political system in 1990. Third, the scale of the violence was such as to generate fears that it could make the country ungovernable, creating the spectre of social breakdown and political fragmentation.
>
> (Guelke 2000: 252)

International and internal mediation in South Africa

Mounting sanctions on South Africa, beginning in 1960 after Sharpeville and increasing in intensity in 1977 (after Soweto, to include a UN arms embargo) and again in the 1980s (most poignantly, with the passage of the Comprehensive Anti-Apartheid Act by the US Congress over President Ronald Reagan's veto in 1996) helped induce ripeness for negotiation. Prior to the upsurge in violence in the mid-1980s, there was little direct engagement by external mediators. However, beginning after the popular upsurge following failed political reforms in 1984, coalitions of international mediators became more engaged. One of the first significant external interventions to facilitate talks was the 1986 Commonwealth Eminent Persons Group, which called for a declaration on the dismantling of apartheid, a de-escalation of violence, the release of Mandela, and "synchronization" of steps by the government and ANC to escape the "first-mover" trap in negotiations (Commonwealth Secretariat 1986: 101–125). While the Commonwealth report itself was rejected by the P.W. Botha government, at the same time the formula – in the Report's terms, the "negotiating concept" – that emerged from the mission was the essential formula that subsequently emerged for the South African peace process.

Most mediation in South Africa to keep the talks on track was internal, led by church and business leaders; in particular, the institutionalization of clerical and business efforts through the Consultative Business Movement was a critical element in allowing domestic mediators to serve as go-betweens.[29] After the June 1992 Boipatong incident – a significant crisis – the UN dispatched Cyrus Vance as a Special Representative of the Secretary-General on a fact-finding mission designed to prevent the talks from going off track. Had the talks gone off the track altogether, it was clear that levels of violence would escalate. Vance met with all the parties, implicitly (but not explicitly) mediating while the talks were frozen and de Klerk and Mandela were engaged in vituperative exchanges of letters blaming one another for the breakdown in talks and engaging in mutual recrimination over the violence.

The Vance mission resulted in the August 1992 deployment of a 60-member UN Observer Mission to South Africa (UNOMSA), which monitored political violence (but was barred from mediation). United Nations monitors were augmented by European Union, Commonwealth, and Organization of African Unity (OAU) observers, about 100 altogether (eventually, UNOMSA grew to about 3,000 observers). The OAU and Commonwealth observers were less constrained by their mandates, and they directly mediated a number of hot disputes, particularly the Hani assassination crisis and in virtual civil war then raging in KwaZulu-Natal. The observers did not directly mediate (it was beyond their mandate), but they were the critically important "eyes and ears" of the international community.

Indeed, there was widespread skepticism about international mediation as the talks wound to a close in early 1994 as the date for an election was to be set and key issues such as the inclusion of white ring-wing parties (who had coalesced under the Freedom Alliance) and the IFP in the elections. Disputes also ran high on issues such as territorial autonomy or a territorial homeland demanded by white right-wing Afrikaners and a strong federalist formula demanded by Inkatha.

Close observers to the negotiations sensed that calls for international mediation were met with widespread skepticism from all but the IFP (a weaker party with ostensible interest in mediator entry to gain concessions from its stronger foe, principally the ANC). Both the government and the ANC were skeptical of international mediation, as then US Ambassador to South Africa Princeton Lyman reports in his memoirs (Lyman 2000: 202–209). Finally, rather than allowing a Japanese mediator clearly advocated by the IFP, the ANC called for the involvement of two eminent persons on the world stage, Lord Carrington and Henry Kissinger.

With the IFP's vowing to spoil the poll and violence escalating in the closing months of the transition, Lord Carrington and Henry Kissinger were eventually brought in to mediate between the NP, ANC, and IFP. The mediation attempt was an unqualified failure; after several days, the two left without agreement on their terms of reference; in reality, despite inviting Kissinger into the process, the ANC (Mandela and Ramaphosa) made the decision that the mediation was off (affirming their skepticism that the mediation itself was a last-minute effort for concessions principally by the IFP). A modest Kenyan professor – Washington Okumu – who was curiously part of the Carrington–Kissinger mission, stayed behind and brokered a last-minute accord on April 19 in which the IFP agreed to contest the poll and accept the settlement. But this was less mediation than face-saving by the IFP (and especially Buthelezi, who claims a religious insight in prayer with Okumu), which had been out-maneuvered in the negotiation and was threatened with political oblivion if it failed to contest the liberation April 26–28 elections. Hastily, poll workers literally pasted an IFP option at the bottom of the ballots for the landmark liberation poll. From Okumu's mediation, little was new with the exception of a promise for future mediation, a deal which the ANC subsequently failed to abide by.

South Africa: political violence, in retrospect

The violence often tracked major turning points in the negotiation process. Violence was used in the negotiations strategically: to derail the peace process, to prove political power, and to destabilize and marginalize opponents. Du Toit argues that the violence was often strategic and instrumental; moreover, it was not directly managed by the highest-level elites, but emanating from mid-level cadres and in direct confrontations by mostly IFP and ANC allied local structures. He writes:

> The very best efforts of Buthelezi, de Klerk and Mandela could not prevent those actors with the intent and coercive means from increasing the levels of violence.... Violence escalated because the structure of conflict (with the profound and basic breakdown of the rules of war) *resulted* in the emergence of coercive units who operated virtually autonomously from political and even military leadership....
>
> At the onset of negotiations these coercive units gained more freedom to act, not less. This was a function of the negotiations process where the lack of explicit commitment to good faith, in the widest sense of the word, perpetuated and even exacerbated the problems of political and military control.
>
> (du Toit 2001: 78, emphasis in original)

Particularly after the Bisho incident, it was clear that the ANC and the NP had made a strategic decision to push through talks despite the political violence. In bargaining terms, the South African protagonists relied on a back-channel of secret negotiations when violence or other deadlocks threatened talks. Patti Waldmeir, who covered the peace process for the *Financial Times*, observed that:

> Even in the dark hours, the ANC and National Party kept their sights firmly on the dawn. While Mandela and de Klerk were trading insults from Boipatong to Bisho, their two young lieutenants – Cyril Ramaphosa, thirty-nine and Roelf Meyer, forty-four – were meeting secretly to look for a deal. Between June and September 1992, they met something like forty-three times in what became known as 'the channel'.
>
> (Waldmeir 1997: 208)

By April 1993, senior ANC officials including Mandela had begun to admit that at least some of the violence was being perpetrated by ANC cadres, and that the ANC would need to adopt new strategies including consideration of an ill-conceived and ill-fated "internal peacekeeping force."

A key aspect of the success of the South African peace process lies with civil society. Many attribute the strength of contemporary civil society in South Africa to the plethora of organizations that spontaneously sprouted during the difficult years of apartheid. Despite the oppressive, exclusive apartheid state that purposefully sought to keep groups apart through social policies such as separate political enfranchisement, housing, and education systems, and in social life through separate religious organizations, progressive anti-apartheid organizations worked against such policies. In neighborhoods and communities, in exile politics and in underground movements at home, civil society groups were geared toward disproving apartheid's premise that separation, not integration, is the solution to multiethnicity.

During the transitional period, these civil society groups emerged as critically important because of the legitimacy they secured from their long and difficult struggle against the apartheid state. Although organizations such as the South African Council of Churches or Congress of South African Trade Unions faced enormous problems as they evolved from liberation organizations to partners in negotiation and eventually governance, they were critical to a relatively smooth transition process. In virtually every arena of public policy, parallel civil society forums emerged as alternative arenas of bargaining in which mid-level and grassroots participants augmented the elite-level bargaining of the formal constitution-making activities.

A report of the Carnegie Commission on Preventing Deadly Conflict titled *A House No Longer Divided: Progress and Prospects for Democratic Peace in South Africa* (Stremlau and Zille 1997) details the comparatively extensive social integration and the pivotal role that civil society actors played in supporting, and at times mediating, in the formal negotiation process. For example, in June 1992, as the negotiations were on the brink of collapse, the South African Council of Churches stepped in to mediate among the political parties; this initiative is credited with keeping the process on track in the midst of extremely damaging political violence.

Another instance of mediation by civil society actors is the experience with the structures of the National Peace Accord, an agreement reached in late 1991 that set up violence monitoring and prevention committees at the national, regional, and local level. The Peace Accord committees were facilitated mostly by non-governmental organizations, and they included a myriad of bargaining arenas in the most troubled areas (such as KwaZulu-Natal and the "East Rand" near Johannesburg) that brought together the police, anti-apartheid neighborhood committees, political parties, church leaders, social workers, and trained mediators. Through the layered peace structures, mid-level elites (particularly the police and local ANC and IFP party activists) had the opportunity to build critical cross-ethnic ties (Gastrow 1995; Collin Marks 2000).

Peace in post-apartheid South Africa

The negotiators reached a broad-based agreement on formal power sharing in the 1993 Interim Constitution. This agreement was a quintessential political pact, or mutual security agreement, in which democratization occurs with the explicit protection of the interests of the incumbent regime and its military and security forces. Such pact-making and consensus-seeking continued after the elections of 1994 and through the period of constitution-making by the elected Constitutional Assembly (which also acted as an interim parliament) until the adoption of a permanent constitution and its eventual certification by the Constitutional Court in October 1996.

Table 4.2 The 1994 liberation election results

Party	*Seats*	*Percentage*
African National Congress	252	63.7
National Party	82	20.2
Inkatha Freedom Party	43	9.8
Freedom Front	9	2.8
Democratic Party	7	2.0
Pan-Africanist Congress	5	1.0
African Christian Democratic Party	2	0.04

The linchpin feature of the interim agreement was the concession by the ANC on a period of transitional power sharing and a pledge to ensure the jobs and livelihood of the civil service, South African Defense Force (SADF, now SANDF) and the police. The power-sharing pragmatism was backed up by political finesse, manifested by the ANC concessions of early 1994 to the right-wing Freedom Front and the IFP.

These concessions to potential spoilers of the pact brought these parties into the GNU at the eleventh hour and averted a bloody showdown during the liberation elections of April 1994. South African political scientist Vincent Maphai summed up the 1993 democratization pact well when he said "we formed our government before we elected it" in the celebrated founding elections held April 26–28, 1994.[30] Table 4.2 shows the final results of the elections, reflecting the percentage of votes and the concomitant seats in the 400-member National Assembly.

Successful political settlement in South Africa was clearly the result of heroic and skillful leadership. Often, rather than exploit concessions as extracted from wary opponents, the negotiators would describe them as victories in pursuit of lofty principles. As a result, the negotiations and the settlement that sealed agreement were not seen as giving in or compromising aims, but as discovering what is fair and just for this long-conflicted society.

The constitution-making process

During the period of formal ANC–NP power sharing (1994–1996), deliberations continued on a new set of post-apartheid political institutions.[31] After two years of deliberations by the Constitutional Assembly, the ongoing negotiations on a permanent charter came to fruition with the adoption of the new constitution of South Africa, which was ultimately finalized in October 1996. The 1996 constitution – designed to serve South Africa into the indefinite future – does not include consociational power sharing. There is no grand coalition and no ironclad minority veto. Voluntary executive-level coalitions are possible, of course, but there is no constitutional mandate that parties not receiving a majority of the vote must be included in executive decision-making. Nevertheless, there are several reasons why the new institutions will have integrative (as opposed to consociational), conflict-ameliorating effects and that neither ethnic nor racial hegemony through the ANC or ethnic meltdown are likely scenarios for South Africa in the long term. Power sharing continues in many non-executive, informal political institutions and arenas in South Africa, along with formal power sharing with Zulu nationalists by the ANC ruling coalition.

Highlights of constitution-making, 1994–1996

- The proceedings were generally open and transparent, with a very high level of public education on the issues, and public input (via mail, meetings, surveys, and contributions on the Internet).[32] The Assembly received and evaluated over 1.9 million submissions during the public comment period. Especially insightful were the inputs submitted by non-governmental organizations, an extensive public relations/information campaign, widespread radio advertisements, and public meetings. People felt like they could and would be heard on the constitutional issues that mattered in their daily lives.
- The IFP essentially boycotted much of the formal negotiating process, insisting that agreements made in April 1994 with the ANC on post-election international mediation be upheld (such mediation never occurred). The party also asserted that regional powers were insufficiently entrenched by the Interim Constitution's principles.
- In general, agreement was reached by consensus; when sticking points arose on specific issues (death penalty, appointment of judges, employer lock-out clause, competence of regions, own-language education, etc.) the differences were ironed out in bilateral meetings between the ANC and NP, or with other parties (such as the Freedom Front on own-language education or the Democratic Party on appointment of judges). This method of negotiation reflects the earlier pattern of deal-making in South Africa.
- Agreement on a Cultural Commission for the Promotion and Protection of the Rights of Cultural, Religious, and Linguistic Communities resolved much of the concern about "group rights." The Commission is purely advisory but has an important "bargaining arena" function. The most important judiciable rights are those relating to non-discrimination on the basis of race, religion, culture, gender, sexual preference, or national origin.
- Careful attention was paid to ensure that the provisions of the constitution were consistent with international law, especially human rights law and humanitarian law.
- The Constitutional Court rejected the initial draft of the charter in May 1996 and sent it back to the Constitutional Assembly to ensure its

conformity with the principles and to safeguard independence of several state institutions (e.g. the Auditor-General and the Public Protector); this was an important, early indication of the power of an independent judiciary.

- The constitution was adopted by a vote of 421 to 2, with 12 abstentions. The IFP did not participate in the final vote.
- The new constitution was signed by President Mandela on December 10, the anniversary of the 1960 Sharpeville massacre (now Human Rights Day).

At the very heart of the constitution-making process in South Africa were the nitty-gritty technical committees, working groups, and in-the-trenches negotiations among the members of the Constitutional Assembly between 1994 and 1996.[33] Although the details of the talks were somewhat tiresome and even anti-climatic, as the May 1996 deadline for the completion of the negotiations approached the parties came close to deadlock on a series of critical issues. Like in the many negotiations that preceded the final days, resolution of outstanding issues – a debate on the right of employers to lock out striking workers and the volatile issue of own-language education – the final negotiations were turned over to what had become known as the ANC–NP "Channel," consisting of negotiators Cyril Ramaphosa and Roelf Meyer, respectively.[34] In many ways, the real explanation of success in South African constitution-making rests in the skill, charm, rapport, and trust that existed between these two men, representing as they did the contending social forces in a deeply divided society. On May 10, 1996, in a warm – and for many, tearful – ceremony, President Nelson Mandela dedicated the new constitution "to the People of South Africa."

Post-apartheid South Africa: ten years toward reconciliation (1994–2004)

A decade of full enfranchisement and governance under the ANC has proven relatively peaceful, with political violence sharply diminished (although, as described below, criminal violence has sharply increased). The 1996 constitution was approved by a wide range of political parties and now enjoys virtually universal acceptance. The country survived the unexpected, early demise of the GNU when the NP withdrew in May 1996. Today, the Democratic Alliance (DA), which once included the NP but now does not, is the official opposition party in parliament.

Several factors have led to a marked decline in political violence in South Africa, especially in the troubled KwaZulu-Natal region. (As Table 4.3 shows, fatalities attributed to political violence have been reduced in South Africa to levels that are common even in states that are not "war-torn," such as Mexico or Brazil.) First is the true commitment of leadership to halt the party-political rivalry that fueled much of the strife; Mandela and

Table 4.3 Post-settlement violence in South Africa, 1997–2003 (number of deaths attributed to political violence)

Year	*KwaZulu-Natal*	*Entire South Africa*
1997	226	470
1998	NA	353
1999	NA	650
2000	NA	20
2001	12	70
2002	7	57
2003	8	24
Total	253	1,644

Sources: Data for 1994–1997 and 1998 (entire) from du Toit (2001). Data for 1999–2001 from the Project Ploughshares Armed Conflicts Report, available at www.ploughshares.ca/acr. For later years, compilation of news and human rights reports. (NA is "not available.")

subsequently Mbeki included Buthelezi in the first several post-apartheid governments. Thus, much of the earlier violence was transitional and much of it was the consequence of elite instigation. Second, after 1994, the police and military were under new command and became increasingly less predisposed to play an *agent provocateur* "third force" role. Third, the violence between 1990 and 1994 was partly a struggle for political territory – geographical areas from which parties could exclude their rivals. Once the election was passed, incentives for violence subsided (although they did not disappear altogether).

Despite the formal end of apartheid more than a decade ago, South Africa continues to struggle with racial and ethnic divisions, particularly around the still-troubled concept of race and its still prominent role despite legislative and policy efforts to make apartheid-era divisions less salient. In public attitudes and popular discourse the language of race – such as "black" economic empowerment or in the debate over the further integration of "white" sports such as rugby and cricket – remains a significant point of social differentiation and an ongoing root cause of conflict. At the same time, ethnic differences within the black community and along a number of other lines are also salient points of social conflict, such that race is embedded in other forms of identity that are at times equally salient. And religious differences are also sometimes a source of conflict, particularly in localized settings.

While South African society has come a long way from its officially racist past, and the government has made considerable strides in redressing social inequalities along racial lines, policy debates are laced with allegations of privilege, of discrimination, or reverse discrimination, of minority grievances, and code words such as "transformation" that underscore the basic fact that South Africa remains a deeply divided society. Differences between President Thabo Mbeki and former president F.W. de Klerk and several white journalists over minority rights and majority prerogatives, which flared in 2005, are reflective of the broader social debate about burying the past, addressing present imbalances, and the future of South Africa as a "rainbow nation" society.

The truth and reconciliation process

In a concerted effort to directly address the atrocities of the past, South Africans borrowed on transition experiences elsewhere (such as Chile) to create the Truth and Reconciliation Commission (TRC) to investigate apartheid-era crimes, consider amnesty for perpetrators who came forward to acknowledge and report on crimes, and to pay reparations to victims of injustices. The TRC was co-chaired by Nobel Peace Laureate Desmond Tutu and a widely respected clergyman and democracy campaigner in South Africa, Alex Boraine. It is clear that part of the explanation of the TRC's relative success in South Africa was the capacity to cast the reconciliation in quasi-religious (mostly Christian) terms; the TRC's proceedings and especially local hearings had ritualistic quality which contributed significantly to the overall social capacity for forgiveness.[35]

The TRC's mandate was to systematically investigate apartheid-era human rights abuses, suggest ways to compensate the victims, and hear applications for amnesty in exchange for full disclosure of facts related to politically motivated crimes. The Commission began work in 1996 and issued a report to President Nelson Mandela on October 29, 1998. In 2001, the Commission concluded its work after processing 7,127 applications for amnesty, investigating 14,000 political killings in the 1980s and 1990s, assigning culpability to the state and liberation forces for abuses, and being a sufficiently public process that has contributed to a broader sense of social healing. In sum, the TRC has mostly succeeded in putting the past to rest, at least in terms of offering a ritualistic or ceremonial pursuit of transitional justice. South Africa is less reconciled, however, on matters of socio-economic "transformation" (Gibson 2004).

Re-evaluating South Africa's peace process

South Africa's story of negotiated transition can be seen in two fundamental ways. One is a predominant view that in this country reason prevailed over fear leading to negotiating a settlement to avert all-out civil war; in this view, much credit goes to leadership such as Nelson Mandela and the many negotiators who persisted in talks despite setbacks, mistrust, and street-level violence. South Africa's "miracle" transition has produced a "rainbow nation of God," or a model multiethnic democracy. More realistically, however, the peace process progressed to settlement because of the mutual dependence of the parties (giving them a symmetry of bargaining power), divisions within the ruling apartheid-era elite that allowed moderate voices to prevail once the fundamental dilemmas inherent in the ideology of separation became overwhelming, the ability of the negotiators to devise innovative rules of negotiation (such as the idea of "sufficient consensus"), and above all, high-quality leadership (du Toit 2001: 85–114). As Mandela said of de Klerk on the day he accepted the Nobel Peace Prize (December 10, 1993):

> He had the courage to admit that a terrible wrong had been done to our country and people through the imposition of the system of apartheid. He had the foresight to understand and accept that all the people of South Africa must through negotiations and as equal participants in the process, together determine what they want to make of their future.[36]

A less salutary interpretation is that the negotiations left economic and social root causes of conflict intact; the tough issues of redistribution were deferred, and not resolved. Political institutions changed, but the society is still beset by deep-seated inequalities, grievances, prejudice, and now disease (HIV). In this view, the negotiated settlement is paper thin. Some believe that within the ANC the compromises reached in the 1990s were strategic, with the second phase of the revolution – dramatic overhaul of the still-capitalist economy – to come.

- South Africa's historical context is full of both high levels of social conflict and remarkable strides toward accommodation and conflict management. Such a history could set the stage for renewed violence as new social tensions emerge, or for continued strengthening and eventual consolidation of democracy. The xenophobic violence that erupted in 2008 – in which hundreds were killed and thousands displaced – is indicative of these underlying root causes of conflict.
- So far, the more optimistic view of South Africa's democratic transition as a just exit from apartheid's conflict is more credible. The depth of support for democracy in South Africa runs high, and the ANC has emerged as a broad-tent political party that now – in an element of true historical irony – includes the leaders of the now-disbanded NP.
- The negotiated transition left many of the more positive elements of South Africa's structure intact: a strong private sector, a functioning banking system, the best physical infrastructure in Africa, a good technology base, and a well-developed system of higher education; to these assets may be added a reasonably good set of political institutions that were the product of well-considered decisions by highly informed negotiators.
- The key question for the future is: Will the compromises reached for peace in the 1990s frustrate the eventual "transformation" of the underlying social and economic inequalities that permeate South

African society? Tough issues of land reform, education reform, workers' rights, and the meeting of basic needs for the impoverished majority mean that history's wrongs will remain challenges well into the twenty-first century South African future.

These root causes of conflict contain the key ingredients to manifest new political violence, instability, and in the worst scenario a total breakdown of government capacity (a failed state). However, it is difficult if not impossible to define every possible way that South Africa's stressed social environment could lead to a sharp escalation of conflict, either along old apartheid-era lines or along new fissures. Indeed, the transition left both a weak state and a culture of violence in South Africa (du Toit 2001: 114). The sources of grievance may well expand in the next ten years as the demographic, social, and material bases for conflict remain or in some instances worsen.

Generally, the linkages between root causes and a sharp escalation of political violence or instability in South Africa are found in the complex linkages between poverty, inequality, and frustration and desperation in stressed township and city environments. Some areas see unemployment of up to 60 percent, with a weak informal economy providing barely subsistence living. The most imminent threat to the country lies in a large cadre of mobilized, disaffected youth in these areas who may cohere around politicized conflict groups – either party-political, criminal, ethnic, or around new radicalized ideologies such as extreme African nationalism. Such groupings, mobilized by a neo-revolutionary mindset, may become very attractive to masses of dejected youth unless the government is somehow able to dramatically expand employment. As the country sees leadership change within the ruling ANC, it is likely that many new such challenges may emerge.

South Africa in the twenty-first century: poverty, inequality, and disease

Estimates of unemployment levels vary greatly, with common expert claims of 5–8 million unemployed; unemployment rates are estimated to be 31 percent nationally but in some areas the rates are as high as 80 percent. Some analysts believe that there are at least 4–6 million South Africans (11–18 percent of the entire population) who are "desperately" unemployed, meaning that they have no access to sustainable livelihood outside of small-scale trading, meager gardens, or charity. It is estimated that these "poorest of the poor" survive on R144 ($24) per person per month. Three children in five live in poor households. Only 11.8 million of the 23.8 million poorest South Africans receive public social assistance according to a 2004 report by the Johannesburg-based Centre for Civil Society.

- Little progress has been made in reducing overall levels of poverty in the last decade, such that the proportion of people living in poverty has not dropped since 1994. In fact, according to the Human Sciences Research Council, those living in poverty have sunk deeper into despair, and inequality – particularly among Africans – has widened.

- Poorer households have not benefited from economic growth. In 1996, the poverty gap was estimated to be 6.7 percent of gross domestic product but by 2001 it had risen to 8.3 percent (the poverty gap is the difference between an average poor household's income and the poverty line).
- The GINI coefficient measuring income inequality rose from 0.69 in 1991 and 1996 to 0.77 in 2001; most new inequality is within the African community; "horizontal inequalities" between racial groups have narrowed in the wake of post-apartheid black empowerment policies. The "empowerment," though, has been differentially felt such that a minority of black South Africans has been able to take advantage of new economic opportunities.
- Regional variations suggest some areas are especially vulnerable to poverty-related frustration and possible social tension: Limpopo and the Eastern Cape are the poorest provinces, with 77 percent and 72 percent of their populations living in poverty, respectively. Poverty is most extreme in rural areas (74 percent) but is also endemic in urban areas (41 percent).
- Poverty rates will grow as HIV/AIDS disproportionately affects working-age people and leads to sky-rocketing dependency rates. The February 2005 report that showed AIDS-related deaths increasing a shocking 57 percent in 2004 reveals a much more significant effect on the economy from the disease than the already dire predictions of its effects. AIDS is differentially affecting three types of groups that are important for understanding the complex linkages between the disease, economic performance and provisions of basic human needs, and conflict vulnerabilities: AIDS orphans, skilled workers, and children and the elderly.

Since the celebrated "liberation" elections of April 26–27, 1994, South Africa has featured a fully functioning democratic system with a fairly representative parliament, a coherent executive branch led by an indirectly elected president (Mbeki), and an independent and sometimes assertive judiciary. Its civil society is vibrant, and its press is independent. At the same time, the government is a de facto one-party state with weak parliamentary opposition; the ANC has increased its majority in the last two elections – 1999 and 2004 – winning with 69.68 percent of the popular vote in the ten-years-after April 2004 poll.[37] Governance is guided by a broadly accepted constitutional settlement that was reached in 1996.

South Africa's post-apartheid government – led first by Mandela until 1998 and until late 2008 by his protégé Thabo Mbeki – faced deep and intense social and economic challenges. All the danger signs of a weak state – high unemployment, rampant poverty, massive inequalities, lingering racial and ethnic divisions, crime, corruption, disease (especially HIV/AIDS), and tensions over land are present in South Africa today. Although it may be the strongest and most economically developed state in Africa, South Africa faces fundamental social challenges that if not addressed, ameliorated, and managed may well create new violent tensions, undermine the transition to democracy, and spell stormy weather for this pivotal state in the region and on the world stage.

Peacebuilding in South Africa

Will South Africa's "miracle" transition succumb to the pressures of extremism, as some have predicted?[38] Clearly racial and ethnic strains are acute throughout society and conditions are favorable for political entrepreneurs to construct or exploit ethnic enmity when rapidly changing social conditions make playing the ethnic card advantageous. Are the newly crafted democratic political institutions capable of non-violently processing social conflict in South Africa's diverse and multiethnic society? In other words, are South Africa's new political institutions "wired" for ethnic conflict management?

On balance, optimism for South Africa is warranted. The culture of bargaining that arose during the 1990–1996 transition from apartheid to non-racial democracy is deeply embedded in many sectors of South African society, including its new political institutions. Remarkably, this culture of bargaining is found in both formal and informal institutions alike. The deep revulsion to race- and ethnic-driven politics that characterized the apartheid era has given South Africa impetus to embrace a vision of democracy in a diverse society that places a premium on tolerance, recognition of difference, and mutual accommodation. Steeped in the necessity of pragmatic moderation that propelled the transition, power sharing that arose as informal institutions during the transition has been sustained into the post-apartheid era despite the overwhelming electoral predominance of the governing ANC. Ethnic conflict clearly remains a long-term threat to this newborn democracy.[39]

As long as the ANC continues to make institutional and symbolic overtures to minorities, and as long as minorities respond favorably to these overtures, South Africa's reconciliation process will continue. The ANC realizes that the power of these groups is not only their electoral strength, but also lies in their ability to spoil post-apartheid social stability and economic development. Balancing the need to keep minorities on board – while delivering results to the majority – is a walk on a political tightrope. With Africanist populist politician Jacob Zuma having taken over as president of the ANC in 2007, the strains within the party are clearly evident.

As rapid social transformation continues to unfold in South Africa, relations among its diverse people are changing quickly. With such socially volatile conditions, it is important that the underlying constitutional bargain should be open for review and revision. Not surprisingly, this need is being recognized already by the most astute observers of the South African scene; some have called for a new process of "post-settlement settlement" negotiations that would continue to adapt institutions and policy-making to the rapidly changing social problems (du Toit 2003). Among the most pressing issues for review are the electoral system, local governance, and socio-economic rights.

Why did South Africa progress to settlement, without extensive, direct international mediation? A common destiny, economic interdependence, high-quality leadership, and external pressures continue to explain South Africa's trajectory toward inclusive, non-racial democracy and sober, pragmatic management of this multiethnic society. Ethnicity is everywhere fluid and multifaceted, and the rapid pace of change in South Africa makes identities in that country unusually volatile and prediction inherently difficult. Such fluidity can be a good thing if it means that coalition-making across identity lines remains possible and politically profitable. There are some early warning signs of incipient conflict, but there are also new, widely legitimate institutions that offer considerable promise in mediating tensions. Would-be populists and ethnic entrepreneurs, who may seek to foment and exacerbate divisions for power-seeking aims, still face an uphill battle as long as the culture of bargaining and the commitment to reconciliation and pragmatism are sustained.

5 Liberia

Leveraging peace by pursuing justice

Liberia represents a case in which extreme elite predation – banal theft – generated armed violence against the state, rendering a state that resembled an organized crime syndicate more than an entity that served the country as a whole or its people. Liberia thus represents a different type of escalatory pattern than South Africa, one which reflects a basis for mobilization centered around economic (and, secondarily, ethnic) grievances, and a pattern of political violence by factionalized militias (and the Armed Forces of Liberia, AFL) that generated extreme deprivation and gross violations of human rights. Consequently, it also reflects then a different kind of peace process in which the international community engaged primarily for humanitarian motives, and in which effective coordination by an International Contact Group of states led to a comprehensive peace agreement in 2003. Following a by-all-accounts successful peace operation by the United Nations (UN), Liberia, by 2005, had through the peace process been given a new chance at state building and democratization.

Liberia's return to civil war in July 2000 after a devastating period of armed conflict from 1989 to 1996 cost an estimated 250,000 lives in a country of only three million; thus, Liberia is equally compelling for analysis of problems of war recurrence following earlier, failed peace processes. Likewise, the Liberia case demonstrates the regional interconnectedness of civil war highlighted in Chapter 1; the Liberia war was complexly interwoven with violence in neighboring Sierra Leone, Guinea, and Côte d'Ivoire.[1] In many ways Liberia was the eye of the storm of this "regional conflict complex," and, consequently, ending the war in Liberia was at least one part of the puzzle in stabilizing the entire region. From mid-2000 to 2003, tens of thousands of additional combat-related fatalities occurred in Liberia before the war was finally brought to an end at dramatic peace talks in 2003.

The Liberian war has many facets, not least of which was the systematic abuse of the state to loot the country of resources and to facilitate the elite predation that was rampant under the rule of former president Charles Taylor, a former rebel leader who after a series of failed peace agreements (the Abuja Agreement, 1995) and transitional governments managed to win the presidency in elections in 1997. Taylor systematically used the state for his personal enrichment, to include the brokering of diamonds from neighboring Sierra Leone and the later plundering of Liberia's national forests in illicit timber sales.[2]

The effect of the war on the Liberian state was pervasive: the security forces under Taylor became a "state within a state," government ministries either collapsed or became mechanisms for rent-seeking and banal graft, service delivery collapsed (especially in ungovernable rebel-held areas), and the country's financial institutions failed to function. Consequently, there was also a deep human-security crisis with widespread recruitment of child soldiers, deployment of landmines and proliferation of small arms, a devastated economic and social infrastructure, and among the lowest human development indicators on the planet (Levitt 2005).

Key states in the region and in the international community formed an International Contact Group on September 28, 2002 to mediate between the government and Liberians United for Reconciliation and Democracy (LURD) and other political factions in the Liberian context. From late 2002 to mid-2003, the Contact Group organized and led the peace process to bring a negotiated end to the devastating war. The logjam in the Liberian imbroglio was broken in June 2003, when during peace talks being held in Ghana Taylor was indicted by the UN war crimes tribunal for Sierra Leone, effectively undermining his ability to survive again by pledging peace while waging war. Further, as the war escalated in mid-2003 and a battle for Monrovia created a humanitarian emergency, the West African regional grouping ECOWAS (Economic Community of West African States) intervened anew to bring the fighting in Liberia to a halt. Following the arrival of Nigerian peacekeepers in August 2003, Taylor was whisked away to exile in Nigeria (from where he was later extradited to Freetown to face justice before an international criminal court). At this stage, it was clear that Liberia had a chance for democracy (Sawyer 2005).

It is very likely that no successful peace process would have been possible without the removal of Taylor's grasp on power. Following his demise, the Comprehensive Peace Agreement was signed in Accra, Ghana, by Taylor's remaining loyalists and the two principal rebel forces, the LURD and the Movement for Democracy in Liberia (MODEL). The agreement paved the way for the long-planned deployment of a significant Chapter VII UN peace operation with a force of 15,000 troops under the oversight of tough-minded UN Special Representative of the Secretary-General (SRSG) Jacques Paul Klein and pledged the parties to a full peace agreement that featured full disarmament and demobilization of the principal rebel forces, the creation of a transitional government, and the move toward elections in late 2005.

The UN Mission in Liberia (UNMIL) was a classic post-Cold War "multidimensional" peace operation that featured an emphasis on military and police security, the creation and strengthening of justice mechanisms, an emergency relief and cash development program, forward-thinking elements such as an HIV/AIDS policy coordinator and a child soldier reintegration program, and an electoral process. In the long run, the outcome of the Liberia peace process was remarkable: through its implementation under the security provided for by UNMIL, the first female African president, Ellen Johnson Sirleaf, was elected to office.

Escalation and recurrence in war-torn Liberia

The Liberian civil war re-erupted anew with fervor in mid-2000 following cross-border incursions by the insurgent group the LURD. In reality, the LURD was an inchoate group of various militias that were driven as much by economic depredation than by a clearly defined political agenda. The LURD was part of a broader regional alliance of foes, including the government of Guinea, to the Taylor regime and its regional allies. Soon after the onset of renewed civil war, there was an oscillating stalemate on the ground, with the rebels occasionally advancing toward Monrovia while at other times the AFL pushed the insurgents into the hinterland and into refuge in Guinea and Sierra Leone.

The origins of the conflict lie in political instability and the advent of warlordism and eventually the capture of the state by warlord *prima inter pares*, Charles Taylor. The 1989–1996 war escalated quickly and within six months Taylor's National Patriotic Front of Liberia (NPFL) had besieged Monrovia. The fighting featured especially gruesome tactics that victimized the civilian population (although not unlike other conflicts of the era, such as Angola, Bosnia, Mozambique, and Somalia). The intensity of the war led to a military intervention under the auspices of ECOWAS, which deployed the Cease-fire Monitoring Group (ECOMOG) not long after some 600 civilians had been massacred by the AFL at St. Peter's Lutheran Church in 1990. ECOMOG's 4,000 regional peacekeepers essentially became a party to the conflict over time as a dozen peace accords were agreed to and broken by the parties from 1990 to 1996. In the meantime, the war left some 200,000 dead and over one million displaced (of a 2.6 million pre-war population). Liberia, rich in resources, was ironically among the poorest countries on earth, with 80 percent unemployment, no running water or electricity throughout the country, and one of the highest rates of infant mortality anywhere (130 deaths per 1,000 births). Malnutrition was widespread, especially among the 43 percent of the population that is below the age of 14.

Evaluating escalation

The root causes of the Liberian war can be considered from two important orientations; a prior understanding of which orientation one finds most compelling, or how the two are mixed, has significant implication for conceiving and crafting a coherent conflict management approach. The first orientation argues that Liberia is symptomatic of a broader pattern of post-Cold War conflicts that stem from devastating effects of scarcity, crime, overpopulation, tribalism, and disease.[3] In this view, under conditions of extreme scarcity coupled with the availability of "lootable" goods, the pursuit of wealth through illicit natural resource extraction created incentives for militias to form as entrepreneurs seek, through force, to capture markets and rent.

An alternative perspective, however, suggests that Liberia's war is part of a longer transition from 150 years of minority rule by Americo-Liberians to full enfranchisement of the indigenous minority. The Liberian war is a symptom of a troubled transition that was hijacked by power-hungry warlords such as Charles Taylor (and earlier, the regime of Samuel Doe). When Taylor's NPFL launched a revolution on Christmas Eve, 1989, it was a response to years of minority authoritarianism and later Doe's narrow ethnic (Krahn) dictatorship. If this view of the conflict's root causes is correct, international intervention could help facilitate the necessary political reform, inclusive rule, democratization, and economic development. With sufficient political will and resources, the international community can see the country through to a new, reconstructed era despite the path of self-destruction that the civil war has unleashed. A synthesis of these two underlying causal explanations of war in Liberia makes sense. Indeed, war in Liberia *was* a result of the country's rule by a regime that has been accurately described as a "dysfunctional autocratic kleptocracy" under the leadership of warlord-turned-president Charles Taylor.[4]

Liberia's peace process 1996–1997: implications and lessons learned

- *War was more lucrative than peace.* The incessant ambition of faction leaders in the Liberian war for personal profit through exploitation of the country's considerable natural resources meant that any post-war attempt to demobilize militias would also result in the disbanding of vast commercial enterprises. With illicit diamond trading by NPFL and United Liberation Movement for Democracy in Liberia (ULIMO) factions at $100 million in the mid-1990s, the incentives to disarm were wholly absent. The lesson learned for peacemaking is to address directly the economic dimensions of the war, a finding that buttresses the March 2001 and May 2002 Security Council resolutions that sought to stem the ongoing diamond and arms trade by the Taylor regime through the UN-monitored sanctions regime.
- *ECOMOG was an ill-considered intervention force.* Although originally conceived of as a peacekeeping force, ECOMOG became a peace enforcement mission. Like in Bosnia, the deployment of forces without a peace agreement was unwise (they quickly become parties to the war), the forces deployed were not trained or experienced in peacekeeping,

and there was no diplomatic or operational oversight by a neutral body such as the UN Security Council. ECOMOG was by no means neutral among the factions or broadly representative of the sponsoring ECOWAS states (it was largely Nigerian dominated). Moreover, ECOMOG also became caught up in the corrupt practices, and it too profited by the war.[5] At the same time, ECOMOG did provide some security for the capital and perhaps brought the war to an end sooner than it might have otherwise.[6] Debate continues on whether ECOMOG's intervention prolonged the war in Liberia or eventually facilitated the Abuja pact. Clearly a review of the ECOMOG track record would inform any consideration of a new international security stabilization force and particular decisions about force composition, mandate, and oversight (reflected in the UNMIL composition).

- *The Abuja Agreement legitimated the warlords as political leaders.* By bringing the leaders of the warring factions into government as the six-member Council of State, the peace agreement legitimized warlords as political leaders and permitted them to contest the presidential elections (a departure from the terms of the earlier peace agreements).[7] The August 1996 Abuja II compromise essentially allowed the armed faction leaders to enter Monrovia with their military forces intact. The logic of Abuja – to include all the major faction leaders with the capacity to spoil the peace – was understandable, yet it curiously excluded ULIMO-J leader Roosevelt Johnson. The power-sharing deal was also criticized because it allowed faction leaders to appoint executive government positions, which led to a dispute among ethnic groups and political parties as to the equitable division of power. Using his manipulative acumen, Taylor eventually out-maneuvered the other leaders to wrest control of the Council of State.
- *Civil society actors were overlooked.* Critical social actors with the capability of bolstering the official peace process, such as the Interfaith Mediation Committee or the Liberian Women's Initiative, were not fully integrated into the formal peace process. That is, there was no apparent linkage between the elite tier of negotiations and the interests of the militia mid-level leaders (especially of the non-NPFL commanders, who were excluded from the reconstituted AFL) and of local communities, civil society interests, and (to the extent that they exist) private sector players (Joseph 1996).
- *The July 1997 elections were held before demobilization was complete.* The principal lesson learned was the elections were held much too early, before there had been sufficient security measures put into place and before progress had been made on demobilization (particularly of the NPFL).[8] Many observers believe that the 1997 vote for Charles Taylor was not a show of support for him personally, but a vote in favor of the candidate most people believed would bring about peace and stability. Furthermore, the entire notion of an election to a powerful president

under the terms of the Liberian constitution (modeled on the US charter) is anathema to post-war conflict resolution.[9]

- *Brutality left deep social scars, which were not addressed in the peace process.* The parties to the conflict were not motivated by ideology, nor were they fighting for the safety and security of their ethnic kin. Instead, the combatants were bloodthirsty, unprofessional militias who conscripted child soldiers, engaged in untold brutality, wreaked well-documented havoc on society, and left a scorched earth behind them. Liberia's collective psyche was deeply scarred, and the social trauma it endured posed a tremendous challenge to reconciliation and development. The 1996 peace agreement, which bolstered the role of the militias and military leaders, did not directly address the need for social healing, reconciliation, and punishment of war crimes. Any durable peace in Liberia would need to directly facilitate truth telling, reconciliation, and forgiveness.

Of all the retrospective concerns about the peace process of 1996–1997, the most enduring is the troubling legitimization of the many warring factions and their leaders as the basis for transition to sustainable peace, and the failure to demobilize or contain the militias before the elections. There may have been no reasonable alternative at the time, but nonetheless the Abuja peace process seems to have set the stage for a renewed civil war in a short time.

- First, the proliferation of warring parties (as many as eight distinct fighting factions) complicated for ECOMOG the process of demobilizing some 60,000 combatants.
- Second, the peace process failed to address the economic incentives of the warlords and strongmen who ran the militias and failed to provide any financial incentive to adapt to peace.
- Third, like in Somalia, the exclusion of any one capable faction meant that a determined, armed spoiler was available to threaten the delicate negotiations.
- Finally, the financial support and manpower required by ECOMOG to undertake the task was not forthcoming, nor was the enlargement of UNMIL.

Within this environment, Taylor was able to circumvent the disarmament process, remake the AFL with former NPFL fighters, and eventually to intimidate the war-weary population into electing him president. As one observer notes, by the end of the civil war

> Taylor's NPFL emerged as the most tenaciously cruel, best funded, and the least scrupulous militia in a war of militias backed by foreign sponsors. Throughout the 1990s, he reneged on a series of peace

deals brokered by regional international agencies and continued his ruthless military campaign.[10]

The 2000–2003 Liberian civil war: causes and characteristics

Flaws in the 1996 peace process and the Abuja Agreement – together with weak implementation – set the stage for the renewal of civil war in Liberia. As Licklider has found, under certain conditions civil war settlements are inherently unstable, especially when the parties retain the capacity to continue to wage war and when there is an inability to resolve disputes and allocate resources in political institutions and processes; in these situations, war erupts among former enemies and allies in the war because war-making is a preferred alternative to peace (Licklider 1995). As seen in Angola, Burundi, Chechnya, the Democratic Republic of Congo, and Sudan, fragile peace agreements, especially ill-considered ones, often collapse with new bloodshed after just a few months or years. Surely President Charles Taylor saw victory in the 1997 elections as opportunity to win at the ballot box what was not definitively won on the battlefield during the seven years of war.

Most egregiously, he then (as president of the state) colluded with the criminal Revolutionary United Front (RUF) in Sierra Leone, under Foday Sankoh, over the systematic looting of Sierra Leone, engaging in the trade of "blood diamonds" and in the process – together with his army – committing unspeakable crimes against humanity in the exercise of what was in effect a joint criminal enterprise with the RUF. Taylor was indicted on 17 counts by the court: in the indictment of Taylor before the Special Court for Sierra Leone, the breadth of his manipulative use of violence in a maniacal chase for wealth and power is chillingly detailed; the Indictment by the Prosecutor, David Crane, reads: "The Prosecutor … charges Charles Ghankay Taylor … with Crimes Against Humanity, violations of Article 3 Common to the Geneva Conventions … and other serious violations of humanitarian law."[11] The counts against Taylor included:

Counts 1–2: Terrorizing the Civilian Population and Collective Punishments
Counts 3–5: Unlawful Killings
Counts 6–8: Sexual Violence
Counts 9–10: Physical Violence
Count 11: Use of Child Soldiers
Count 12: Abductions and Forced Labor, Enslavement
Count 13: Looting and Burning
Count 14–17: Attacks on UNAMSIL Personnel

On August 11, 2003, wearing a white safari suit, serenaded by a ululating chorus, and seen off by his supporters (including vice-president Moses Blah, who assumed control of the shattered state), Taylor waved good-bye to his war-torn land with a white handkerchief as he accepted the invitation of Nigerian president Olusegun Obsanjo for exile in Nigeria. He said to his audience, "History will remember me kindly."[12]

War in Liberia, 2000–2003

The escalation and conduct of the 2000–2003 civil war reaffirms its characteristics as a recurrence of the earlier war. The LURD was a reconstitution of Taylor's defeated opponents, drawn particularly from the erstwhile ULIMO-J (United Liberation Movement for Democracy in Liberia, Krahn-led) and ULIMO-K (Mandingo-led) factions. Some of the regional alliances are also the same. A careful look at the lessons of the earlier war and its peace process informed the approach for handling the recurrent conflict.[13] However, understanding the interpretations of root causes of the earlier conflict and the present recurrence is important to the present.

Predatory and corrupt governance since 1997 is a principal and immediate cause of the current insurgency against Taylor's regime. Taylor's reign as president of Liberia was the antithesis of inclusive, transparent, competent, responsible governance. Unlike South Africa's Nelson Mandela, when Taylor won at the polls he abandoned any modicum of conciliation and ruled Liberia as a personalized autocracy, using the power of the state to exclude and oppress ethnic and other political opponents and to maximize profit for himself and his loyalists. Infiltration into Liberia by the LURD began in earnest in mid-2000 although there had been some four earlier outbreaks of anti-regime violence.

What were the essential characteristics of the 2000–2003 war?

- *Taylor's autocratic regime.* Virtually any opposition or resistance to complete control of the state by Taylor's faction was met with oppression, intimidation, and violence. Ethnic Mandingo and Krahn citizens faced arbitrary arrest and violence based solely on their identity. Students, journalists, and human rights organizers were targeted; the government contended with other elements of civil society as well, including the Liberian Catholic Church. The human rights abuses of the Liberian armed forces – especially the Anti-Terrorism Unit and the Special Operation Division – are well documented. The abuses include war crimes, recruitment of child combatants, violations against civilians seeking refuge, attacks on civil society groups, exacerbation of religious and ethnic tensions, and cross-border destabilization of Sierra Leone.[14]
- *Corruption and rent-seeking.* Having been sanctioned by the UN Security Council for arms-for-diamond trade, Taylor shifted his commercial ambitions to trading timber for weapons using the same network of international smuggling.[15] Some have reported that Taylor made at

least $75 million annually in that natural resource trade. At the same time, the state had virtually no domestic sources of legal revenue, iron mining virtually ceased, and the historically important Firestone rubber enterprise operated at a minimal level of production. The state garnered about $13 million per year in royalties from maritime flagging and about $2 million per year flowed into Liberia in repatriated funds from the Diaspora communities. Corruption was rife in the state and civil servants had no pay for seven to 14 months, including the security forces.

The ethnic dimension

Liberia's conflict also had an undeniable ethnic undercurrent. Although moderate political and civil society leaders often assail tribalism, clearly ethnic identities have been closely associated with various political parties and factional militias. Taylor's ties to the Gio and Mano ethnic groups of Nimba County were juxtaposed against perceptions that the Krahn and Mandingo groups were the regime's enemies. Ethnic enmity between the Kru and Sarpo in Sinoe County and between the Mandingo and Lorma in Lofa County were heightened by the civil war.

The "ethnicization" of the Liberian war is understandable when understood against the finding that wars harden ethnic identities as people retreat to the social grouping in which they can find security and allies whom they can trust. Further, various political leaders – like elsewhere – played the ethnic card to advance personal political interests. Liberian moderates argued against tribal arithmetic in forging a conflict resolution strategy. Nevertheless, as in Afghanistan, Ethiopia, or even clan-based Somalia, reconstitution of a legitimate state requires a rough ethnic balancing of appointments, military, police, civil service, and in the distribution of state resources … all absent in the Liberia case.

Military dynamics

The military dynamics of the Liberian war affected the prospects for peace and set the stage – *sans* Taylor – to broker a peace deal despite the lucrative nature for some of the war economy. Truly reliable military assessments were impossible to determine given the lack of information from and access to the country's impenetrable interior. However, the overall "unwinnability" of the war was evident by mid-2002.

- *A fluid balance on the ground.* Although AFL saw successes in September 2002 in pushing the LURD back across the northern borders of Lofa and Bong counties (following the retaking of Tubmanburg in mid-July 2002), the LURD demonstrated its ability to infiltrate and launch attacks, occasionally reportedly striking close to Monrovia. Reports in late 2002 suggested that the LURD began a dry-season offensive in the northern towns of Kolahun, Foya, and Voinjama and the northwestern provincial towns of Fassama and Gorlu.[16] New attacks by the LURD in early 2003 provoked panic in the capital and seriously undermined the confidence of Taylor's various armed units.

- *A stalemate.* Most observers agreed that the AFL did not have the capacity to definitively defeat the LURD. The reactivation of pro-government militia groups from the 1989–1996 era, along with the creation of new forces such as the Jungle Warriors, was an indication that Taylor's armed forces were preparing for a more intense war. At the same time, the insurgents did not have the military might to topple Taylor and the AFL; an indication of the LURD's operational weakness was its unwillingness or inability to hold territory (although this could equally be explained in terms of Maoist insurgency strategy).
- *Highly disparate military units* complicated military analysis, especially among the government forces. Analysts of Taylor's security forces cited the internal differences and tensions within the AFL as a significant factor in understanding the conflict. Internal reshuffling by Taylor of top commanders suggested he was wary of a military coup and the shadowy former RUF henchman Sam "Mosquito" Bockarie, and an estimated 200 former RUF combatants further complicated analysis of palace politics. Finally, within the government security forces there was what the International Crisis Group called "a confusing proliferation of military groups" to include at least seven special forces and a host of other armed factions, some of whom were involved in the forcible recruitment of child soldiers.[17] Reports also suggested that the military factions were not regularly paid, and that they subsisted by "self-financing" through looting and extortion of the civilian population.

Two implications for conflict management strategies flow from the analysis above.

- *The humanitarian situation was acute, explaining the depth of international commitment to intervene.* The situation on the ground rapidly deteriorated in late 2003 without early warning as the dry season began and the militaries began campaigns. A rapidly deteriorating situation is a motivating factor for the parties in conflict to seek a cease-fire if they believe the further escalation of violence holds greater risks than the preservation of the current balance of power.
- *Unilateral, military victory was unlikely and undesirable.* The Liberian people could not be well served by a military victory of one side or other. The danger of such a swift victory in such a volatile environment would have been even more extensive crimes against the vanquished, including the possibility of genocidal retribution or "vicarious punish-

ment" for specific ethnic groups. Furthermore, a definitive military victory could only have been the result of a more protracted war with its end game inevitably playing out in the streets of the capital Monrovia, portending devastating humanitarian consequences.

Bargaining for peace in Liberia

The warring parties in Liberia were essentially caught in what is known as a "conflict trap" from which there is no self-escape – a proverbial "thieves' dilemma." That is, even though the parties would gain from exchanging war for cooperation, they could not because they knew that adversaries would cheat; peace would leave them vulnerable. Despite the pledges by Taylor and the LURD political representatives that they sought to end hostilities through peaceful means, international mediators proceeded with the presumption that these parties and other armed elements did not yet prefer to seek a verifiable cease-fire and negotiated settlement of the war. Statements of a willingness to negotiate a cease-fire by Charles Taylor were seen as playing to the gallery of Western powers and international organizations.

The incentives for Taylor were certainly not to settle. For him, there was no reason to exchange certain power for the uncertainties of an internationally monitored peace process; the presumption was repeatedly tested by the defection by the Taylor regime to international overtures to peace. The rebels, too, were not inclined to accept a cease-fire while Taylor was on the scene. That is because without the assurances and acceptance of a robust external peacekeeping force there was no basis for the insurgents either to credibly commit to any agreement. One analyst described well the situation then:

> What we have in Liberia today is a classic case of the 'prisoner's dilemma, or shall we say the 'thieves' dilemma.' All armed groups are keenly aware that none has operated under any informal system of rules that is based on trust, honesty, principles, and respect for law and order. Indeed each leader has so much blood on his hands that none believes the others are capable of using power for the common good.[18]

In the absence of such a force the international community must rely upon weaker levers of influence for peace, namely pressure, sanctions, and purchase.

For this reason, vigorous and highly assertive leverage by the international community, coordinated by the International Contact Group on Liberia, was needed for Liberia's tragic civil war to end. The international community appreciated the urgency of action in Liberia. With the creation of the International Contact Group in September 2002 and the appointment of UN SRSG Ahmedou Ould-Abdallah for West Africa, global powers and regional brokers appear poised to engage with unity and determination. In addition, the UN Secretary-General Kofi Annan's appointment of former UN High Commissioner for Refugees (UNHCR) regional head Abou Moussa to head the UN Peace-building Support Office in Monrovia (and a one-year extension of its mandate) laid the foundation for on-the-ground international engagement. These developments signaled a new consensus among a coalition of external actors to correct what was described by the August 2002 International Crisis Group report "Liberia: Unravelling" as a "muddy" international approach in recent years. Action against by the United States was further ratcheted up when in May 2003 Special Court Prosecutor David Crane alleged that Taylor had links to *al-Qaeda* and *Hizbollah*, bringing him under the aim of the US post-9/11 "war on terror"; Crane said Charles Taylor is "not just a regional troublemaker; he is a player in the world of terror and what he does affects the United States and Europe."[19]

The Contact Group, consisting of representatives from the UN, the European Union, African Union, ECOWAS, the United States, the United Kingdom, France, Senegal, Nigeria, and Morocco, included the key organizations and states with influence in Liberia and the region. Members of the group consistently called for a cease-fire between the government forces and the LURD. Senegalese president Abdoulaye Wade, chairman of ECOWAS, and Mobamed Ibn Chambass, executive secretary, pressured the Taylor government to negotiate with the LURD while at the same time suggesting Nigerian president Olusegun Obasanjo as a specific interlocutor. In the end, the choices and strategies were wise as a military stalemate on the ground, combined with a clever tactic to remove Taylor, and a credible promise of the international community generated a chance for peace in Liberia.

Indicators of "ripeness" for meaningful negotiation in Liberia, early 2003

Military stalemate

The primary motivation to settle arose from a perception that the conflict had reached a military stalemate that was mutually hurting for both sides. For the *Taylor regime*, the status quo was costly in terms of the UN sanctions regime, the damage inflicted by the LURD in outlying areas, the possibility that the AFL might quickly crumble or disintegrate in widespread defections to the LURD, and the risk of a public outpouring of opposition to the war that could not be contained. For elements of *the LURD*, it became clear that despite their ability to strike at government forces and to occasionally hold strategic outlying towns for a few days, their capacity to quickly defeat the well-funded and battle-hardened AFL (and eventually take Monrovia from them) was limited.

- *Coherent leadership.* Parties that are divided and incoherent do not make for good bargaining partners, and much of the assessment on whether the conflict is ripe for negotiation depends on the nature, intent and capacity of government and rebel armed forces. This was a critical concern in Liberia and took considerable attention by international mediators. The machinations of Charles Taylor in manipulating the many security force factions under his control revealed that he distrusted soldiers he put into action over the years. Reports of defections among the ranks of the AFL seriously called into question the coherence of the government and the ruling National Patriotic Party as a credible bargaining partner. So, too, the LURD was apparently quite divided (although they did send a capable diplomatic delegation to the Ouagadougou, Burkina Faso meetings convened by the Bukinabe government and the International Republican Institute (IRI) in July 2002). The backing received by the LURD – more implicitly than explicitly – from the Liberian opposition political parties was also critical in giving it legitimacy to bargain.
- *An exit process.* For a ripe conflict to be turned into an agreement to cease fire, the parties need a clearly defined exit process. The "prenegotiations" related to cease-fires in civil wars are essentially about the security issues: how to resolve the key dilemma that stopping the fight leaves them vulnerable to attack by their opponents (Smith 1995). Given the uncertainty of political support among the Liberian factions, and the sour history of the 1997 elections that brought Taylor to power, a pre-election pact that assured each party a place in a transitional parliament/national conference was a necessary part of the formula for settlement.
- *Public "exhaustion" factors.* In Liberia's context, with a society exhausted by war a useful strategy was to mobilize that aversion and public demand for peace through programs of civil society. A key to the sealing of a cease-fire in Liberia was surely the existence of a population – particularly in Monrovia – which decried the regime and was weary of war, and which the weak government was incapable or unwilling to further repress.

With humanitarian motivations driving action, the political will arose in the international community to intervene and end the Liberian conflict. United Nations Security Council resolutions 1343 (March 7, 2001) and 1408 (May 6, 2002) imposed diamond-trade, arms, and travel sanctions on the Liberian leadership, reflecting an acute awareness of the rationale for extensive intervention to halt the civil war and the awareness that war economy of wealth and weapons drove facts on the ground. On December 13, 2002, the President of the Security Council issued a statement endorsed by the Council's members that cited violations of these resolutions and called upon "a comprehensive strategy" for international mediators to seek a solution to the Liberian war.[20] The international community was aware that to end the violence in Liberia it would be called upon to further increase its diplomatic, monitoring, and military intervention strategies to stabilize the situation and to facilitate or manage an extended peace process.

Civil society and the peace process

In addition to cohesion internationally, programs implemented during the war also helped create the basis for a peace process in Liberia. In 2001 and 2002, there were extensive efforts abroad and regionally in multitrack diplomacy, including an internal, regime-led national reconciliation conference in 2002 in Monrovia (this conference was not attended by the most significant major opposition figures, however). More important to the peace process were those that occurred outside Liberia, especially the concave in July 2002 in Burkina Faso facilitated by the IRI in which prominent exiles, opposition figures, and rebel leaders met with interlocutors of the government.

These channels of communication, neither of them fully representative of the Liberian political spectrum, were critical to the multilateral mediation effort in two important ways. First, they facilitated consensus-building around key issues, such as participation (or not) in the planned 2003 elections, and, second, they served as a "focus group" for the international community to gage the attitudes of Liberians with regard to the war and the country's political future. ECOWAS's engagement to promote initial cease-fire talks was useful, with chairman Abdoulaye Wade having met with Taylor on November 27 and later with the LURD.[21] This channel established direct negotiations between the warring factions, coordinated through the ECOWAS Mechanism for Conflict Prevention, Management, Resolution, Peacekeeping, and Security.

At the national level, efforts such as those of the Liberian Leadership Forum were also invaluable to developing a basic consensus about the steps required for the transition phase and for the long-term future of Liberia. The Forum met, as mentioned above, in July 2002 in Ouagadougou, Burkina Faso and was attended by a wide range of opposition elite and at least one representative close to the Taylor regime. It built on earlier meetings in 2002 that brought together Liberian civil society and political party representatives, and there had been an attempt by the Taylor regime to convene an internal dialogue process on national reconciliation.[22] Key internal conciliators in these meetings included the inter-religious council of Liberia, various civil society groups, and the prize-winning Mano River Union women's peace network.

The general recommendations of the Forum were highlighted in the so-called Ouagadougou Declaration, which outlined a broad consensus on the need to end armed hostilities and for a process of national reconciliation. From the official declaration and the observations of the facilitators, the following conclusions and recommendations emerge for the transitional phase of Liberia's peace process.[23]

- *Civil society and the LURD.* The LURD was termed a legitimate party to the conflict and the armed group was backed implicitly by key opposition parties, especially those tied to the Mandingo and Krahn ethnic groups. There was considerable underground support for the LURD's political aims among leaders of Liberian civil society.
- *Civil society and ECOWAS intervention.* There was deep skepticism among civil society groups about the ability of an ECOWAS force to be neutral; there was strong preference among civil society for a UN force. There was no consensus on whether the peacekeeping force should oversee the disarmament process or how it would deal with Taylor's armed forces.
- *Political party consolidation.* Political party leaders and exiled figures appeared to be able to cooperate in advance of elections. In 1997, Liberians agreed to a Special Election Law that allowed for proportional representation but that retained a directly elected president; the election system needed to be designed to provide incentives for political party coalescence, but in the end the prior electoral law was retained.

The relative success of these forums suggests that facilitating consensus among political social leaders in Liberia was critically important to the official peace process. Among the most important civil society actors at the national level are the Liberian religious organizations such as the Catholic Church, the independent media and human rights organizations, women's groups, and youth representatives.

Negotiating peace in Liberia: the Accra agreement

The most critical element of the peace process in Liberia was set into motion in January 2002, when the Special Court for Sierra Leone, established by the UN Security Council, arrived at statutes that eventually provided the basis for an indictment for complicity in crimes against humanity if sufficient evidence of Taylor's support for the RUF was available to the UN-appointed Prosecutor. The Statute of the Special Court for Sierra Leone reads:

> Article 6
> Individual criminal responsibility
> 1. A person who planned, instigated, ordered, committed or otherwise aided and abetted in the planning, preparation or execution of a crime referred to in articles 2 to 4 of the present Statute shall be individually responsible for the crime.
> 2. The official position of any accused persons, whether as Head of

> State or Government or as a responsible government official, shall not relieve such person of criminal responsibility nor mitigate punishment.

Clearly the simple act of indictment – signed by the Prosecutor on March 3, 2003 and unveiled on June 4 (see above) dramatically and quickly changed the political dynamics of Taylor's regime in Monrovia.

In July 2003, the UN Secretary-General appointed the former US general Jacques Paul Klein as his Special Representative for Liberia, and this move (combined with the scene set by the court) proved to be decisive in bringing the Liberian war to an end; Klein, with a deserved reputation for toughness and coercive diplomacy skill, took over the peacemaking and, eventually, peacekeeping efforts needed to provide credible commitment in the chaotic Liberian context. Likewise, the US government exerted pressure, with President George W. Bush suggesting several times in 2003 that Taylor "must leave" Liberia. The efforts of the international community to leverage for peace in Liberia made progress in the talks in Accra, Ghana, in June 2003; there, a cease-fire agreement was signed but not taken seriously by the protagonists as fighting continued on the ground. The United States and Nigeria sent military teams to assess the peacekeeping needs that would be required to provide credible commitment for the Liberian peace talks taking place among the political parties, militia leaders, and the erstwhile followers of Taylor. Taylor's exile on August 11, 2003 provided the turning point in the Liberian negotiations.

The Accra negotiations

The crisis that drove peace talks in Liberia was the siege of Monrovia in July and August 2003, as forces of the LURD and MODEL overcame sagging AFL troops and pressed in on the capital. Beginning in June 2003, rebel forces took the offensive and began to press in on Monrovia, routing the AFL in skirmishes and engaging in attacks on villages. Thousands of civilians were killed in a campaign that lasted through to August and September of that year. By August, ECOWAS deployed a peacekeeping force into Monrovia, which was eventually replaced by the UN force within six weeks.

The siege of Monrovia cost more than 1,000 deaths according to the estimates of international relief agencies, who struggled to provide emergency services in the midst of chaotic fighting in the lawless environments. According to an Associated Press report, the fighting in the capital "killed over a thousand civilians outright and left hunger and epidemics raging among the 1.3 million residents and refugees."[24] The only relief agencies reporting from the ground were those who virtually never leave: the International Committee of the Red Cross and *Médecins Sans Frontières*. In July, UN Secretary-General Kofi Annan met US president George Bush to discuss the terms and modalities of sending in a humanitarian force as new engagements in and around the capital came in from military monitors.

In the context of this dire humanitarian emergency, negotiators were induced to join the peace process by the Contact Group acting under the aegis of principal ECOWAS mediator and former Nigerian head of state General Abdulsalami Abubaker. Talks critically involved regional leaders such as Guinean president Lansana Conte, the LURD's main patron in the region. On the ground, a Joint Verification Team was dispatched to eye the military situation and to prepare for a full-scale international intervention in concert with the signing of a peace agreement. As the talks unfolded in late July and early August, the focus was on earlier agreements made in the June 17 cease-fire agreement and the details of forming an interim government. Taylor's exit had the government negotiators agreeing that Vice-President Blah would quickly stand down to an interim government with participation by mostly "technical" administrators. Militarily, ECOWAS pushed forward with immediate plans to deploy troops to stabilize Monrovia while planning proceeded apace at the UN for a major peace operation, "along the lines of what we are doing in Sierra Leone," according to Annan.[25]

With the full focus of the international community in leveraging the parties into agreement, talks in Accra led to a quickly sealed peace agreement in August 2003 to cease fighting, create an interim government, and allow deployment of the UN mission to backstop the pact. As the talks took place in Accra on August 14, 2003, the points on the table included the date of surrender of power by Blah, appointment of interim government administrators with no putative ties to the warring parties, and the delivery of humanitarian relief (especially Monrovia with the handover of the port to ECOWAS forces). The 78 days of negotiation that would be the penultimate chapter in the ending of the Liberian war reached fruition.

The peace pact, the Comprehensive Peace Agreement, was finally formally signed on August 18, 2003 by the government, the LURD, and MODEL.[26] The nearly two-and-a-half month peace negotiations process came to fruition within a week of Taylor's exile. Abubaker, the mediator, said: "Liberia does not need liberators anymore but nation builders and developers. Those responsible for signing this document must take their responsibilities seriously. The international community is getting impatient with the Liberian crisis."[27] The interim government (National Transitional Government of Liberia) was to be headed by Episcopalian religious and business leader Gyude Bryant, who declared "My government will be an all inclusive one.... The only one out is Charles Taylor."[28] Importantly, the pact spelled out in Annex 3 a clear set of benchmarks for a UN peace operation-guided process of demilitarization and a transition to democracy in transition-culminating elections.

Violence on the ground followed the signing of the pact in Accra, as the last skirmishes of the war played out as first ECOWAS and then UN peacekeepers deployed throughout the country. In hotspots such as Bong County, just days after the agreement was signed and as humanitarian workers and peacekeepers arrived, clashes continued between AFL troops and rebel forces of the LURD. Days later, fighting erupted between the AFL and LURD fighters at the border of Guinea and at the airport between Monrovia and Buchanan, generating new waves of refugees fleeing the fighting.[29] Although the agreement had called for troops to remain in their locations, clearly widespread non-compliance with the pact occurred.

Motives for the peace-agreement fighting were found in the precarious situation of the AFL, especially, as they foresaw a demobilization campaign that would leave them open to retribution by civilians and former rebels alike as well as possible indictment in processes of transitional justice. Likewise, because so many of the forces included children, many of them failed to know, understand, or trust that a cease-fire had been negotiated. Finally, as looting was the only means of survival for the balkanized forces ostensibly under Taylor's prior control, there were no incentives to stop; indeed, survival suggested accumulating as much as possible prior to the arrival of the international troops.

UNMIL: a case study in credible commitment

United Nations Security Council Resolution 1509 in September 2003 established UNMIL, the United Nations Mission in Liberia, with a wide-ranging mission to implement the Accra accords, to disarm and demobilize fighters, to provide humanitarian relief, and start the long process of rebuilding the country's shattered economy. UNMIL deployed with overwhelming force: 15,000 personnel comprised of military troops, UN Civilian Police, and a legion of international civil service and humanitarian relief workers.

As the peacekeepers deployed, post-agreement violence subsided. ECOMIL (as the ECOWAS force was known) negotiated with a myriad of rebel and AFL commanders to lay down arms and enter into encampment areas. While ongoing fighting in the countryside delayed deployments in Liberia, over September through December the UN force gradually grew in size and expanded its footprint through the country. Key to success of the UN's providing credible commitment was the clear, repeated signal sent from the cigar-chomping UN SRSG General Klein; the UN envoy took a tough stance, clearly signaling its intent to deal forcefully with any potential spoilers to the peace pact.

In the beginning, Klein made clear that he foresaw UN provision of security as the key to managing violence: he argued that deployment of peacekeepers and disarmament was essential to the "demilitarization of the country and the creation of a stable security environment, without which peacebuilding efforts cannot begin."[30] The key to the strategy was a signal to all potential spoilers: the UN meant business and would respond aggressively to any act of non-compliance. Klein asserted in November 2003 that those violating the agreement were "thieves, murderers and criminals.... They will continue to rob, they will continue to steal, until we're in charge. It's a tragedy for the people of Liberia that these people, who signed a peace agreement, continue to violate it."[31]

Despite the fact that it took several months, into 2004, for the UNMIL forces to deploy throughout the country, over time the UN was able to extend its authority and security to even the most far-flung and remote areas of the country. With the support of key states such as the United States which provided $50 million for the UN-managed DDR process (disarmament, demobilization, and reintegration program), over time the Liberia process would be seen as an example of successful management by a blue-helmet led peace operation of a successful implementation of the Accra agreement. UNICEF became involved with the specifics of addressing the needs of child soldiers; nearly 10 percent of all demobilized soldiers were children, numbering nearly 11,000.

By November 2004, some 103,000 Liberian fighters had been disarmed by the UN (twice as many as expected), which in turn allowed UNHCR to begin its program of repatriating refugees and internally displaced persons in much of the country.[32] The median age of the demobilized soldiers was 24, and 24 percent of them were female (to include 2,500 girls). Despite considerable success in stabilizing the country and in the disarmament and demobilization tasks, UN peacekeeping in Liberia was not without peril. In October 2004, three days of rioting by disgruntled demobilized AFL troops left more than a dozen people dead and 400 wounded as UN troops defended their positions and stores of supplies from the demobilized troops.

Building peace in post-war Liberia: pursuing human security

Tenacity in providing credible commitment through the DDR process and through the volatile period of post-war elections yielded full implementation of the peace process in Liberia. The presidential election on October 11, 2005 (first round) and November 8 (second round) reveals a dramatic process that is significant because it shows that – at the end of the day – the essentially peaceful outcome of the elections was *sui generis*: Liberia's first post-war elections ended peacefully because of sheer luck combined with fortuitous agency. In the first round of elections, former Champions League football star and youthful populist George Weah won a plurality of votes (28.3 percent) and the next most winning candidate was Johnson-Sirleaf with a first-round tally of 19.8 percent. In the second round, however, voters clustered around Johnson-Sirleaf such that she was able to win 59.4 percent of the total votes cast compared with Weah's 40.6 percent. Remarkably, both rounds of elections went off peacefully, in no small measure attributable to the widespread deployment of international election observers and the ability of the UNMIL force to provide security.

In a moment of high drama, however, it was not clear that Weah's supporters would accept his loss in the second round, and indeed protests in

Monrovia following the poll featured the chant "No Weah, No Peace"; into December of 2005 Weah claimed that due to fraud in the second round he had won the presidency. By mid-December, however, Weah conceded the presidency and the inauguration of Johnson-Sirleaf went off without considerable violence. Despite speculation that Johnson-Sirleaf would appoint Weah to her cabinet in an act of voluntary power sharing, she declined to do so; Liberia would enter its post-war period without power sharing.

In the parliamentary elections, however, Weah's party (the Congress for Democratic Change, CDC) gained a plurality in the House of Representatives. Moreover, in the House and in other posts are a range of former rebel and government of Liberia commanders and, indeed, Charles Taylor's wife (from whom he was legally separated) and a host of other erstwhile Taylor loyalists. Thus, the Liberian outcome is similar to Afghanistan's: the inclusion through the legislative arena of a number of factions involved in the war who have either emerged as "warlord" figures or whose hands are not clean in terms of the widespread atrocities that occurred. Indeed, several members of the new parliament are on lists of possible indicted individuals in the Sierra Leone war crimes court; among them too are erstwhile warlords such as Prince Johnson, who was responsible for the murder of Samuel Doe in September 1990 who won elections as a Senator from Nimba County. Perhaps the one positive side of the legislative outcomes in Liberia is the relative balance of ethnic interests reflected in the results. Thus, serious problems may lie ahead in the functioning of the parliament as state-(re)building occurs in earnest, foremost among them factionalism, incoherence, and a number of legislators with a long history of rent-seeking and corruption.

Despite the well-founded concerns about the nature of the Liberian parliament and the possibility of a Taylorist revival, the fact that Liberia was able to move toward a more legitimate state through the election of the widely popular Johnson-Sirleaf is a positive first step toward the enabling of state institutions. Liberia remains a tenuously balanced society with deep insecurities resulting from the devastation of the wars and neglect its people have suffered. Ethnic tensions will continue to bedevil efforts to build a strong state, especially in the military and in addressing tensions that occur around the return of refugees and the internally displaced.[33] With regional instability emanating from Côte d'Ivoire, a proliferation of small arms, a culture of conflict, and a myopic scale-down of the UN peacekeeping force, Liberia remains at risk for recurrence of conflict. Nonetheless, comparatively, the peace process and implementation of the agreement has indeed imbued the state with a new legitimacy that for the first time in many years may give Liberia an opportunity to rearrange an erstwhile predatory state's relationship with its people.

6 Burundi

Empowering the fragile center

The civil war in Burundi, which began in 1993 but with many prior antecedents of violent confrontations, cost some 300,000 mostly civilian lives in a country of just over eight million; over one million have been displaced. Since Burundi's independence from Belgian mandatory rule in 1961, the country has become synonymous with ethnic strife, in part because the tensions between the country's long-dominant Tutsis (14 percent) and the Hutus (85 percent) are parallel to the strife in its erstwhile colonial partner territory, Rwanda, where genocidal strife between these identity groups occurred nearly simultaneously with Burundi's own ethnic crisis.[1] Indeed, the act of violence that was *the* precipitant of the Rwandan genocide in 1994 – the downing of an airplane on April 6 carrying the country's president Juvenal Habyarimana – also killed the Burundi president, Cyrian Ntayamira, who along with ten others aboard the aircraft were returning to Kigali from peace talks held in Arusha, Tanzania. Ntayamira, a Hutu, had taken over the presidency of Burundi following the assassination of his predecessor, Mechior Ndadaye, who had been killed in a military coup by Tutsi military leaders in October 1993. Ndadaye's killing precipitated Burundi's slide into civil war, which saw 100,000 deaths in violence in its first 12 months.

Through more than a decade of war, Burundi's elite at the same time sought to negotiate peace. Talks to reinstate a power-sharing pact among the country's two principal ethnic groups continued through the war, but only with considerable regional and international engagement (particularly by the United Nations (UN)) was the war settled in a series of peace agreements. On January 29, 2007, the last of the Burundi rebel factions was finally brought into the mechanisms created to secure peace – the so-called Joint Verification and Monitoring Mechanism (JVMM) – under the watchful eye of international monitors. The hold-out rebel force, the Palipehutu-FNL (*Parti pour la libération du peuple Hutu* – Front for National Liberation), had been engaged in ongoing negotiations in Dar es Salaam, Tanzania, for months on the modalities of cease-fire and especially the future of its rank and file absent an agreement for their safety and livelihood if their guns were to fall silent. Rebel spokesperson Pasteur Habimana said, "Words are wasted on a starving man and … the Palipehutu-FNL combatants have a right to be provided with food."[2] The January 2007 agreement was the final plank in a prior pact – unimplemented – that had been reached between Burundi's government and the FNL faction in September 2006. This agreement, however, also broke down in 2007; fighting erupted anew in Burundi in early 2008 with more than 100 dead in renewed violence.

The peace process in Burundi has been characterized all along by a concerted push by regional and international mediators to bring peace to the troubled Great Lakes region of Africa; in this context, the Burundi talks are intricately linked to post-genocide peacebuilding in Rwanda and the stabilization of eastern Democratic Republic of Congo (DRC). Burundi is one piece in a larger Great Lakes of Africa process of war termination and stabilization. Talks that began in 1998, brokered first by former Tanzanian president Julius Nyerere and then subsequently by former South African president Nelson Mandela and later Thabo Mbeki, led to a pact on power sharing that led to the transitional government headed by a Hutu, Domitien Ndayizeye, in April 2003 and eventually to the celebrated Pretoria Protocol of October 2003 followed by the Global Ceasefire Agreement sealed at a summit of African leaders in November 2003. With the FNL still a spoiler, violence continued to reign in Burundi despite general compliance by the CNDD-FDD (*Conseil national pour la défense de la démoratie-Forces pour la défense de la démoratie*) and the transitional government to the terms of the pact.

Deployment of a 5,500-strong UN force (United Nations Operation in Burundi, ONUB) provided the credible commitment and disarmament process that led to the transitional elections of August 2005 that brought the erstwhile rebels of the CNDD-FDD into power in the person of President Pierre Nkurunziza. ONUB officially disbanded on December 31, 2006, to be followed on by a longer-term peacebuilding effort by the UN and regional leaders through the engagement of the UN Peacebuilding Commission and the on-the-ground presence of the UN Integrated Office in Burundi.

While the peace process has ostensibly run its course in war-torn Burundi, the road ahead is fraught with peril. Underlying root causes of conflict remain rife, ethnic tensions in the military and police, and in parliament, threaten power sharing, and a truth and reconciliation commission will test the country's ability to address openly the horrors of the past. Regional destabilization in the DRC also continues to have deleterious effects on the consolidation of peace in Burundi. Nonetheless, the lesson of Burundi's peace process is the need for considered, sustained, and engaged peacemaking by regional and international mediators and military men. Precisely because of Burundi's violent past, and the specter of genocide if the peace process fails, the international community galvanized to pressure the parties into peace because of, not in spite of, the continuation of violence on the ground.

The Burundi civil war: ethnic asymmetries in a climate of fear

Like many conflicts in Africa today, at least part of the story of current ethnic tensions lies in the close conjuncture between pre-colonial patterns of social organization and the imposition of colonial rule that reinforced and even exacerbated ethnic tensions. This is surely the case in Burundi, which for centuries prior to the arrival of the British explorers and later German and Belgian occupiers had seen a quasi-feudal system of rule by Tutsis over the demographic majority Hutus in the unified kingdom of Urundi and Ruanda. In 1899, the territory became part of German East Africa, was officially colonized by the Kaiser in 1903, and after the defeat of the Germans in World War I the territory was given over to Belgium as a League of Nations mandate.

Post-independence: turbulence in a minority dominant state

At the moment of independence in 1962, when Burundi emerged from tutelage as a UN Trust Territory (a continuation, in effect, of the League mandate) it appeared as a monarchy under the Tutsi king Mwambutsa IV. Violence escalated sharply among the ethnic groups in 1963, creating mass migration of Hutus out of Burundi and heightening insecurity among the dominant Tutsi. The first post-independence parliamentary elections yielded a Hutu majority, but Mwambutsa demurred in appointing a Hutu prime minister (despite the fact that Hutu politicians won 23 of 33 seats). On October 18, 1965, Hutu leader Gervais Nyangoma fomented a coup, ousting the king, and in short order the Hutu-dominated police force began pogroms against Tutsis in the countryside. Parallel violence occurring in Rwanda also heightened ethnic tensions in Burundi, a classic case of the contagion of fear.

A young Tutsi minister of defense, Michel Micombero, mobilized the Tutsi military and reclaimed power in a coup in what would become a pattern of control by Tutsi military elites. The monarchy was steeped in history but failed in legitimacy, and it did not last: in November 1966, Mwambutsa's son, Ntare V (who had himself deposed his father), was deposed by Micombero and the dominance of the Tutsi military was affirmed. Ntare V, first exiled in West Germany, was lured back to Africa by Ugandan dictator Idi Amin and then returned to Burundi to be imprisoned at Gitega where he was executed during the swirl of events that was the genocide of 1972 as ethnic tensions and killing spiraled out of control.

Indeed, in 1972, Burundi's "first genocide" played out, precipitated in part by the Ntare assassination. Beginning with Hutu insurrection organized from within the police, violence between the ethnic groups grew wildly with Hutu insurgents killing every Tutsi and moderate Hutu they could find, thus constituting genocide. In response, Micombero declared an emergency and the Tutsi army responded with its own genocidal frenzy; the 1972 genocide in Burundi was clearly planned, orchestrated, and implemented by the Tutsi army armed with weapons but also with detailed lists of targeted individuals. The genocidal violence left some 100,000–150,000 dead and about half a million fled in exodus to neighboring countries. Among the fatalities in the 1972 orgy of violence was the father of Pierre Nkurunziza, a Hutu rebel leader who would be elected president in 2005.

The genocide itself was clearly part of a broader strategy of Tutsi elite to retain control of the country despite their minority status: Lemarchand and Martin argue that

> "Prophylactic violence" thus became a major element in the strategy of counter-insurgency adopted by Tutsi authorities to deal with the Hutu problem. The aim was to decapitate not only the rebellion but Hutu society as well, and in the process lay the foundation of an entirely new social order.
>
> (Lemarchand and Martin 1974: 18)

Many prominent Hutu leaders were among the hundreds of thousands killed by Tutsi military units.

Competition within the Tutsi military elite perpetuated political turmoil in Burundi; Micombero fell to Jean-Baptiste Bagaza in 1976, and Bagaza was in turn ousted by Pierre Buyoya in 1987. Bagaza's rule was rife with corruption and mismanagement and the ill-considered efforts to make Burundi a one-party state. While overseas, Buyoya mounted what would be the first of his two successful coups d'état in Burundi, promising ethnic conciliation and clean government. In fact, Buyoya did seek to reconcile the country, appointing voluntarily Hutus into cabinet positions, including a prime minister, and he began to broaden the ethnic base of the military. Hutu frustrations, however, again produced mutiny in Ntega during which a rebellion led to the deaths of several hundred Tutsis, after which in reprisals by the Tutsi military some 20,000 Hutus died in what some consider a second wave of genocide.

Buyoya, however, goes into history as a conciliator, although his conversion to national unity came as a result of considerable pressure from the international community. Following the 1988 violence, he led efforts to draft and implement a Charter of National Unity that was supported in a national referendum in May 1991 and a new constitution adopted in March 1992 which was approved by nearly 90 percent of the voters. *La constitution Burundaise* was thoroughly consociational, dedicated to the principles of national unity and ensuring that the country's majority Hutu would be fully represented in an entire range of power-sharing features.[3] More extremist Hutu groups such as the rebel force Palipehutu opposed the constitution. With the new constitution in hand, and with a wave of multiparty democratization sweeping across Africa, Buyoya fatefully announced multiparty, presidential and parliamentary elections for June 1993.

The assassination of Mechior Ndadaye: precipitant of civil war

In the context of the run-up to elections in Burundi in 1993, it became clear that the poll was emerging not as a simple electoral contest for political power among elites, but as a proverbial "ethnic census." The principal Hutu opposition party, FRODEBU (*Front démocratique du Burundi*), led by Mechior Ndadaye, mobilized as the principal challenger to the Tutsi-dominated UPRONA (*Union pour le Progrès national*). The presidential contest was a three-way affair as Buyoya faced Ndadaye of the FRODEBU and a third candidate, Pierre Claver Sandegeya, ran for a small splinter party on a "royalist" platform. Given Buyoya's attempts at national unity, and his control over the central government, there was strong expectation that Buyoya would prevail and the democratization gamble would pay off in political continuity. However, Ndadaye prevailed in the presidential poll with nearly 65 percent of the vote in an election considered generally free and fair by international observers (Reyntjens 1993). In parliamentary elections later in June, FRODEBU won overwhelmingly, garnering nearly 70 percent of the vote and more than 80 percent of the seats in the National Assembly. Thus, the stage was set for a historic shift in Burundi to Hutu-majority rule.

For his part, Buyoya complied with the results of the election and handed over power to Burundi's first Hutu president, Ndadaye. Ndadaye set about putting together a unity government despite the election results, aware of the tenuous nature of his hold on power despite the election outcome, reaching a power-sharing pact with UPRONA that lasted for only three months. Rumblings of a coup began within days of the elections, even though the head of the military initially pledged allegiance to the newly elected president. Burundi's transition to democracy was doomed to failure. As Reyntjens narrates:

> On 21 October, 1993, the Tutsi-dominated army staged a coup and killed a number of FRODEBU leaders, including Ndadaye. Massive violence immediately erupted all over the country. Tutsi and even Hutu sympathizers of UPRONA were killed, while both the army and local Tutsi attacked Hutu and FRODEBU members. By the end of the year, about 50,000 people were dead, more or less as many Hutu as Tutsi.
>
> (Reyntjens 2005: 117)[4]

The assassination of Ndadaye, who was killed in his presidential palace by Tutsi paratroopers, together with many of his ministers, was the precipitant of the Burundi civil war. FRODEBU and other Hutu groups split and many leaders moved into the countryside and into then-Zaire (now DRC) to mount an armed rebellion.

The moment of crisis and escalation in Burundi was not lost on the international community. Shortly after the assassination, and fearing an escalation of violence that could reach the level of genocide, UN Secretary-General Kofi Annan appointed Ahmedou Ould-Abdallah his Special Representative, charged with the task of preventing genocide in the country as the civil war escalated dramatically.[5] Peacemaking saw progress during this period because of the deft diplomacy of Ould-Abdallah, who carefully mediated among the Burundian parties, leveraging them using the moral authority and practical power of the UN, and carefully coordinating among the various states, the Organization of African Unity, and engaged international powers (in particular, the United States and the European Union and non-governmental organizations (NGOs) such as the Carter Center).[6] The 1994 pact that emerged from Abdallah's mediation has been criticized as an ill-considered power-sharing formula that heightened ethnic differentiation and set up a zero-sum game between the protagonists; Lemarchand has argued that the pact "carried the logic of power sharing to an extreme … and with extremely dysfunctional consequences. Rather than cohesion, the result had been to foster paralysis at every level of government" (Lemarchand 2006: 9).

In mid-1994, the CNDD formed as a Hutu-based political party, and an armed wing, FDD, emerged as the military wing to confront directly the Tutsi-led armed forces. In the early months of the war, too, Palipehutu-FNL and other rebel groups challenged the government forces and the prolonged civil war began in earnest. Peace talks in Arusha, Tanzania were convened and proceeded together with the talks on ending the civil war in Rwanda, and in April of 1994 the death of Ndadaye's successor, Natayamira, deepened the political crisis. The event stimulated more internecine violence in Burundi, leading to continued ethnic violence and more refugees.

Confirming the pattern of politics in Burundi, in July 1996 the Tutsi military again seized power from a weak and ineffective coalition government, and once again Pierre Buyoya was proclaimed president. Although the coup was denounced internationally and economic sanctions were imposed on the already impoverished country, Buyoya's prior moderation earned him some time to consolidate power and to begin the process of prenegotiation with the Hutu rebels and Hutu moderates (to whom he appointed positions in his cabinet in a voluntary power-sharing arrangement); among these moderates were Domitien Ndayizeye, a FRODEBU politician who served as Buyoya's vice-president and who succeeded him as head of a transitional government that held power following the Pretoria agreement of 2003 until the transition-capping elections of 2005.[7]

From Nyerere to Mandela: eminent persons mediation

With Buyoya in power at the head of the Tutsi-dominated state, and in the wake of the Rwandan genocide and subsequent humanitarian crisis in

Zaire/DRC, the international community – with warnings of new genocidal violence in Burundi – stepped up its efforts to mediate the Burundi war. In early 1996, the Great Lakes Initiative, a global effort involving former Tanzanian president Julius Nyerere, former US president Jimmy Carter, former president of Mali Amadou Toure, and South Africa's Archbishop Desmond Tutu, chose Nyerere as the principal mediator.[8] In prenegotiation talks, Nyerere had engaged Buyoya and the leader of the CNDD-FDD, Leonard Nyangoma, in secret talks. At the same time, the Burundi military stepped up its counter-insurgency campaign, adopting the controversial strategy of placing Hutu civilians in "regroupment" camps that many alleged were essentially gulags. For their part, Hutu rebels used bases in the refugee camps of Tanzania to launch assaults on the regime's military forces.

1998: the teacher as mediator, Julius Nyerere

The Nyerere mediation initiative began in earnest in June 1998, backed by a wide range of regional actors and backstopped as well by the governments of the region (especially Tanzania and Kenya, together with the new African National Congress-led government in South Africa). Nyerere was a classic soft mediator: hesitant to employ much leverage and insistent primarily on the broadest possible inclusion of the Burundi parties in talks. In the mediation, he lived up to his nickname, Mwalimu (teacher), and was often condescending toward the Burundi protagonists. Tutsi elite, to include Buyoya, however, regarded Nyerere with suspicion because of his alleged bias toward the Hutus; indeed, in the negotiations Nyerere likened the situation in Burundi to South Africa, drawing parallels between the Tutsi minority and the Afrikaners and contending that the strategy of talks was to convince the minority elite that they should voluntarily adapt to the realities of demography.[9] Likewise, the Burundi government was concerned about the use by the rebel factions of refugee camps from within Tanzania and argued that the government should be able to control its borders. At the Arusha talks, differences among the Hutu rebels (including a split for a while within the principal group, the CNDD-FDD) meant that the talks were never inclusive of the FDD and Palipehutu-FNL rebels and thus were destined to have only partial success in mitigating violence in the country.

2000: Mandela as mediator

The sudden passing of Nyerere in October 1999 raised questions about the future of the Burundi peace process. The situation was urgent and violence escalated: Jan van Eck, a former South African member of parliament, observed the talks for the NGO community; he wrote in November 1999: "The Burundian security, economic, and political situation is fast deteriorating and fragmenting, the specter of a new and more disastrous regional war (one with even more pronounced ethnic overtones), is looming larger by the day."[10]

By all accounts, Nyerere's successor as mediator, Nelson Mandela – confirmed by African heads of state – took a different approach. Although he, too, saw the root cause of the Burundi war in patterned discrimination and exclusion and he retained the facilitation team that Nyerere had created, Mandela was impatient with Burundi factions. While he called the rebels "freedom fighters" and acknowledged the legitimacy of their struggle, he berated them for human rights abuses and the killing of civilians. Mandela was particularly tough on the Tutsis, however, accusing them of "playing games" and of holding on to power unrealistically. Mandela saw early success in reversing the government's regroupment camps and in building confidence among the Tutsi military elite. At the same time, Mandela met bilaterally with the spoilers outside the process, Palipehutu and the FNL. As a result, Buyoya as a moderate was constantly under threat from spoilers within the Tutsi military elite: he faced apparent coup attempts in both April and July of 2001.

Mandela's mediation bore fruit. Working in concert with regional leaders and the international community, he leveraged the parties into an agreement – the Arusha Accord – reached at the Arusha regional initiative on July 23, 2001. In the accord, key elements of security and power sharing were brokered. On the security front, the agreement called for the reform of the security sector (especially the army and police) and it was agreed that an African peacekeeping force, led by South Africa, would deploy (involving key concessions by the Tutsis); in a bid to ease Tutsi fears of the Hutu majority, a power-sharing pact was reached in which Buyoya would be retained as president as head of a unity coalition government during an 18-month transitional period followed by Domitien Ndayizeye as president for the second 18-month period ... leading up to new elections. A transitional constitution was developed, and the new government was formed in October 2001.

While all sides of this debate agree that in many ways Mandela and the strong leverage of the broader international community imposed peace upon Burundi at Arusha, there exist two distinct perspectives on Mandela's role as mediator. Some regard the Mandela role favorably, seeing the process in terms of "Madiba Magic" (Madiba is a diminutive nickname for Mandela in South Africa) whereby the elegant leader used his moral stature, key interpersonal skills, and sense of social relationships to broker a settlement to an intractable conflict. For example, South African scholars Bentley and Southall found that

> Burundi politicians admit that without Mandela they would not have reached any agreement, nor so quickly. He was tough, exacting but fair, and ultimately seen as disinterested. His experience gained during

> the South Africa transition process was crucial both in knitting a deal and convincing delegates of the viability of its outcome.
>
> (Bentley and Southall 2005: 212)

Others, such as Daley, suggest the contrary, that Mandela's

> lack of understanding of the Burundian situation meant that he could be manipulated by the Burundi government, to which he made concession, forcing the Hutus, particularly the Frodebu leadership, to compromise – an action that may have led to their party's loss of power to the CNDD in the July 2005 elections.
>
> (Daley 2006: 154)

International mediation in Burundi: providing credible commitment

One of the most critical, early steps by external mediators in the Burundi peace process was to provide some level of credible commitment to this pact – recalling prior failures, not least of which the assassination of Ndadaye in 1993 – and especially direct protection for the Burundi moderates who participated in the power-sharing pact. Spoilers from the Tutsi army and the Hutu rebel forces remained outside the accord. The threat of violence to Burundi's top political elite was clearly a result of their having made progress in talks, in agreeing to terms that seemed suicidal from the extreme Tutsi perspective and unjust from the vantage of the long-excluded Hutu. The arrival of South African military personnel to guard the Burundi political leaders was an essential providing of credible commitment by external actors: the first contingent of the SANDF-led force arrived on October 29, 2001 ... two days before the transitional government took office (Reyntjens 2005: 118).[11] Mandela stepped down as mediator two days after the transitional government took office with the words: "Your country has bled enough. It and its people now deserve peace."[12]

Clearly the strategy of the mediation team was that palpable progress on the political front was essential for demonstrating to the spoilers, the remaining Hutu rebels, that the international community would provide credible commitment to the Arusha pact. Mark Bomani, Mandela's principal representative for the talks, said: "If they [the armed rebel groups] have doubts on whether the agreement reached here will be honoured, I think the answer is that the agreement will stick."[13]

Escalation and negotiation: from Arusha to global cease-fire

The Arusha agreement, unfortunately, did not bring immediate peace to Burundi even though the basic terms of Arusha did in fact "stick." In military confrontations in December, clashes between the Burundi military and rebel forces escalated, and on Christmas Day major clashes occurred near Bujumbura in which the army claimed to have killed 500 rebels. The offensive was related directly to the peace talks; the fighting was a classic case of violence as a beyond-the-table tactic. "The BBC's Prime Ndikumagenge in Burundi says that there are hopes that the rebel defeat might encourage them to enter negotiations with the reconciliation government, which was sworn in last month," the news service reported.[14] As the violence waged on the ground, the peace process continued to progress in the political arena as the transitional government was further established and Jean Minani, a Hutu of FRODEBU, was elected to guide the transitional National Assembly. Peace and war were unfolding in Burundi side by side.

Throughout July clashes between the government and rebel forces outside of the transitional pact – the FDD and Palipehutu-FNL – continued while talks went further under Mandela's auspices in Arusha. A sharp escalation of violence in July 2002 and a failed cease-fire between the FDD and the government, which led to newly intensified clashes in early 2003, reflected the obstacles to a sufficiently broad settlement needed to end the violence. Certainly, the parties did not perceive a settlement and indeed the rebels launched a major offensive in July 2003 in which a reported 300 rebels and 15 government troops died and as a result of which an estimated 15,000 were thrust into displacement from their homes as rebels shelled parts of the city. Still, the transitional government held during this volatile period and Buyoya – true to form – agreed to step down at the appointed hour of his relinquishing the presidency of the transitional government in April 2003.

By early 2003, mediation of the Burundi peace process had been turned over in full to South Africa, particularly President Thabo Mbeki and then-deputy foreign minister Jacob Zuma; Zuma (later fired by Mbeki over corruption charges) especially mediated day-to-day in the context of the broader regional efforts to achieve a comprehensive end to hostilities among the Burundi parties and in particular efforts to bring the FDD and Palipehutu-FNL into the peace process itself. With the former, Zuma was successful in clinching a critical power-sharing pact that furthered peace in Burundi, the Pretoria Protocol of October 2003. In this agreement, the parties agreed to sweeping security sector reform, and a comprehensive power-sharing deal that would broaden the transitional administration to include the CNDD-FDD. In mid-July, the rebels entered Bujumbura peacefully, led by Pierre Nkurunziza, a military leader in the process of metamorphosis to politician (and eventually to president). Critical to the Pretoria agreement was a security pact: the CNDD-FDD would get 40 percent representation in the officers' corps and 35 percent in the police.

By October, the Zuma-mediated talks led to agreement in principle in Pretoria on a cease-fire, and then further rounds of negotiation led to the Global Ceasefire Agreement sealed in November 2003 in Dar es Salaam, formally bringing the CNDD-FDD into Burundi's cease-fire and military integration efforts. Progress on power sharing continued, even after the interim government's term ostensibly expired, which eventually led to a subsequent agreement in August 2004 that formalized a new constitution and constituted the basis of a near-complete settlement to the Burundi war. Indeed, the 2003 Global agreement and the 2004 power-sharing pact left only the Palipehutu-FNL in the field to wage violence against the consolidating transitional government and state, a fact that was not lost on the UN Security Council when it explicitly named the group in a presidential statement as the last remaining spoiler to the peace.[15] The interim constitution, which enshrined power sharing, and the referendum which affirmed it in February 2005, marked milestones in the substantive bargaining phase of the Burundi peace process.

The blue helmets in Burundi

The United Nations Operation in Burundi (ONUB) was authorized in May 2004 and was essentially a handover (on June 1, 2004) from the previously deployed African Union (AU) peacekeeping mission. The AU troops had been deployed since 2003 to implement the 2002 Arusha cease-fire agreement and subsequently the Global Ceasefire Agreement of 2003. Still, the UN deployed its peacekeepers into the situation with most of the major protagonists in the Burundi conflict, with the principal and significant exception of the FNL.

The advent of the UN peace operation and the appointment of a new Special Representative of the Secretary-General (SRSG) (Carolyn McAskie of Canada) signaled a new push for peace in war-torn Burundi (the AU mission continued to be deployed alongside UN troops). The mandate of the UN mission (with an authorized force level at 5,650 troops) set about disarmament and demobilization efforts, security force reform, delivery of humanitarian aid, and continued diplomatic pushes to garner the inclusion of the FNL in the peace accords. By the end of December 2004, the UN troops had made considerable progress in the demobilization campaign and had brought a sense of relative normality to Bujumbura.

Especially, ONUB made considerable gains in working with other UN agencies (particularly the UN High Commissioner for Refugees, UNHCR) to begin the process of repatriating refugees and returning internally displaced persons together with the essential tasks of disarmament, demobilization, and reintegration (DDR) and of security sector reform. During the time of UN deployment, violence continued to threaten the peace; in June, just as the UN was arriving, Hutu rebels (an act claimed by the FNL) attacked and killed 160 Congolese Tutsi (Tutsi Banyamulenge) in a refugee camp near the border with the DRC. The UN commenced disarmament and demobilization of the rebel forces and commensurate furthering of security sector reform in late 2004, and by 2005's elections had already made significant progress in the demilitarization of politics prior to the polls.

Peacebuilding in Burundi

A turning point in the Burundi talks was the announcement in April 2005 that, in accordance with the vision laid out in the negotiations and consistent with the power-sharing terms of the peace pacts, the country would turn again to elections to legitimize the peace agreement and to launch a new, democratic government. First, municipal elections would be held in June 2005, followed by parliamentary polls in July and indirect elections of the Senate and President. The specter of 1993 hung gloomily over the preparations for the poll. However, as Reyntjens argues, the conditions in 2005 were much different from the failed, early attempt at ethnic conflict management through democratization. The political landscape was more multipolar, allowing for more fluid, cross-ethnic coalition-making, the parties were exhausted by war and averse to violent deadlock, the army and security forces had been significantly reformed and broadened, and ONUB provided credible commitment. In the run-up to elections, UN SRSG McAskie initiated lines of communication with the FNL to bring the last spoiler into the electoral process. At the same time, much of the violence was between the FNL (allied to FRODEBU) and CNDD-FDD cadres as they competed for Hutu votes and for local control.

Local elections yielded considerable success for the CNDD-FDD at the expense of FRODEBU, with the clear outcome that the Hutu majority itself was internally divided to the benefit of stability in the country. In the parliamentary elections, the CNDD-FDD again proved electoral success, and, fortuitously for the country, the CNDD also included (as required in the constitutional agreement) a number of Tutsis on its proportional representation lists; the outcome was that 30 percent of CNDD-FDD winners in the parliamentary elections were Tutsi. In the indirect presidential elections, then, Pierre Nkurunziza, rebel-turned-statesman and a Hutu, was voted into the presidency by the National Assembly. To balance out the overall picture of the parliament on ethnic and gender terms, the Electoral Commission constitutionally adjusted the composition of the National Assembly through appointment to ensure that the 60–40 Hutu-Tutsi ratio was secured and that a minimum of 30 percent of all parliamentarians were women; the added members were spread equally over the three parties that had fared best in the poll (CNDD-FDD, FRODEBU, and UPRONA, the primarily Tutsi party).

While the elections did not create the departing train scenario that could bring the FNL on board, the new realities of power in Bujumbura meant that the rationale for Hutu resistance to the government quickly lost logic. In September, after the election, the FNL rejected peace talks but less than a year later, in June 2006, persistent mediation efforts by regional leaders finally yielded a government-FNL deal to a cease-fire. *Times of Zambia* reporter Betniko Kayaya captured the moment in his narrative of the crucial talks:

> The stand-off persisted with neither side willing to back down on their demands. Closed-door negotiations and consultations led by Mr Mbeki and his facilitator Mr Nqakula then intensified late into the night until the following day when a compromise breakthrough was announced. And this was that the Burundi government and the rebel Palipehutu-FNL would sign a peace accord that would bind and pave the way for a comprehensive ceasefire in two weeks time.
>
> Announcing the development before a weary but anxious audience, Tanzanian president who is also vice-chairman of the regional peace initiative Jakaya Kikwete said the history of Burundi was strewn with blood and violence and it was now time to bring reconciliation and lasting peace to the country. The Tanzanian president observed that the impact of the civil war on life and property in Burundi was incalculable. Mr Kikwete however paid glowing tribute to Mr Nkurunziza and the rebel FNL for choosing to tread the path of reconciliation at long last, adding that war cannot be used to prevent another war.[16]

The 2006 Accord was finally signed and sealed in September at a ceremony witnessed by Ugandan president Yoweri Museveni, Tanzanian president Jakaya Mrisho Kikwete and South African president Thabo Mbeki; the pact spelled out terms for the cease-fire and created a Joint Verification and Monitoring Mechanism to ensure commitment. However, negotiations dragged on for several more months in Dar es Salaam as FNL leaders bargained for more assurances for their troops in the DDR process, release of political prisoners, and about their own future in the government. Finally, international mediators pulled the plug on financial support for the rebel leaders while negotiating, forcing the two years of negotiation that culminated in a May 2008 deal that, ostensibly, will finally bring the FNL into the demobilization and power-sharing peace process.

The lesson of the Burundi peace process is very much the ways in which the international community has played a concerted, coordinated, and persistent role in leveraging the parties into peace. Especially, the African regional power brokers have used persuasion, shame, and leverage into bringing the ethnic tragedy of Burundi to a more sustainable basis for national coexistence and integration. The international community has consistently backstopped the peace process, through leverage, aid, expertise, and financial backing, but in the driver's seat has been the African leadership and in particular the Tanzanians and the South African state under Thabo Mbeki. Peace in Burundi was ultimately sealed, too, by the UN deployment of ONUB in 2004, although challenges of armed conflict remained through the balance of the transition that was ostensibly furthered by the inclusion of the FNL in the negotiated cease-fire reached in 2006; this has meant a change in the UN presence as the operation moves from peacekeeping into the first test of the UN's new Peacebuilding Commission to provide long-term commitment.

Today, the task of peacebuilding in Burundi is clearly a long-term one. The UN Peacebuilding Commission has developed a comprehensive plan for post-settlement implementation and economic renewal in Burundi, yet fear of renewed conflict is pervasive as demobilization challenges for the rebels and security sector reform frustrate a stable peace.[17] The Nkurunziza government has turned out to be challenged by its own transformation from rebel force to ruling party, and the economy is devastated by years of war-induced "development in reverse" from infrastructure devastation, lost investment, and economic embargo. There have also been creeping authoritarian tendencies on the part of the government which has been accused of significant human rights violations in its efforts to stamp out dissidence and secure its grip on power.[18] Certainly, Burundi remains vulnerable to the bane of its post-independence existence: a military coup; the Tutsi officers have not fully given up power over the military (especially the army). Likewise, Burundi's opportunities for peacebuilding are fleeting as the country faces new elections in 2010 that could again engender and inflame ethnic tensions.

7 Sri Lanka

Mediating without power

The collapse of Sri Lankan peace negotiations in Geneva in late October 2006, which was preceded by a presumed Tamil Tiger suicide bomb attack on a Sri Lankan bus convoy a week prior that killed more than 90 navy personnel, represented the latest iteration in the see-saw between violent encounters and settlement negotiations in the country's post-independence history of protracted ethnic conflict. The Geneva talks, brokered by Norwegian mediators who had been patiently engaged as interlocutors since achieving a landmark cease-fire agreement in 2002, ostensibly collapsed over the means of delivering humanitarian relief: the Tigers wanted overland shipment to the besieged Jaffna peninsula, whereas the Sri Lankan government insisted on delivery of aid by sea. But, indeed, there was no success in even reaching agreement in these talks, and in the end the failure was chalked up to mistrust, to the on-the-ground strengthening of both sides for a new major military encounter, and the unwillingness or inability of the international community to leverage the parties into making progress. Consequently, despite a cease-fire on paper, deaths in the Sri Lankan conflict in 2006 topped more than 3,000 and the protracted war carried on; the "peace process" was more hope than reality. The war recurred and indeed intensified into 2007 and 2008, and the parties appear determined (again) to pursue a military victory.

Events like these characterize the peace process in Sri Lanka, which has failed to progress toward settlement despite myriad negotiations and no small measure of international intervention and mediation. The major escalation of violence in Sri Lanka since 1983 has been accompanied by numerable efforts to negotiate early a formula for settlement that bridges the Tigers' claims for an independent Tamil state ("Eelam") and the government's offers of weak autonomy within the confines of the majority-Sinhalese state. The 2006 stumbling of peace talks for war-torn Sri Lanka and the subsequent withdrawal of official Norwegian mediation efforts highlights the unsavory fact that in Sri Lanka efforts to find common ground among moderates committed to coexistence under mutually agreed upon rules of interaction are accompanied by, and beget, new violence. In this case, pre-talks violence (the October bombing, one over several during 2006) was ostensibly perpetrated by the Liberation Tigers of Tamil Eelam (LTTE) as a signal of strength, motivation, and capacity to fight, an all-too-common occurrence of tragedy in Sri Lanka's halting efforts to find peace.

Since 1983, Sri Lanka has been embroiled in a civil war between a Sinhalese-led government and Tamil separatists principally but not exclusively represented by the LTTE. The mostly Hindu Tamil minority is 18 percent of Sri Lanka's 20.2 million people, the majority of whom are Buddhist (74 percent).[1] Tensions grew in the post-independence era (1948), following Sinhalese cleric-inspired intolerance of Tamil language rights and educational opportunities. Violence flared intermittently in 1958, 1977, and 1981, with seemingly "spontaneous" (but in fact mobilized for and orchestrated) ethnic riots. Myriad attempts at peacemaking have failed, even when they feature strong military intervention by a powerful, interested, neighboring state: India, and especially in the neighboring kin state of Tamil Nadu.

The brutal civil war in Sri Lanka has claimed some 74,000 victims (1983–2006), and Tamils have been "cleansed" from some areas of formerly mixed living. The Tamil-majority area of northeast Sri Lanka has for some time been in the de facto control of the LTTE. In both Sinhalese and Tamil, as well as among other communities (Muslims, who generally speak Tamil, are another distinct ethnic community at 7.6 percent of the population) in the affected regions of the country (to include, occasionally, within the capital Colombo), insecurity prevails among all the country's vibrant and diverse society.

Certainly a central factor in the failure of successive peace processes in Sri Lanka has been deleterious, bitter, internal disputes within the parties; barriers to settlement lie as much within each group as between them. Within the Sinhalese, the appeal and influence of extreme nationalism has prevented more moderate, peace-negotiated elites to secure a bargain. Within the LTTE, the question of internal leadership looms large, and in particular whether the reclusive leader Velupillai Prabhakaran is capable of bargaining a change in identity from rebel to political leader (as did Alfonso Dhlama in Mozambique, for example) or will remain comparable to figures such as Jonas Savimbi of Angola or Pol Pot in Cambodia who died unreconstructed in their roles.

The Sri Lanka case reveals significant insights into the effects of violence on peace negotiations. Clearly, in the course of the more than two decades of war, violence has been used by all sides – bombings by the Tigers, offensives by the state – as a means of bargaining: principally to signal to the opponent that full military defeat of the other is impossible and that power not lost on the battlefield will not be traded away at the table. The Tigers are a very special case: they have perfected the practice of suicide bombing as a way to reveal the ultimate depth of motivation, and to communicate that the very heart of the state – the denizens of power and politics at the pinnacle of power – are vulnerable to violence. The "intractability" of the conflict in Sri Lanka finds its roots, then, not necessarily in the ability of the protagonists to imagine a settlement (based on some form of quasi-sovereign autonomy, like Northern Ireland; see final section of this chapter), but instead in the ways in which the prior, extreme use of violence by the parties has undercut any ability to trust the other to abide by peace. Resolution of the problem of memory, insecurity, and commitment is thus the task for peacemaking in Sri Lanka.

Sri Lanka and the "invention of enmity"

As the story typically goes, the principal ethnic, linguistic, and religious communities lived in relative harmony for centuries in Sri Lanka prior to independence and the revival of Sinhalese nationalism in the wake of colonial rule as the country achieved independence from British colonialism on February 4, 1948. Like in other colonial situations, the British had a significant effect on the structure and nature of post-colonial ethnic relations. Although English had been made the official language in 1833, the political economy of colonialization had led to the transnational importation of labor, Tamils from southern India, to toil in the tea, coffee, and coconut plantations; these migrants subsequently became known as the "Plantation Tamils," and indeed their arrival had a significant effect on the growth of a counter-nationalist sentiment to stress that the Sinhalese community is more nativist.

Thus, Sinhalese chauvinists have at times appealed to what Malay nationalists termed *bhumiputra*, the concept of the "sons of the earth." One of the first acts of post-independence government was to disenfranchise the Plantation Tamils, setting the stage for grievances of inferior "relative group worth" that could have been addressed early – but failure to do so has contributed to the development of a protracted civil war (Horowitz 1985).

Although a controversial thesis because it ruffled the feathers of many Sinhalese, Little argues that the conflict in Sri Lanka was "invented" by political elites who together with religious authority (particularly, Theravada Buddhist monks) articulated and created the underlying rationale that provided an injunction to intolerance of the Tamils; in turn, a counter Tamil nationalist revival stressed Hindu roots.[2] Thus, the story of the roots of post-independence conflict in Sri Lanka is deeply rooted in complex historical narratives that, in part, demand interpretation of deep religious canton and often heroically described interpretation by myths of past glory. The deeply ideological and ultimately social-psychological basis of nationalism and counter-nationalism is a leitmotif of the Sri Lankan conflict, even as the day-to-day waging of the conflict involves rational cunning of military strategy, modern financing and banking, and the attack and counter-attack struggle of the fighting.

The historical narrative of conflict in Sri Lanka: a tale of escalation

Analysis of the deep-seated basis of conflict in Sri Lanka requires tools of both historical and political evaluation – such as the focus on the institutional and elite factors that shaped the rise of a chauvinistic nationalism and a counter-reaction by Tamil nationalist elite, especially from 1948 into the late 1950s (DeVotta 2004, 2005). The 1956 election of Solomon Bandaranaike and his Sri Lanka Freedom Party (SLFP), riding the crest of Sinhalese nationalism, is marked as a turning point in the deterioration of social relations which set the stage for the protracted nature of the civil war. The antecedents of contemporary antagonisms lies in these pivotal moments, when the societal relations began to enter into a spiral of deterioration that produced over time a classic "social trap" (see Chapter 2). With Bandaranaike's inflammatory initiatives – the "Sinhalese Only" language policy especially – the society began a downward spiral away from coexistence from which it has not yet escaped.[3]

On May 25, 1958 when the train to Batticaloa was derailed at Polonnaruwa, Tamil passengers were identified and attacked; the riots began and spread both around the country and in their intensity. Rioting was especially acute in the capital, Colombo, and in implicit support for the bloodshed the Bandaranaike government declined to issue a state of emergency and act against the mobs. As well, the pogroms resulted in "ethnic cleansing," with nearly 5,000 Tamil farmers being ousted from their land in the northern and eastern provinces.

Ironically, or perhaps not surprisingly (given other cases in this book), Bandaranaike's assassination in 1959 was perpetrated by a fanatic within his own community (in this case, a Buddhist monk). As a consequence of factional struggles within the SLFP,

> On the morning of September 25, 1959, Talduwe Somarama Thero called on Bandaranaike by appointment at his residence at Rosemead Place. Just when Bandaranaike was in the act of paying obeisance to the Buddhist monk, Somarama whipped out a revolver and shot at the Prime Minister, hitting him in the stomach at point blank range. It was later revealed that the disillusioned monk, the assassin, was manipulated by former supporters of the Prime Minister. On September 26, Bandaranaike succumbed to the gunshot injuries.[4]

As David Little observes, "Here were the Buddhist *bhikkhus* [monks], sworn to nonviolence and to a life set apart from worldly temptations, committing murder in pursuit of earthly prestige and wealth" (Little 1994: 72).

Again, violence marked a turning point in the heightening conflict between the two communities. The periods of power by Bandaranaike's widow, Srimavo, furthered the gulf between the Sinhalese and Tamil communities, the latter witnessing deep deprivation in economic opportunity and, perhaps more importantly, in their fundamental equality as members of a common society (for example, in changes in university admissions and civil service posts). The political economy of "horizontal inequalities" both reflected and furthered the evolution of ethnic enmity in Sri Lanka, as struggles over employment, land, and education left the Tamils in a distinctly inferior position as a class, justified in sacred terms of superiority by the more extreme Sinhalese monastic orders. Riots erupted again in 1971, although this episode was primarily government suppression of rebellion Sinhalese ultra-nationalists. Following the 1971 episode of violence, however, the government moved to shore up its nationalist credentials and the declaration in the constitutional amendments of 1972 that Buddhism is the country's primary religion seemingly sealed the fate of Sri Lanka as a protracted ethnic conflict.[5]

The language and constitutional changes were accompanied by profound economic changes that overlapped identity boundaries: in sum, the patterns of horizontal inequalities were reversed. As Stewart argues,

> When the Sinhalese gained power, they sought to correct the horizontal inequalities perceived as disadvantageous to them – through educational quotas, the use of Sinhalese as the official national language, and regional investment policy.... From 1963 to 1973, the incomes of the Sinhalese rose while those of the Tamils fell sharply.
>
> (Stewart 2001: 21)

The creation of the Tigers in 1976, a reaction to the 1972 constitutional changes, marked a counter-balancing turning point in the conflict. As a consequence of the initial success of the Tiger insurgency, they were able to establish a war economy in which they assumed monopolistic control of the territory, resources, labor, and markets. Together with the capacity to articulate an ideology of Tamil "organic" nationalism, the LTTE has created an economic system within the territory it controls through which it creates sufficient rent not only to rule, but to prosper. Likewise, the Tamil community in exile, the Diaspora, has been generous in its contributions to the cause of the Tigers in Sri Lanka. Gunaratna has dissected the Tigers' economic base in terms of its reliance on overseas donations, domestic taxation, and illicit business such as the narcotics trade, arguing that there are few tools available to the international community to curb the rebel's rent-seeking machine (Gunaratna 2003). Thus, the economic capacities that exist today, even after the implementation of international sanctions to strangle the cross-border financial flows, also have their antecedents at the very beginning of the escalation of the ethnic struggle. Sri Lanka shows well how the dynamics of difference combined with war economics can create conditions through which protracted conflict becomes possible.

Pivotal in the evolution of conflict in Sri Lanka is not just elite manipulation, predation, and capture, but also direct social antagonisms manifested in deadly riots and suicide bombings. While historical narratives of nationalist claims and economic structures of struggle can explain well the broad dimensions of conflict, understanding the role of violence in Sri Lanka and how a protracted conflict evolves and persists must also take into account the individual dynamics of rationalization, recruitment, and – to be blunt – brainwashing that occurs. The LTTE's "Black Tigers," or suicide bombers, have been pivotal in the violence–negotiation interaction in Sri Lanka given the use by the leadership of such bombers as a deliberate tactic in the conflict.[6]

On the political front, it was also significant that in the political sphere separatist-oriented political parties (the Tamil United Liberation Front, TULF) prospered during elections, winning in 1977 all the seats in Tamil-majority areas in the parliamentary elections of that year. Related to the political mobilization was the re-eruption of direct social violence in 1977. In the election that ensued, J.R. Jayawardene of the United National Party (UNP) captured power initially on pledges of improving ethnic relations (and thus winning Tamil electoral support) but was quickly undermined following tensions between Sinhala and Tamil youth in Jaffna. The 1978 constitutional reforms represented important early concessions to Tamil interests; however, the government's internal divisions prevented many of the promises from becoming reality. Likewise, the adoption of the notorious Prevention of Terrorism Act in 1979 contributed to the Tamil sense of insecurity and vulnerability.

As Rotberg suggests, by the time the war began the Sri Lankan society had become "irredeemably polarized" (Rotberg 1999: 7). Tamil frustrations grew, sporadic incidents of violence heightened deteriorating relations, and violence in 1983 spread into Colombo; hundreds of Tamils died in the conflicts, killed by Sinhala mobs with the tacit tolerance of security forces.[7] From India, prime minister Indira Gandhi took measures to train and finance the newly emerging Tamil guerillas. The 1983 riots were prompted by reports that in Jaffna the LTTE had ambushed and killed 13 Sri Lankan army personnel on July 23. The Sri Lanka soldiers retaliated the following day, killing 44 Tamils in a rampage in Jaffna. Funerals for the dead Sri Lanka Armed Forces (SLAF) men were held in Colombo in the ensuing days, setting the backdrop for what would be a firestorm of deadly ethnic riots. As Horowitz has observed, such events provide "an occasion for violence" and the "social environment for killing" (Horowitz 2001: 268–373). These events launched the civil war.

The onset of civil war in Sri Lanka was an orchestrated event. Human Rights Watch, in a comparative study of how political elites mobilize for violence, reported the following in relation to the 1983 riots that followed the Tiger attacks:

> In Colombo, police and soldiers stood by and watched as Tamils were attacked. In some cases, they perpetrated the acts themselves. The violence was well organized and politically supported. High ranking

> officials, including government ministers, were accused of orchestrating the violence.... When President Jayawardene finally made a public statement regarding the July 1983 riots four days later, he clearly showed his support for a Sinhalese majoritarianism which was not concerned with the plight of the Tamils. He did not condemn the violence against Tamils, but rather focused on violence perpetrated by the Tamil separatist movement.
>
> (Human Rights Watch 1995: 88–89)

As Horowitz argues, by 1983 the mutual antagonism of protracted war had been well laid as in social-psychological terms the justification for violence:

> It is clear that rioters are inclined to attack groups they believe to be aggressive, and a long period of violent conflict can bring groups ... under the rubric of people prone to be cruel and violent, as the Tamils, by 1983, were certainly thought to be.
>
> (Horowitz 2001: 242–243)

Contributing to intractability: a history of failed peace talks

There were early and immediate efforts to settle the rapidly escalating conflict through a settlement. Halting peace talks in 1985, hosted in Bhutan under the guidance of Rajiv Gandhi, failed to make progress (Smith 1999: 18). Like many civil wars, the Sri Lankan conflict quickly settled into a stalemate: the Sri Lankan government, although ostensibly more militarily powerful than the rebels, was unable to definitively defeat the movement despite by 1987 having pushed rebel forces into their stronghold of the Jaffna peninsula. If Sri Lanka is a history of many "missed opportunities" to realize peace and to de-escalate violence, perhaps the most significant of all such moments was the inking on July 29, 1987 of the Indo-Sri Lankan Agreement and the subsequent deployment of the 50,000-strong Indian Peacekeeping Force (IPKF).[8] The agreement reaffirmed the plural nature of Sri Lankan society and pledged "a multi-ethnic, multi-lingual, multi-religious plural society, in which all citizens can live in equality, safety, and harmony." Substantively, one of the principal achievements of the agreement was the creation of new decentralized councils as a way to provide de facto autonomy and rights in the Tamil areas in the north and east.

Again, internal divisions doomed progress toward peace.[9] Left-wing nationalist and Sinhalese extremist forces mobilized against the presence of Indian troops and the concessions for decentralization in Tamil areas. This period saw, ominously, the advent of the Janatha Vimukthi Peramuna (JVP) as the principal Sinhalese spoiler not only to the 1987 Indo-Sri Lanka accord, but to the subsequent prospects for peace throughout the 1990s and into the 2000s. The JVP launched a death squad campaign in which backers of moderation among both communities (Sinhala and Tamil) were systematically targeted.[10] From the Tamils, tensions over Indian hegemony stimulated an insurgent LTTE reaction to the force – importantly, the LTTE had not been party to what was an international agreement – and the IPKF mission collapsed in a debilitating armed confrontation between the Indian soldiers and the LTTE.

The only silver lining was the cooperation of the government of then-prime minister Ranasinghe Premadasa and the LTTE in 1989 to oust the foreign peacekeepers, but this cooperation was short-lived and the hope for peace was illusory: the war between the regime and the LTTE resumed thereafter. Equally, Premadasa sought to tame the JVP. Certainly, the implication of the LTTE in the brazen assassination of Indian president Rajiv Gandhi by a 17-year-old female suicide bomber (Thenmuli Rajaratnam) in Tamil Nadu on May 21, 1991 obliterated any perception that it was possible to make peace with such a fanatical group. On the other hand, in the mythology of the Tigers and their movement, Rajaratnam was venerated as a heroic woman who had revenged her virtue (she had allegedly been raped by Indian soldiers) and that of the similarly abused Tamil nation.

A window for peace: the Kumaratunga initiative

Assassination by the LTTE's "Black Tiger" suicide machine touched another victim on May 1, 1993, where at a May Day rally President Ranasinghe Premadasa and 23 others were killed by an LTTE cadre who had infiltrated the president's entourage. The Premadasa assassination and the political vacuum his murder set in motion ironically set the stage for a moment of ostensible opportunity in the conflict: Chandrika Kumaratunga, daughter of Bandaranaike and his wife Srimavo, came to power with a mass sentiment that through negotiation she would pursue an end to the war. Indeed, by then, it had become clear that the war was unwinnable for the government and that the conflict was costing the government dearly, not only in reputation terms but practically, for example in shaving up to two percentage points off the annual gross domestic product of the early 1990s.

The Kumaratunga initiative

The LTTE had entered into negotiations with the Kumaratunga government beginning in October 1994, which resulted in an agreement to cease fire by January 1995.[11] Direct talks between the LTTE and the government of Sri Lanka began in early 1994, following the assassination of Premadasa. As elections approached for November 1994, ruling UNP candidate Gamini Dissanyake was killed by a suicide bomber, along with 51 others; the blast was attributed to the LTTE. Nevertheless, or perhaps because of the violence, Chandrika Bandaranaike Kumaratunga won elections on a peace platform. After her election, direct talks with the LTTE led to a January 8, 1995 cease-fire agreement, with broad agreement that the government would eventually devolve significant power to the Tamils.

By April 1995, however, the LTTE broke off further talks and threatened to resume the armed struggle. The peace plan unveiled in August 1995 was an attempt by the government to circumvent and undercut the LTTE's base by appealing directly to moderate Tamils and by retaining the support of a small pro-government Tamil party in the legislature. The peace plan offered to provide for greater autonomy by giving Tamils legislative powers over their own affairs in areas of law and order, land, and finance. Elements within both communities opposed the peace process. Chauvinist Buddhist monks and the Sinhalese nationalist JVP worked to undercut the search for moderation. Notably, the agreement was also strongly opposed by hard-line elements within the Kumaratunga cabinet, as well as by elements within the LTTE, likely including enigmatic leader Velupillai Prabhakaran.

The government of Sri Lanka, since the failed Indian attempt at peace, has consistently rejected external mediation or other forms of intervention (with the exception of the International Committee of the Red Cross and the United Nations (UN) High Commissioner for Refugees for relief work assisting the internally displaced). However, in 1995 Kumaratunga sought the mediatory assistance of the government of France. The French refused to mediate, but offered the services of eminent person François Michelle, who would be working in his private capacity. The LTTE rebuffed the government's effort, however, to allow third-party intervention and Prabhakaran insisted that any mediator represent a government and not act as an individual. With the exception of the work of Western ambassadors to keep the cease-fire, no other serious effort was mounted when elements within the LTTE continued terrorist attacks in April through August and the talks collapsed as a result.

Political violence during the nascent period of peace talks undercut the ability of Kumaratunga, despite her electoral mandate, to continue talks with the LTTE. It was clear that the cease-fire of January 1995 was a momentary pause in the war, and that talks failed to progress beyond very initial and preliminary steps. As Shastri notes, "The government promise to devolve substantial power to the provincial level was insufficient to the LTTE, which was committed to the establishment of an independent Tamil state" (Shastri 1997: 158). In early August 1995, Kumaratunga unveiled the long-awaited peace plan to end years of cyclical upsurges of ethnic violence in her country through a detailed, well-considered, and by external judgments reasonably fair plan for peace talks and devolution for autonomy. Kumaratunga's devolution plan for Tamil areas in November 1995 reflected an effort to woo Tamil moderates away from the LTTE and to possibly split the organizations. Hard-liners within her government and the Sinhalese majority rejected the plan as generous, and the devolution scheme failed to gather momentum.

The following day, the LTTE responded to the plan: the Black Tigers killed 21 people in an attack on a government building in Colombo. Equally, the bloody attack was on the peace plan itself, the key plank in Kumaratunga's efforts to build a moderate core of Sinhalese Buddhist and Tamil constituencies to support the peace plan's aims and provisions. The early August blast was followed by a sharp upsurge in bloodletting – both between the government and rebels, and within the rebel movement itself. Justice minister G.L. Peiris declared "now the government is at war with the LTTE.... In those circumstances we cannot confuse the picture by entering into any process of negotiation."[12]

Resurgence of war

In late 1995, the Sri Lanka military launched a massive offensive that wiped out much of the LTTE's real estate holdings, although the military was not able to "mop up" in the country's jungle terrain. The SLAF recaptured Jaffna, however; the military operation (code-named Operation Sunshine) created a new sense of victimization by the Tamils and directly contributed to renewed resistance by the Tigers' supporters (Wilson 2000: 162). Many Tigers fled the island, gathering strength to return to the fight. But they responded to might with might: in 1996, the Tigers once again unleashed bombs in Colombo, leading the government to once again declare a state of emergency and by 1997 it had launched yet another futile military offensive against the recalcitrant, and well-entrenched, Tigers. The government's interest in war was the hope, but not the realistic expectation, that it could definitively defeat the Tigers. As Saravanamuttu writes, the government adopted a "war for peace" strategy:

> Following the LTTE's unilateral resumption of hostilities in April 1995 and early success in inflicting damage, the government of Sri Lanka felt it had to restore the military balance in its favor as a task of the utmost urgency and as the necessary prerequisite for the employment of other means of conflict resolution. This included the resumption of negotiations. This situation of the strength/negotiation from strength rationale came to be frequently used by the government, and the very real concern for not being duped or seen to be duped by the LTTE again conditioned its attitude toward conflict resolution.
>
> (Saravanamuttu 2000a: 203)

At the same time, on the political track, Kumaratunga launched a major political reform initiative designed to woo moderate Tamil political leaders away from the Tigers and potentially to grasp a viable "internal" settlement with them. New efforts at reform featured prominently in the 1997 constitutional reform initiative, which offered power sharing at the center and revised efforts to invigorate with some power local councils in Tamil-majority areas.

The January 25, 1998 bombing of the sacred temple complex, the Buddhist Temple of the Tooth Relic, in Kandy – timed in anticipation of the 50th anniversary of independence – further communicated that for the Tigers peace negotiations and violent encounters could easily unfold side by side. Stalled efforts to encourage the Tigers to openly pursue peace led by March 1999 to another big, and another futile, push by the government to achieve military victory: Operation *Rana Gosa* (Battle Cry) was a major offensive of the Sri Lankan government to obliterate the LTTE on the ground. With massive investments in an effort to solidify the recapture of Jaffna, the military made significant gains against the rebels but could not ultimately defeat them. The offensive seemed at the time to have been a turning point in the see-saw of advantage between the contending sides, however the gains were temporary and fragile as the Tiger military was able to resist and eventually recapture lost ground by the end of the millennium.

A deeply unfortunate event occurred in mid-1999: the assassination on July 29 of Neelam Tiruchelvam, known throughout the world as a peace-maker and human rights campaigner, the kind of moderate Tamil who could be a potential partner with the government in creating a new centrist core of those seeking peace.[13] Indeed, the moderate coalition in Sri Lanka lost one of its finest leaders when a suspected LTTE suicide bomber assassinated Tiruchelvam, member of parliament and founder of both the International Centre for Ethnic Studies and the Law and Society Trust, a human rights research and advocacy organization. Tiruchelvam had, perhaps more than anyone else, devised an approach to constitutional reform that had emanated from the 1985 agreement on principles in the failed negotiations held in Bhutan in that year.

The Tigers also tried to kill President Kumaratunga, on the last election rally in the run-up to the late 1999 presidential elections[14]; a female LTTE suicide bomber detonated an explosive at Colombo City Hall that injured Kumaratunga's left eye. Two weeks later, in a landmark interview with the BBC, she reiterated her commitment as a messenger of peace but also demurred that Prabhakaran has "an obsessive fear of peace."[15] Kumaratunga was re-elected in the elections with 53 percent of the vote; she reiterated her commitment to talks, despite the assassination attempt, as long as the LTTE "jettisoned terror and secession" (Saravanamuttu 2000b: 223).

Between cease-fire and settlement, 2002–2006

The new century opened in Sri Lanka with yet another opportunity for peace: a series of events on the ground and at the table created a moment of possible ripeness in the conflict in which a constellation of external and internal developments pointed to the possibility that the structural and dynamic elements of the situation could lend themselves to the realization of a new peace agreement. In February 2000, following an extensive number of secret unofficial or "track-two" initiatives held in Bergen, Norway accepted invitations by all sides and entered as an official mediator in a new bid for peace in Sri Lanka.[16] The new government turned to Norway as a mediator because of the country's success in brokering the Oslo pact in the Israeli–Palestinian case, and for its identity as a neutral facilitator that would not embarrass or yield leverage for the government to concede anything to the Tigers; on the other hand, the LTTE needed legitimacy badly, and having recognition from an upstanding UN member state such as Norway (whose policies tend to favor engagement even with international scofflaws, such as Hamas) would help achieve this. The Tigers continued linking the bargaining process with the military struggle: by April 2000, they gained a major military advantage by retaking the strategic Elephant Pass that links Jaffna to the main part of the island.

In October 2000, President Kumaratunga and her People's Alliance were again re-elected in general elections, but the weak coalition flailed and within a year she was forced to dissolve parliament as intra-Sinhalese coalitional struggles once again undermined peace efforts. In December 2001, Ranil Wickramasinghe – a deeply antagonistic foe to Kumaratunga – formed a new cabinet featuring the return of the UNP to power; with Wickramasinghe as prime minister and Kumaratunga as president, the government fragmented into rival camps, seriously impeding its ability to present a coherent front at the negotiating table. In the meantime, Norway reinforced its role as an ostensibly pure and neutral mediator: Erik Solheim and Vidar Helgesen served from 2000 to 2005, despite opposition of some actors within Sri Lanka (and a few in Norway) against their involvement. As Solheim remarked,

> Remember, Norway has no way of imposing peace in Sri Lanka: we have no marines to send; we are not a military power; we do not even have any meaningful way of putting diplomatic pressure on them. We can only assist them if they wish.[17]

Progress emerged from persistent facilitation and unexpected events. One of the myriad consequences of the attacks on September 11, 2001 was the Tigers being declared a terrorist organization by the United Kingdom in new anti-terror legislation seeking in part the end of the transnational funding flow for the Tigers emanating in the Diaspora community. Likewise, in the United States the Tigers fell (albeit as a sideline) in the Bush Administration's "war on terror" and faced de-legitimization in the broader international community as the full weight of international financial sanctions was put to bear to dry up Tiger access to cash and weapons. "After September 11 [the Tamils] had no choice … they don't have anywhere to run their international operations," commented K.T. Raasingham, an exiled Tamil journalist.[18] External events reinforced pressures for peace as they solidified the stalemate locally and created urgencies – especially for the Tigers – to consider a negotiated exit from the struggle. Surely, the Tigers were motivated by the need to avoid the fate that befell other supporters of global terror, especially the Taliban and *al-Qaeda* (to which there are no known affinities or relations).

Norwegian mediation: good intentions, little leverage

One manifestation of a moment of ripeness in Sri Lanka was a landmark Permanent Ceasefire Agreement in February 2002, ostensibly creating a moment of peace in which words could replace war as the basis of interaction to resolve the underlying conflicts. In March through May 2002, there was tangible progress toward peace. The nominal decommissioning of weapons commenced, the Elephant Pass road was reopened for the first time since the late 1980s, and civilian air traffic into Jaffna was resumed (offering hope for economic revival in the besieged city). Talks held in Sattahip, Thailand in September 2002 yielded further progress and a hope for peace. The government lifted the ban on the LTTE (which had been a key Tiger demand), prisoners of war were exchanged (the first set of exchanges in the conflict's history), and – critically – the Tigers mooted the possibility of settling for less than a separate state.

By December 2002, talks were progressing in peace negotiations in Oslo in the shadow of the awarding of the Nobel Peace Prize for that year to peacemaker/mediator ex-US president Jimmy Carter. The government and the LTTE agreed in principal to a substantive settlement that began to outline a formula for peace to accompany the process of direct talks: power sharing and minority autonomy. Another round of talks ensued in Berlin in February 2003 with peacemakers reporting moderate progress in the negotiations. In these talks, the Norwegians clearly adopted a policy of facilitation, not mediation per se; "We are not driving the agenda," they said; "We don't have a blueprint which we feel would be the best solution" (quoted in Martin 2006: 112).

Table 7.1 highlights the major known sessions of negotiation between the government and LTTE during the period immediately following the cease-fire. These talks were initially encouraging: they covered the principal issues of power sharing, federalism and devolution (i.e. the terms of autonomy), development finance and aid, child soldiers, and in Japan in March 2003 a possible joint charter of human rights.

Perils of politics and the failure to progress

Significant progress in finalizing a comprehensive peace settlement ended in April 2003, when the Tigers "suspended" their participation in talks, claiming they were being marginalized. Indeed, the United States had excluded direct representation of the Tigers at a planning meeting prior

Table 7.1 Overview of the Sri Lankan peace talks, 2002–2006

Cease-fire talks
Session 1, Geneva: February 22–23, 2006
Session 2, Geneva: October 28–30, 2006
Peace talks
Session 1, Thailand: September 16–18, 2002
Session 2, Thailand: October 31-November 3, 2002
Session 3, Norway: December 2–5, 2002
Session 4, Thailand: January 6–9, 2003
Session 5, Germany: February 7–8, 2003
Session 6, Japan: March 18–21, 2003

to the convening in June 2003 of the Tokyo Conference on Reconstruction and Development of Sri Lanka, at which the four co-chairs (Norway, the European Union, the United States, and Japan) emerged as a quartet leadership of the subsequent Contact Group of states that pledged to support the peace process.

The problems of the time were not only across the table – trust in the implementation of early agreements, willingness to take the final compromises necessary to reach convergence on the details of autonomy and decentralization – but within the parties as well. Part of the problem was with the jingoist press in Colombo, which consistently criticized the Norwegian mediators as biased busybodies bent on appeasing LTTE terror.

Within the government, the tensions between Kumaratunga and Wickramasinghe escalated to breaking point in November 2003; disputes over the conduct of the peace process led Kumaratunga to dismiss three UNP ministers and to employ her presidential authority to suspend parliament. Although the constitutional crisis was averted following two weeks of negotiation within the political elite, the casualty of the moment was talks with the Tigers, which were shelved. Within the Tigers, in March 2004 a renegade faction under a commander known as Kiruna split from the LTTE, leading to intra-rebel battles that highlighted the factionalization within the LTTE and in particular the dominant role of Prabhakaran at the top of the rump LTTE. The event underscored a long-running thesis about the reclusive LTTE leader: that he is a maniacal, personalistic ruler whose cult-of-personality grip on the organization is total and whose interests by no means rest with peace. Smith writes that "while Prabhakaran remains in control of the Tamil Tigers, the chances of a negotiated settlement are virtually nonexistent" (Smith 1999: 37).

The political crisis in Colombo further frustrated Norwegian efforts to keep up momentum in talks. Early elections in early 2004 led to the defeat of Kumaratunga and the inauguration of Mahinda Rajapakse into the presidency. The Tigers, in turn, re-engaged in politics not through the talks, but rather through their more common method of signaling intent:

in July 2004, the putative voice of the Black Tigers returned in yet another suicide blast in Colombo, the first since 2001.

December 2004 brought disaster to Sri Lanka as the most deadly tsunami ever recorded thrashed the eastern shore of the island, leaving an estimated 30,000 dead in the wake of the deadly waves; thousands more were displaced. Initially, the natural disaster may have reinforced moves toward peace, leading to negotiations in which six months later (June 2005) a bargain was reached among the government and leaders of the various ethnic communities to share in the allocation and distribution of the nearly $3 billion in humanitarian relief pledged by the international community. The tsunami relief effort also brought in droves of international humanitarian relief workers who sought to distribute aid in a way that reinforced pressures for peace. Yet progress on the humanitarian aid distribution front led to a familiar, devastating result for peace negotiations. The Sinhala nationalist JVP responded by pulling out of the Rajapakse-led coalition, setting the stage for a subsequent political crisis and new elections that once again inflamed ethnic enmities.

In the run-up to the elections, the Tigers voted again with bullets: this time killing foreign minister Lakshman Kadirgamar; he was gunned down by a sniper on August 12, 2005, blocks from his home. "It's the Tigers," Inspector General of Police Chandra Fernando told reporters on the day following the attack.[19] Indeed, Kadirgamar had proven himself a tough opponent for the Tigers in talks as a close confidant of Kumaratunga and it is clear that he and the Tigers knew each other well; the murder was a clearly strategic one, directly related to talks themselves. The implications of the attack were not lost on the electorate: Kumaratunga's tenure as president would come to an end in the November 2005 elections, leaving the task of negotiating peace with the Tigers to a more hard-line Rajapakse, who won in a poll boycotted in the Tamil-majority areas (and the LTTE had prohibited participation in any event); Rajapakse had pledged to deny Tamil autonomy claims and had claimed to "review" the 2002 cease-fire agreement. Likewise, he hinted that he may terminate the welcome extended to the Norwegians by Kumaratunga.

That talks would resume in February of 2006 was evidence that despite the election of a new government, there was continuing interest of both the government and the Tigers in giving the appearance of pursuing a negotiated settlement. In Geneva, both sides re-dedicated themselves to the 2002 cease-fire. However, on the ground, throughout 2006 there was a clear and marked escalation of the violence while talks were ostensibly continuing through the Norwegian facilitated channel. Explosions in Trincomalee in April 2006 were followed by suicide bombings against the Sri Lankan military in Colombo and escalating attacks on the government's naval operations; in May, an LTTE attack on a naval convoy near Jaffna was counted as a "clear violation of the ceasefire" by the European monitors. In June, the Tigers struck again and by mid-June the LTTE's

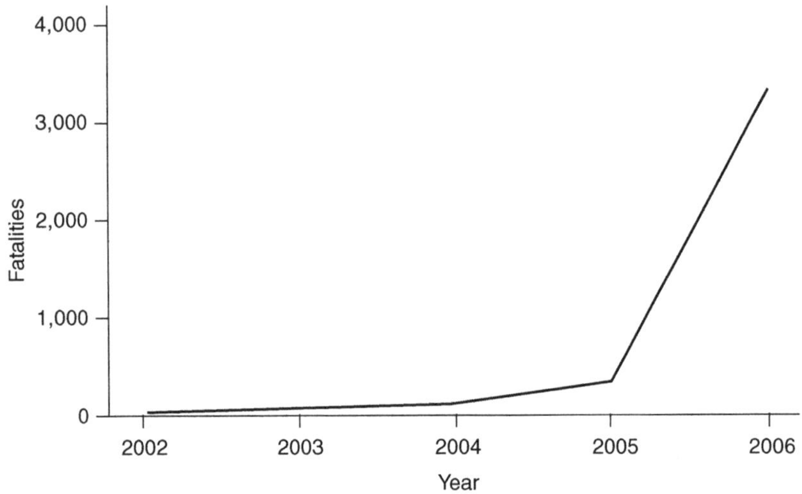

Figure 7.1 Post-cease-fire "terrorist" violence in Sri Lanka, 2002–2006 (source: Institute for Conflict Management (Delhi), South Asia Terrorism Portal; http://satp.org/satporgtp/countries/srilanka/database/index.html).

and government forces were caught up in direct military engagements, particularly in northeast provinces and in Trincomalee. The price was paid in thousands of lives lost in 2006, hundreds of thousands of refugees and internally displaced persons (roughly 350,000 in 2006), and renewed allegations that both the Tigers and the government continued to recruit and abduct new child soldiers in violation of general and explicit international commitments. Figure 7.1 illustrates the demise of the cease-fire and the rise in violence that characterized Sri Lanka's descent back into civil war.

Progressing to settlement in war-torn Sri Lanka

Imagining the parameters of peace in Sri Lanka is possible: territorial autonomy through a renegotiated federal bargain in Sri Lanka, institutional and developmental ties with India, a new social compact based on religious and ethnic coexistence, tolerance, and equality of dignity and worth, implementation of global norms on human rights, and a process of legitimization and inclusive democratization at all levels and particularly within the long-disadvantaged Tamil-majority areas. Nor is it difficult to imagine how such an agreement would yield a peace dividend for the whole country, whereby Sri Lanka's economic performance without civil war would yield mutual prosperity as the country benefits from its role as integrated emerging market in a global economy.[20] Certainly, given the country's youthful demographics, its literate and capable population, and the propensity toward tolerance that its religious orientations could provide, it is also not difficult to imagine that in a generation the society could experience reconciliation and even forgiveness after more than two decades of open war and a half-century of ethnic tensions.

Yet the prognosis for Sri Lanka's future is bleak. The 2002–2006 window of peace, now closed, sustains the assertion that cease-fires without settlements are inherently unstable. With the official end of the cease-fire on January 16, 2008, both the government and the Tigers have returned to bargaining with bullets, as the government seeks to definitively defeat the insurgency and the rebels, in desperation, return to guerilla war and asymmetrical violence (e.g. suicide bombings). Associated human rights and humanitarian crises are mounting.[21] As the Sri Lanka Monitoring Mission (SLMM) departed in the aftermath of the government's revocation of the cease-fire, the head of the departing team, Lars Solvberg, warned: "The SLMM is absolutely convinced that this complex conflict cannot be solved by military means."[22] The sad reality of Sri Lanka's renewed war is that even if the government were to defeat the Tigers on the battleground, which is unlikely, there would still be the need for a sustained period of peace negotiations to define a constitutional reform and economic pact to redress the serious questions of autonomy and minority rights and of the lessening of economic inequalities on ethnic lines.

The collapse, again, of peace negotiations fuels perceptions that in Sri Lanka the trust can never exist, that opponents cannot credibly commit, and that essentialist attitudes of enmity will not change. The government claims to be pursuing a strategy of talking while fighting, but the reality is one of all-out pursuit of military victory. On the one hand, there are continuing factors favoring the "ripeness" of the conflict in Sri Lanka; at the same time, there are counter-vailing factors that prevent the war from being terminated through a negotiated settlement (Table 7.2). Clearly, the

Table 7.2 Ripeness in Sri Lanka?

Factors favoring ripeness	*Factors preventing ripeness*
• A mutually hurting stalemate • Relatively cohesive politics in Colombo under the Rajapakse presidency • Compromise outcome is known and indeed the details also are fairly fully developed • The Norway channel: Norway, despite being "asked to leave," remains engaged	• Sunk costs in civil war • Political elites: the LTTE's Prabhakaran • Essentialist demands for the Eelam state and rejection of federalism leave little bargaining space • Lack of guarantor to provide credible commitment to agreements reached

balance today is stronger against renewed talks, and even among the most patient, persistent, and indeed headstrong-for-peace Norwegian mediators there is a palpable sense of despair on the possibility of imminent resolution and the prevention of renewed, open, escalating war.

Obstacles to the negotiated end of Sri Lanka's tragic civil war prevent much optimism that peace will arrive soon. Principal among these obstacles today is the lack of ability by international interlocutors to provide for credible commitment to agreements reached. Neither the regional power broker, India, nor external actors like the UN have demonstrated the willingness and capacity to deploy sufficient peacekeeping resources; arguably, credibly committing to a peace agreement in Sri Lanka would require tens of thousands of international peacekeeping troops, resources which are unlikely to materialize in the present international context. Likewise, external mediators seem unable or unwilling to leverage the parties into peace. Especially, leverage on the Tigers is limited; at the far end of the spectrum, it is not fanciful to think that a strong mediator could raise the possibility of an International Criminal Court indictment for the LTTE leadership for the role in crimes against humanity as a way to leverage parties into talks. It may well be that the real blockage to peace lies not in intractable communal enmity, but in the inability of the rebel leader to envisage a role in a post-settlement future; in Angola, for example, it took the battlefield death of the rebel leader, Jonas Savimbi, to create the necessary conditions for peace. While such a move would scuttle incipient peace talks – which, as this analysis shows, are not progressing in any event – the very threat of indictment before the world court could be the kind of leverage to stimulate progress in war-torn Sri Lanka (as in Liberia, Uganda, or Sudan/Darfur).

Over the long term, the economic incentives of aid will have to either surpass, or replace, the economy of war that fuels the Tigers and leaves them less amenable to positive incentives; thus, closing down cross-border funding flows and reinforcing aid and pledges (especially to the government) of encouragement for foreign direct investments is a critical element of peacemaking. Even at $4.5 billion in pledges at a donor's conference in early 2007, the incentives to exchange war for peace still appeared insufficient.[23]

For the government of Sri Lanka, international mediators are right to focus on an internal dialogue among the Sri Lankan elite in Colombo to achieve a common platform in talks that bridges the deep gap between the SLFP and the UNP together, to the extent possible, with "hard option" factions within the Sinhalese political elite. Yet until a true coalition for peace emerges on the majority side of Sri Lanka's ethnic divisions, there is little prospect of a negotiated solution.

Substantively, it is unlikely that in the foreseeable future the island of Sri Lanka will be partitioned, if "partition" is meant as a two-state solution;

neither global powers such as Russia or China, nor regional hegemonic power India, would agree to such an outcome. Thus, the outcome of the conflict lies in the reiteration of principles that have been at the heart of negotiations since 1985: power sharing, autonomy, religious tolerance, and local democratization. They include commitment by the government of Sri Lanka – encompassing the consent of ruling and opposition groups alike, in rejection of spoilers – to a meaningful multiethnic polity; this means a renewed clearly articulated commitment to Tamil respect, protection, participation, and the reduction of horizontal inequalities. As Chadda observes:

> Majoritarian democracy turned out to be a recipe for civil war in Sri Lanka. The proposed consociational formula did not lead to agreement, and the control model failed equally to end the civil war. The reason for this was not the collapse of democracy, but the establishment and implementation of a majoritarian democracy.
>
> (Chadda 2004: 111)

While at the institutional level devolution and autonomy are necessary, the principles themselves are insufficient; indeed, the details of such a new power-sharing pact should emerge in a new constitution-making process that eschews unbridled majoritarianism and unilateral decree that has constitutional solutions to the conflict in the past. Likewise, autonomy and devolution are problematic in Sri Lanka if the terms lead to legitimating the authoritarian control of the Tigers in the areas they control without the ability to ensure tolerance and protection of human rights. Commensurate with institutional change is the necessity of economic development to alleviate years of horizontal inequity and deprivation by the Tamils. Finally, compliance with global norms of human rights – and in particular solutions to the problems of child soldiers and attacks on civilians – are essential elements of peace.

The missing element for peace in Sri Lanka is not imagination on how the problems of sequencing, preconditions, venues, and participation can be resolved, however acute these roadblocks to talks may be. Surely there *is* a problem of international commitment to attain a settlement: as the International Crisis Group noted in November 2006, "The international community has a key role to play in restraining both sides and pushing for serious discussion of a political settlement. However, rather than engendering a new level of engagement, the resumed fighting has led to frustration."[24] Instead, the missing element lies in the perceptions of the parties themselves: as long as the parties perceive greater gain, or minimally protection of the status quo, from violence, progress in talks will be elusive. Thus, today, Sri Lanka remains mired in a conflict trap for which the exit path may be known to the parties but they are simply unable or unwilling to take the choreographed steps necessary to travel toward peace together. Because of the human rights and international spillovers from this conflict, the time for more assertive peacemaking in Sri Lanka has arrived.[25] In the meantime, the protagonists in this conflict will continue to bargain on the battlefield in futile pursuit of mutual submission.

8 Kashmir
The power of imagination

The conflict over Kashmir is a highly complex, internationalized dispute involving India and Pakistan reaching immediately back to the design and moment of the partition of British colonial India in 1947, when Hari Singh, Maharaja of Kashmir, decided to accede in India and not seek independence or to join Pakistan; poignantly, Singh made the decision in the face of Pathan tribesmen spilling into the territory from the Northwest Frontier.[1] Today, the conflict is synonymous with global concerns about a possible nuclear war in South Asia as both India and Pakistan have well-developed capacities for mutual annihilation. Indeed, if Kashmir is seen as anything internationally, it is as the world's most conflict-vulnerable "flash-point," where miscalculation, accident, or uncontrolled escalation could precipitate a nuclear exchange that would have devastating, global implications.[2] Three of the four wars fought between India and Pakistan were over Kashmir (1948, 1965, and 1999).

Kashmir is further representative of a seemingly irreconcilable problem in international affairs in the post-World War II world: the balance between territorial integrity and the right to self-determination. In this vein, since the long-promised but never held United Nations (UN) plebiscite over the disputed territory to the present negotiations over scenarios for settlement, a key issue has been determining a balance between the rights of states to their sovereignty juxtaposed against the will of some "self" to exercise the right to self-governance and internationally recognized sovereignty. Thus, as an international dispute, Kashmir is perplexing because of the competing claims of two member states (India and Pakistan) to Kashmir, exacerbated by the fact of the territory's split along a Line of Control (LoC) monitored by a small UN force. From the repulsion of the tribesmen by the Indian army to today, Kashmir has remained the bone of contention in the enduring international rivalry that has become India–Pakistan relations in the years and wars between the two states since partition.

The LoC from the 1948 armistice has created a bifurcated territory of historical Jammu and Kashmir and has resulted in a standoff between the two states, each with claims on the other. Since 1989, however, Kashmir has also become a major armed conflict within India. This conflict within India finds its immediate origins since 1989 in what has become known as the Kashmiri *intifada.* The violence in the Valley has sent development into reverse and has escalated at times to the level of civil war as a multitude of various militant groups, often with cross-border support emanating from Pakistan, have challenged the Indian military and border security forces from within.

In its core characteristic, Kashmir bears some resemblance to the long-running conflict over the sovereignty of eastern Cyprus (the putative Turkish Republic of Northern Cyprus), Timor-Leste, Northern Ireland, and Kosovo. While there have emerged no clear guidelines or best practices to resolving these types of conflicts – indeed, each is so unique that good generalization is impossible to find – it is clear that resolution of territorial sovereignty through negotiation has become one of the most difficult types of disputes for the international community and domestic protagonists to resolve (Chesterman *et al.* 2001).

An estimated 40,000–60,000 people have died in the violence from 1989 to 2006.[3] Peace negotiations on Kashmir within India have been explored since the early 1990s, but only with the more formalized détente between India and Pakistan beginning in 2003 has significant progress been made between coalitions of Kashmiri parties and the central government in Delhi. Today, there is a dual peace process: one between Pakistan and India to resolve the question of international sovereignty and cross-border issues in the management of violence, and one within India and Kashmir over the future of the Valley (assuming that in any plausible final status scenario India will not relinquish at the table what it has not lost on the battlefield, namely sovereignty over the Kashmir Valley itself to include the retention of all governance in the capital, Srinagar).

This chapter evaluates the escalation of the conflict in Kashmir and the patterns of violence that have accompanied various initiatives to secure peace. As the international process between India and Pakistan unfolds, so, too, has a process within India to address issues of autonomy, minority of individual and group human rights, migration, democracy and devolution, economic redevelopment, and reconciliation, religious tolerance, and cultural identity that are the agenda for the peace process. The most significant challenge for Kashmir, like in other ongoing conflicts such as Sri Lanka, is not necessarily to envisage possible scenarios for settlement; as important as such exercises are in illuminating points of common views or interests, they are secondary. Indeed, the most challenging aspect of peacemaking in Kashmir is imaging a process through which negotiation political elites can find mutually acceptable solutions. Thus far, it has been difficult for the Kashmiri separatists in the Valley to garner the support of a population that has invested so much in the violent pursuit of a cause such as independence or accession to Pakistan that is, at the end of the day, unachievable.

Contemporary Kashmir: a prisoner of the past

On January 19, 2007, some 2,000 protestors poured onto the streets of Islamabad to protest statements by the Pakistani president Pervez Musharraf that, conceivably, Pakistan could back away from its claim to the reunification of Kashmir as it was constituted prior to independence and that the LoC could conceivably, and finally, consolidate the borders in the volatile South Asia subcontinent. Protestors chanted reaffirmation of the imperatives of *jihad* to liberate Kashmir, and they denounced Musharraf's mooted concessions with chants of "No to the LoC."[4] The rally, attended by supporters of Kashmiri militant groups and banned Islamist organizations, revealed public support for opponents of any change in long-standing Pakistani policy that Kashmir rightfully and forever should be given the right of self-determination through a referendum and that a majority of the people in the reunited territory would opt for union with Pakistan, reconciling the wrongs committed during the partition of India and the lines drawn on the map by Lord Mountbatten during the fateful months of 1947 and 1948. Spoilers (both within Pakistan and potentially within India) will exist in any effort to negotiate a mutually acceptable outcome to the final status of Kashmiri territory; with more than 50 years of deliberate mobilization by the state of Pakistan to declare Kashmir's future non-negotiable, it is no surprise that the state will not easily demobilize constituencies that have been so deeply socialized for the conflict.

Conflict in Kashmir: competing historical narratives

Like many contemporary wars, in Kashmir there are deeply differing historical narratives as to the origins of the dispute and these inform the contending ideologies that frustrate the realization of peace today. While Kashmir is not exceptional in this fact, at the same time there are few conflicts whose historical roots cast such a long shadow over the present. For this reason, events, incidents, and decisions made more than 50 years ago continue to be the basis for enmity today. The contending historical narratives revolve much around those critical events in 1946–1948 in which Kashmir's place in a disintegrating British colonial empire was to be decided. Efforts by Sheikh Abdullah to reclaim Kashmiri independence led to his arrest and to the imposition of martial law in 1946. Disputed elections in January 1947 generated new grievances among those who sought to reclaim independence from Delhi, and just after the official independence of India and Pakistan secessionist tendencies in the province of Poonch led to a rebellion that encroached upon Srinagar, the Kashmiri capital in the famed heart of the "Vale of Kashmir." The Pooch rebels established "Azad" (free) Kashmir. On the fateful day of October 26, 1948, the Maharaja (Hari Singh) signed instruments of accession (in exchange for military aid to oust the rebels); within a month full-scale war had broken out in the Valley between India and Pakistan.

Debate continues to swirl around the legitimacy of claims from the Azadis and from the legal interpretations of the accession agreements, as well as the human suffering of divided families that were a consequence of the war. After the matter was taken to the UN, the Security Council established in January 1948 a Commission and in April it adopted the now-famous Resolution 47 that declared the disposition of the territory according to a "democratic method of free and impartial plebiscite." On the first day of 1949, a cease-fire went into effect that established the present LoC which left India occupying most of the Vale and the provinces of Jammu and Ladakh with Pakistan occupying "Azad Jammu and Kashmir" (AJK) and the so-called Northern Territories. Through negotiation the LoC was later codified as the boundaries of effective sovereignty and within India, Kashmir's place as an autonomous territory within the asymmetric Indian federation was enshrined in Article 370 of the Indian Constitution. In 1951, the UN established an observer mission on the high-altitude frontier, the UN Military Observer Group in India and Pakistan (UNMOGIP), which continues to operatc today.

The history of Kashmir since the fateful days of the late 1940s is one of failed efforts to mediate peace and of war and tension between India and Pakistan over the territory. International initiatives include the 1950 Dixon Plan and talks in Geneva in 1952 under UN auspices together with direct talks in 1953–1960 between Indian and Pakistani foreign ministers (leading to the Indus Waters Treaty). In this period, too, the border between China and India has also been the subject of dispute, leading to a brief war between the two states in 1962 that ended in de facto defeat for India and a cease-fire agreement.[5] Following cross-border infiltration of fighters into Indian-controlled territory, the second Indo-Pak war broke out in September 1965, which was eventually settled in a cease-fire through UN Security Council intervention; following Russian mediation in late 1965, the status quo was affirmed anew in a cease-fire agreement (the Tashkent Agreement). Although Kashmir did not feature significantly in the fighting of the third Indo-Pak war (over the secession of East Pakistan, now Bangladesh), the 1972 Simla Agreement included negotiations that upheld the cease-fire line and which created the nomenclature "Line of Control" and which pledged the parties to resolve their disputes through peaceful means.

The advent of India as a nuclear power in 1974 dramatically changed the calculus of war in South Asia; so, too, did the further entrenchment of Indian claims to Indian Jammu and Kashmir (IJK) territory with the negotiation between Sheikh Abdullah of the "Kashmir Accord" reaffirming India's claim to unending and unfettered sovereignty. In response, Kashmiri exiles in London established the Jammu and Kashmir Liberation Front (JKLF), a cofounder of which was subsequently hanged by Delhi on charges of murdering an Indian diplomat in London. Thus, the present tensions in the Valley can be marked to this turn of events in the 1970s. As Kaur observes:

> Many Kashmiris in IJK lost faith in their political leaders as champions of their interests after a number of opportunistic deals with New Delhi governments. These include the 1974–1975 accord between Kashmiri leader Sheikh Mohammad Abdullah and Indira Gandhi, and the connivances of the sheikh's son Farooq with Rajiv Gandhi's government to rig the 1987 IJK state assembly elections. This political background inspired separatists in the Kashmir Valley to resort to the gun in 1989, fighting variously for a plebiscite, outright independence, or accession to Pakistan.
>
> (Kaur 2006: 13–14)

The Kashmiri intifada

The immediate antecedents to civil strife within the Valley find their origins in widespread Hindu–Muslim communal strife in late February 1985, leading to the imposition of emergency rule and a growing secessionist struggle among the majority Muslims (especially in Srinagar).[6] The precipitant of further escalation, marking the advent of the so-called Kashmiri *intifada*, was the strikes and occasional attacks carried out by the JKLF in late 1988 and 1989 (following the disputed state elections of 1987 in which pro-Delhi parties prevailed).[7] The exact origins of the escalation are well described by Asia Watch in a 1993 report:

> After the elections [of 1987], militants of the JKLF and other groups – many of whom openly admitted that they received arms and training in Pakistan – grew bolder, detonating bombs at government buildings, buses and the houses of present and former state government officials, and enforcing a boycott of the November 1989 national parliamentary elections. One month later, JKLF militants abducted the daughter of Home Minister Mufti Mohammad Sayeed then freed her when the government gave in to demands for the release of five detained militants. That event, together with a surge in popular protests against the state and central governments, led New Delhi to launch a massive crackdown on the militants.
>
> (Asia Watch 1993: 21)

Escalation of the crisis and entrapment into violent conflict had begun: in the following weeks, hundreds were killed by Indian security forces and militants in turn stepped up their attacks. Civil war began in the serene Valley of Kashmir. Indo-Pak negotiations in 1990 failed to yield progress on the conflict, in part because the militants in the Valley were acting autonomously from control by Islamabad.

At least one of the obstacles to calming the tensions in Kashmir was related to the centralizing tendencies within India, as an effort to keep not just Kashmir but also other restive regions (Punjab, Assam, Nagaland) from breaking free of the federation. As Bajpai observed with regard to Kashmir:

> India's handling of problems in Kashmir exemplifies what had become a familiar pattern in its borderland regions: granting autonomy in theory but going back on it in practice; being unresponsive to normal agitational politics; negotiating with caution and turning to repression as agitation mounts; and finally, resorting to a massive use of force to beat down rebellions and bring about a return to political normalcy.
>
> (Bajpai 1997: 69–70)

Early efforts to negotiate a settlement within the Valley also did not bear fruit. In addition to the back-channel talks between Delhi and the JKLF, and diplomatic entreaties between India and Pakistan, track-two diplomacy efforts by outsiders revealed a lack of agreement on the process of de-escalation (e.g. through new elections) and a sharp disagreement on the overall formula for settlement ("final status" of the Valley itself).[8] Violence and negotiation unfolded side by side in the early years of the conflict, and especially in 1992–1994. Government offensives such as "Operation Tiger" in 1992 were met with insurgent bombs and targeted killings; abuses were reported on all sides, particularly by the somewhat irregular Indian Border Security Forces and by the increasingly terrorist tactics of the Kashmiri militants. Further, the *intifada* began to take on a more Islamist tone with the rise of the *Hizbul Mujahideen* in 1993 (with strong backing from the Pakistan intelligence agency, the ISI (Directorate for Inter-Services Intelligence)) as a major fighting force in the Valley (eclipsing to a certain extent the JKLF, which was subsequently banned by the Indian government in 1996). Significant developments also included the formation of the All-Parties Hurriyat Conference (APHC) in March 1993, which sought to unify the myriad of organizations in the Valley that sought independence for Kashmir.

In September 1996, the government of India sought to forge a solution to the crisis by clamping down on security (in addition to the JKLF ban, the government also banned *Hizbul Mujahideen* and *Harkat-ul-Ansar*, another militant group) and holding state government elections to form a Kashmiri government. Violent attacks accompanied the poll despite efforts by the Indian military to provide security and to compel residents to vote; the election resulted in the re-election of Farooq Abdullah (who had prevailed in 1987's elections, widely acknowledged as rigged) as Chief Minister of IJK.

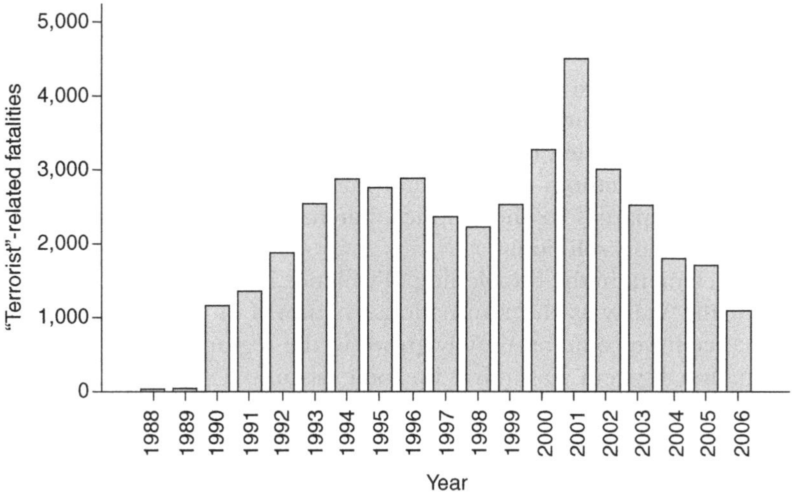

Figure 8.1 "Terrorist" violence in Jammu and Kashmir, 1988–2006 (source: Institute for Conflict Management (Delhi), South Asia Terrorism Portal; http://satp.org/satporgtp/countries/india/states/jandk/index.html).

Violence in the Valley

The ebb and flow of the Kashmiri struggle reveals that at a fundamental level it, too, has evolved into a stalemate among the various parties to the conflict. Although data are unreliable, Figure 8.1 provides some sense of the levels of violence in the Valley from sources that are reasonably trusted. From the perspective of India, massive troop deployments in the Valley, a concentrated counter-insurgency campaign, and efforts to negotiate an "internal" settlement with moderate or at least Delhi-allied Muslims (such as Farooq Abdullah, son of Sheikh Abdullah) have failed to pacify the region. Likewise, Pakistan has seen little return on its years of investment of arms, resources, and diplomatic support for the militants in Kashmir other than destabilization of its rival, India. Clearly driving the conflict also are linkages to transnational Islamist groups, operating beyond the control of Islamabad and sponsoring militias such as the *Jaish-e-Mohammad* and *Lashkar-e-Taiba* with their aim of replacing the traditional tradition of tolerance in the Valley – known as *Kashmiriat* – with Shari'a law. The indigenous Kashmiris, Sufis who are more inclined to tolerance, have been caught in the middle of the conflict and have borne the brunt of the violence; the conflict has indeed led to "development in reverse" in Kashmir, which despite natural resources and beauty is afflicted by grinding poverty, isolation from the world, and more than 15 years of a climate of fear.

Protagonists in the Kashmir conflict

Understanding the protagonists in the Kashmir dispute reveals a complex set of interests and players whose complexity has no doubt contributed to the perplexed nature of realizing peace; variously, groups have ties to governments such as India and Pakistan, and to other networks such as *al-Qaeda* and Taliban-allied leaders in Afghanistan.[9] The conflict is multidimensional, with a plethora of actors and internal divisions within each of the various core parties to the conflict that have undermined efforts to achieve a conciliatory solution.

A salient element in the broadening of violence in Kashmir is the Islamicization of the Valley as the international networks of Islamic revivalism and resistance have commensurately grown in the region, and throughout the international system. Kashmir is for some Islamists a showcase for *jihad*, a place to demonstrate commitment to the creation of a new Caliphate, to sacrifice blood in a civilizational battle with the infidel. Materially, factors of linkages to broader Islamist networks include the linkage to Kashmir as the end point in a network of interaction running through Azad Kashmir and into Afghanistan and Central Asia. Second is the proliferation of new Islamist influences in the Valley, reflected in the building of new mosques and the spread of Wahabist teachings in an area where more moderate Sufi traditions and institutions have prevailed. Yet each of the principal Islamist insurgent groups in Kashmir has its own peculiar networks, and its own set of targets for violent pursuit of essentialist aims.[10]

Kashmir: the political players

- *National Conference.* As the holder of power – off and on – for nearly 55 years in Kashmir, the NC is associated as being the party of the Abdullahs and at times closely aligned in deals with the Indian government. In 2002, the party won a plurality of seats but lost executive power to the PDP/Congress coalition.
- *People's Democratic Party.* The PDP is a newly formed party that contested the state assembly elections in 2002; it has taken a more moderate approach, advocating for the demands of the people (such as curbing security force abuses).
- *Congress.* The Indian National Congress's representation in Kashmir reflects the long-standing goals of nation-building and integration of Jammu and Kashmir into the broader national life.

All of the principal political players have at times been targets of militants; individually, they are all vulnerable to attacks on their lives.

Kashmir: the independence movement

- *The All-Parties Hurriyat Conference/Alliance.* Riven by factionalism for much of its existence, the APHC is the broadest coalition of parties that seek independence for the Valley but understand that the LoC is likely to remain the international frontier. Intense factionalism has limited the ability of the APHC to substantiate its claim to representation of authentic Kashmir voices. Although the leadership of the APHC clearly includes a number of prominent Kashmiri elites, actual support for the platform of independence has never been tested, nor has the popularity of the organization in electoral competition.[11] Moreover, there are repeated reports of splits within the APHC over the very question of negotiations with Delhi.

- *Jammu and Kashmir Liberation Front.* Formerly the premier nationalist insurgency, the JKLF has significantly faded in importance and now works as a (splintered) faction within the APHC.

Kashmir: the Islamist militants

- *Hizbul Mujahideen.* Of all the Islamist movements, *Hizbul* finds its support from within the Valley, although it is principally based in Muzaffarabad. The organization has been minimalist in defining its goals beyond ousting India from Kashmir, staying vague on the question of accession with Pakistan or independence. Although accused of significant acts of violence, *Hizbul* is widely seen as a potential partner in the peace process as opposed to a spoiler.
- *Harkat-ul-Mujahideen. Harkat,* on the other hand, is generally viewed as a clearly rejectionist Islamist faction and as a potential spoiler. Its prior behavior – including abducting foreign tourists in the Valley – has put it on the US list of terrorist organizations.
- *Lashkar-e-Taiba and Jaish-e-Mohammad.* Now banned by the government and shut down on the Pakistani side after 9/11, these former militant factions were responsible for attacks on the Indian parliament in 2001 and on Musharraf's life, respectively. These groups have not gone away, however, and have either renamed and reformed or have joined a wide range of smaller factions that have claimed responsibility for attacks over time. Militant groups allegedly cooperate in the so-called "United Jihad Council."[12] Of all the militant organizations in the Valley, these factions (which continue to evolve and reconstitute rapidly over time) are the most significant spoilers in the current peace process.

The Islamist militants are primarily based in Azad Kashmir and conduct cross-border operations. While prior insurgency had a nationalist orientation (such as the JKLF campaign), insurgency in the Valley is primarily an Islamist struggle, not one of liberation.

Internal Kashmiri divisions are wide. Given their time apart, communities in Azad Kashmir and in the IJK have developed more separate identities. The Azad Kashmiris, caught between a rock and a hard place, have clearly developed their own perspective. On the one hand, they are wholly dependent on Islamabad; on the other hand, they are restrained from all-out struggle given the costs of escalation from within its territory to the Pakistani regime. Thus, cross-border violence is believed to be closely controlled by the government in Islamabad – and in particular the ISI – although much dispute exists over the extent to which government elites in Pakistan "turn the tap" of violence in Kashmir through the enabling or limiting of cross-border support for the Kashmiri insurgents. The Azadis' preferences for settlement are difficult to know for sure; most of them, beholden as they are economically to the government of Pakistan, probably support accession. However, in their hearts it may well be that many Azadis prefer independence for Kashmir even as they fear expressing the sentiment in the current environment.

Like any protracted armed conflict, Kashmir has developed a war economy that for many makes the continuation of violence a lucrative enterprise. India has poured significant amount of aid into parties allied with the state government in an effort to redress economic marginalization and to promote allegiance to the state. Cash reaches the Valley through support for militants from Pakistan, institutions in the broader Islamic world, and through Islamist-held criminal networks in the global drugs trade. According to an Indian customs official, "The militants get involved in narcotics for two main reasons.... One is to give to their fighters during suicide attacks, to give them courage and to take away the pain. The second reason is fundraising. Narcotics are very profitable."[13] Consequently, many protagonists in the Kashmir conflict have a vested financial interest in the prolongation of the conflict (Habibullah 2004).

International monitors have likely frequently cited the effect of the conflict on security in the Valley, and the vulnerability of society to abuses both by the security forces and police and by the militant targeting of civilians. The conflict has led to the mass exodus of minorities from the region, notably the Pandits, Buddhists, and Ladakhis who have over time been driven from the Valley by the violence. While they are not active participants in the conflict on the ground, these minorities' interests will require accommodation at the peace table.

The Kargil crisis: focusing the mind

The dual nuclear tests of India in 1998 (May 11 and 13) and those of Pakistan (May 28 and 30) marked a moment of new urgency in the Kashmir crisis as it became clear that continued antagonism over the territory could lead to an uncontrolled escalation in the region. The UN Security Council's Permanent Members responded quickly, urging in Resolution 1172 that the sides address the root causes of tension "including Kashmir." International pressure also emerged from the meeting of the G-8 in that year that renewed calls for a dialogue on Kashmir; this international activity, and the prospect of mutual destruction that the nuclear tests reinforced, drove the parties to negotiate: in February 1999, tensions were eased as limited access across the LoC was allowed and the parties agreed to the Lahore Declaration which again committed the parties to the principle of a negotiated solution to the Kashmir conflict.

Yet again, however, the cross-border nature of the Kashmir insurgency undermined these initial efforts at peace. As the snows of winter thawed in spring, militants based in Pakistan crossed over the LoC and were sighted by the Indians near Kargil; direct military engagements between Indian and Pakistani forces ensued, and the escalating conflict led to open war high in the Himalayas. The Kargil crisis, as the event became known, was perhaps the closest the two South Asian neighbors have come to an all-out nuclear exchange. Intervention by the United States, especially, and the active involvement of President Bill Clinton to negotiate de-escalation, led to the Pakistanis backing down in Kargil, with Pakistani president Nawaz Sharif taking efforts to curb cross-border militancy along the frontier and to withdraw his country's troops from Kargil.

In December 1999, other events reinforced the depth of conflict over Kashmir. In a dramatic incident, militants of *Harkat-ul-Ansar* hijacked an Indian airliner, forcing the jet's landing in Kandahar, Afghanistan (then under the Taliban); the ensuing crisis resulted in the release of three of their cadres from Indian jails, but did little to further negotiation. Indeed, within the Valley in 2000 the insurgency grew and attacks by the militants on state targets sharply escalated. In October 2001, a militant attack on the legislative assembly in Srinagar further deepened tensions and frustrated back-channel negotiations to de-escalate tensions within the Valley. This incident, which ended with a massive Indian military assault, led to further violence.

Militants of the *Lashkar-e-Taiba* faction from the Valley struck in Delhi later in the year, attacking parliament on December 13, an event that killed 22 and once again brought India and Pakistan to the precipice of war. Five militants stormed the parliamentary complex just after noon, with bombs strapped to their bodies in a maniacal suicide mission. India blamed Pakistan for the attack and withdrew all forms of bilateral cooperation, to which Pakistan responded in kind. India began preparations for striking militants across the LoC in Azad Kashmir. The further polarization of the conflict within the Valley was seen again in May 2002, when Abdul Ghani Lone, the prominent leader of the People's Conference (which had been engaged in back-channel dialogue with Delhi) was assassinated in Srinagar by suspected pro-Pakistan extremists.

Again in October 2002, the Indian government held elections under the heavy hand of the Indian army, resulting in defeat for Farooq Abdullah's National Conference at the hands of a pro-Delhi coalition of the Indian National Congress and PDP. Mufti Muhammad Sayeed became Chief Minister of Kashmir following the 2002 elections. This effort at internal settlement, like others, is only partial in its putative success. While the elections did yield an authoritative government in Srinagar, without the participation of the APHC the government lacked key legitimacy. Negotiation within Kashmir has much to do with the terms and possibilities of widening participation in the official parliamentary structures to allow erstwhile excluded parties – even former militants and terrorists – to participate in political life. The progress to settlement in Nepal, while a much different conflict, may give some imaginative ideas to the protagonists in Kashmir on how to resolve critical problems of demilitarization and inclusion.

India–Pakistan détente and the peace process in Kashmir, 2003–2006

The onset of Indo-Pak détente in 2003 and early 2004 has set the stage for the beginnings of convergence of the two sides over the Kashmir question and the willingness to consider new initiatives and alternatives within the Valley and across the LoC. Evolution in the bilateral relationship has also generated new opportunities for intra-Kashmiri dialogue and for direct negotiations between the various Kashmiri factions – in particular those parties represented by the APHC which stayed out of the 2002 state elections – and the government of India. Yet the process remains vulnerable to security dilemmas that characterize the bilateral relationship, political instability within each country (and particularly within Pakistan), irreconcilable positions on core issues in dispute, and acute vulnerability to spoiler violence emanating from the *jihadist* groups in Pakistan and their client colleagues in the Valley.

A hand of friendship

In landmark speech in Srinagar on April 18, 2003, Indian prime minister Vajpayee took the remarkable step of offering "a hand of friendship" to Pakistan and explicitly calling for extensive talks; the negotiations led to some progress in the relationship, with the conclusion of a cease-fire agreement on November 26 along the LoC and the Siachen Glacier. In the speech, Vajpayee also opened the door to direct negotiations with the Kashmiris, saying "Not only our doors – but also our hearts – are always open for you. You [can] come to us with your grievances; no guns but only brotherhood can resolve the problems."[14] The détente was realized in a set of clear concessions on both sides that were choreographed in talks: India restored diplomatic relations and sport contacts (especially cricket), and renewed air links; Pakistan banned three militant groups, proposed a cease-fire on the LoC, and made concessions on the demilitarization of the Siachen Glacier.

This agreement was bolstered by the full embrace of the two neighbors on a range of confidence-building measures to include the restoration of transportation links, new track-two diplomacy initiatives, and the furthering of regional cooperation efforts through the South Asian Association for Regional Cooperation (SAARC). By January 2004, these talks had led to the restoration of the peace process through which détente in principle was translated into practical measures to prevent another war. In a calculated but significant concession, Pakistan's Musharraf announced on December 18, 2003 in an interview with Reuters that Pakistan would revisit its long-standing claim to full implementation of UN resolutions on Kashmir. He said:

> We are for UN resolutions, however now we have left that aside.... The basis for everything, the basis for a reduction in militancy ... is moving forward on a process of dialogue. If that political dialogue doesn't come about, who wins and who loses? It is the moderates who lose and the extremists who win, and that is exactly what has been happening.[15]

The Musharraf concession on Kashmir also set the stage for a widening of negotiations on a wide range of issues between India and Pakistan, from monitoring of the maritime border to tariffs and trade to possible military cooperation in managing militancy in Kashmir. Especially, Musharraf's willingness to concede the core plank in Islamabad's negotiation strategy for more than 50 years, namely implementation of the UN plebiscite resolutions, set the stage for the January 2004 declaration to launch the peace process to include discussions on the final sovereignty status of the former Jammu and Kashmir.

Confidence-building measures

The peace process further gathered steam in early 2004, beginning with a joint statement from India and Pakistan – the Islamabad Declaration – which emanated from side talks at the SAARC meeting held in the Pakistani capital. The Declaration directly addressed the problem of cross-border support for the Valley's militants, and the need to develop economic ties in the region as a way of increasing interdependency, as well as confidence-building measures (CBMs) such as the establishment of hotlines between the two respective foreign ministers and affirming refrain from additional nuclear tests to augment those previously established between military commanders. From February to June 2004 – remarkably, during the Indian election campaign of May 2004 – negotiations proceeded on a wider range of CBMs, developing in detail a wide range of measures to reduce uncertainty and resolve some of the security dilemmas that had historically plagued bilateral relations.[16]

In September 2004, Musharraf and newly elected Indian prime minister Manmohan Singh met on the sidelines of the opening of the General

Assembly meetings in New York, furthering the process of détente and giving support to incipient moves to dialogue among Kashmiris on settlement of the dispute. These negotiations led to the celebrated opening of a bus service between Muzaffarabad and Srinagar on April 18, 2005, an important symbolic moment in the peace process. Not surprisingly, militants attacked a building holding passengers for the bus service in a direct signal of threat to civilians "participating" in the peace process. Further talks took place in April 2005 on CBMs, to include agreement on a new list of measures that would feature additional bus services across the LoC, commercial truck traffic, and humanitarian measures such as providing space and opportunity for families long divided by the conflict to be reunited at specific locales along the border.[17]

The Delhi–Kashmiri and intra-Kashmiri dialogues

The resolution of the Kashmiri question, however, involves much more than the de-escalation of tensions along the LoC and the prevention of war between Pakistan and India, however important these measures may be. The most opaque of negotiations in the dispute involves those that have occurred within India in the Delhi–Kashmiri talks and among the Kashmiris in track-two diplomacy meetings held as an unofficial complement to the more authoritative talks. Negotiations between India and the Kashmiris took place on at least two major occasions in 2004 and 2005. In January 2004, talks between India and Kashmiris involved, for the first time, decision-makers at the highest level of the Indian government.

On September 5, 2005, Manmohan Singh held meetings with the APHC in Delhi. Though no formal agreement was reached, India agreed to reduce force levels within the Valley if cross-border insurgency diminished and levels of violence were reduced. The continued militancy is clearly seen as an integral part of the bargaining strategy of the APHC: Samii writes that

> the persistence of the militancy is at least partially attributable to its strategic utility to Pakistani strategists and separatists in IJK ... pro-Pakistan militants have been Pakistan's most reliable political lever in IJK. Strategically, Pakistani support (whether tacit or explicit) helps to convince Indian strategists that Indian forces cannot impose a military solution on the Kashmir conflict.
>
> (Samii 2006: 236–237)

As important as these Delhi–APHC negotiations are, in unofficial negotiation considerable progress has been made in evaluating the potential process and terms of the peace process for Kashmir. Among the most important stumbling blocks to progress in talks have been divisions – sometimes violent – among the various Kashmiri factions. Idris reports that:

> Both cease-fire and dialogue initiatives have been impeded by divisions among Kashmiri militant and political groups. *Hizbul Mujahideen*'s cease-fire announcement in 2000 drew strong criticisms from other militant groups in IJK, who actually intensified their attacks. Indeed, ninety-three people, including a group of Hindu pilgrims and their mostly Muslim porters, were massacred across IJK within a twenty-four hour period during the cease-fire.
>
> (Idris 2006: 209)

Likewise, there have been efforts to create channels for dialogue between the Kashmiri independence groups and the government of Pakistan, and the leadership in AJK. In a major step forward, on June 2, 2005, a delegation of the APHC traveled across the LoC for talks in AJK and Islamabad. Participants in the delegation featured the top leadership of the alliance, to include Balal Ghani Lone (daughter of Abdul), Professor Abdul Ghani Butt, and Mirwaiz Umar Farooq. As tragedy struck the region shortly thereafter, these initial efforts were put to the test. The significance of this event in the India–Pakistan peace process cannot be overlooked. It is reflective of a deeper process of bargaining with the Kashmiri independence-movement leaders; according to analysis by the Delhi-based Institute for Peace and Conflict Studies,

> The Union government's engagement with the Hurriyat in particular has been uniform in the recent months. The Congress persisted with the services of N N Vohra, Wajahat Habibullah and A S Dullat to reach the Hurriyat leadership. It also roped in Saifudin Soz, a senior Congress leader believed to be an important link in the current round of negotiations between the moderates and Manmohan Singh. The moderates had two rounds of high-level discussions with L K Advani earlier. Having encouraged Track II level contacts between the moderate Hurriyat leadership and its interlocutors, the Congress government allowed them to visit PoK [Pakistan-Occupied Kashmir]. Undoubtedly, the moderates' visit to PoK, and later to Pakistan was a crucial breakthrough in the internal peace process.
>
> (Chandra 2005: 8)

The October 2005 earthquake affected AJK particularly, although the humanitarian tragedy did not have the same long-term conflict-mitigating effect as the 2004 tsunami had in Aceh or the short-term effect it had to promote peace in Sri Lanka (see Chapter 7). It did, however, lead to an increase in crossing points on the LoC from one to five (to allow delivery of relief supplies) and both India and Pakistan contributed to relief efforts on both sides of the cease-fire line. At the same time, the bombings in Delhi on October 25, 2005 caused Indian leaders to retrench from talks: during the feast of Diwali, three bombs exploded in a coordinated massacre that killed 59 and injured some 200. A Kashmiri militant group, believed an offshoot of the *Lashkar-e-Taiba*, claimed responsibility for the horrific blasts.

At the intra-Kashmiri level, in addition to the 2005 visit by APHC to Pakistan, the most important venue has been a series of three track-two initiatives run by Pugwash, a Nobel Peace Prize-winning organization dedicated to reducing the risks of nuclear war. In dialogues in December 2004, April 2005, and March 2006, Pugwash has convened individuals representing a wide range of views on the Kashmiri question, to include representatives close to all the major factions except for the most extreme of the Islamist militants. These processes have generated a number of understandings, including broad agreement that the present circumstances are intolerable, especially the problem of violence. In the report on the March 2006 meeting, for example, it was agreed that

> there is still a high level of violence [in the Valley] where confrontation between terrorists, armed militias, and mighty state security forces claims innocent lives daily. Beyond human rights violations, such a climate of destruction and insecurity impedes any meaningful socio-economic development in a context where societal conditions have only degenerated in recent years.[18]

As the Kashmir peace process inches forward, it approaches a perilous point in the negotiations. Beyond important but interim measures such as the bus travel, the Kashmiri talks will soon reach the point of needing to make progress on – and directly address – concessions small and large (especially over sovereignty). At this moment, too, it becomes clear that the maximalist goals that the protagonists have been fighting for – from independence to access to Islamic rule – will not be realized. This moment of truth will increase incentives of spoilers to employ violence to sabotage talks, as was also the case in Northern Ireland in the late 1998 Omagh bombing by the "Real IRA." As Sidhu observes:

> Although the round of comprehensive dialogue revived in January 2004 was described as 'irreversible' by the principal interlocutors, it remains to be seen whether dialogue will sustain. The challenge, however, remains not only in sustaining this dialogue but also in ensuring that it is insulated from the day-to-day setbacks (in the form of terrorist attacks, for instance) that have often derailed the process in the past.
>
> (Sidhu 2006: 3)

Imagining settlement in Kashmir

The possibilities for peace in Kashmir appear as close now as they have been in the more than 50 years of conflict over the disputed territory. The moment of ripeness, however, is fleeting as the volatility in Pakistani politics continues in the wake of Musharraf's duster in 2008; internal politics within Pakistan may well curtail the possibility of comprehensive peace on the national-identity issue of Kashmir. "Spoilers" – those who by virtue of their belief or interests opposed a negotiated settlement – abound in this context, and those willing to use violence to bring down a peace process clearly exist within Pakistan (such as within the intelligence services), within India (such as those inexorably opposed to compromise on the LoC as the international frontier), and among the indigenous *jihadist* groups within the Valley itself; as Sakia notes, "spoilers in Kashmir wear many faces."[19]

However, the Kargil crisis and the backing away of both states from nuclear war and historical enmity – symbolized by the March 2004 tour of Pakistan by the Indian cricket team, the first since 1989 – have reinforced the possibility that peace is not only desirable, it is possible within the parameters of current political sentiment in the two countries. Within Pakistan, it is clear that Musharraf saw the benefit of resolving the crisis that has damaged his country's legitimacy on the international stage for years, but particularly in the post-9/11 era in which his government has come under US and European scrutiny for allowing or abetting cross-border *jihad* flows from Afghanistan, the tribal regions of Pakistan, and Azad Kashmir to join the fight in the Valley against the Indian forces. Within the Valley, levels of violence diminished dramatically after the détente, as have reports of cross-border infiltrations.

During afternoon rush hour on July 11, 2006, seven bombs detonated nearly simultaneously in Mumbai, killing 209 and wounding some 700. The blasts hit seven first-class cabins in trains ferrying commuters away from the city center. The bombs were attributed to Kashmiri separatists, and again India pointed the finger at Pakistan claiming that the ISI had used militant group *Lashkar-e-Taiba* to perpetrate the crime.[20] Two days later, India suspended talks claiming that Pakistan had failed in its commitments to end cross-border terror. Musharraf, however, responded that the suspension of talks would reward extremists who sought to derail the peace process, calling the event "a despicable act of terrorism."[21] The meeting of Musharraf and Manmohan Singh on the sidelines of the Non-Aligned Summit in Cuba at the initiative of India in January 2007 revealed an important insight by the South Asian leaders: the peace process imperatives are stronger than those of retrenchment that emerge during times of violence-induced crisis. Likewise, there are increasingly moderate voices in Kashmir from within the militant community calling for support for the peace process and cautiously endorsing an end to armed struggle.[22]

Imagining a peace settlement for Kashmir involves the close linkage between a process of negotiation and the formula for settlement.[23] That is, prior to agreement on the sequences of the peace process on the two principal axes of negotiation – the India–Pakistan axis and the Delhi – Srinagar (and intra-Kashmiri) talks – prior agreement on an overall formula for settlement is required. Like similar situations (such as Kosovo or Cyprus), there are a wide variety of possible autonomy and cross-border institution-building proposals that could be seen as a way to acknowledge simultaneously the reality of a divided Jammu and Kashmir that reifies the LoC as the international boundary and the need for a proliferation of autonomy institutions that can achieve the desperately desired self-governance. There is no shortage of outcome options to the conflict, which have been enumerated carefully in a variety of ways, from the map-based scenarios of BBC News[24] to the detailed plans laid out by various participants in the Pugwash Dialogues. Outcome scenarios that are most plausible seem to suggest a "Northern Ireland" solution, which witnessed the proliferation of bargaining institutions across borders and involved a "North-South, East-West" approach which has proven a way to potentially reconcile competing and mutually exclusive claims to sovereign control.

The principal problem is a classic one of sequencing: one side, Delhi, requires that violence end before talks can progress, while the Kashmir independence leaders claim they are unable to control passionate violence until the terms of a just settlement are in hand. Among the key elements of a peace process in Kashmir are measures that have been seen in other conflict settings to have contributed to the management of ongoing violence; measures to create opportunities for process and outcome options to further evolve; and measures to address the grave and immediate human security consequences of the conflict. Among these, as applied to Kashmir, are:

- Measures to improve human rights, such as repeal or revision of the Disturbed Areas Act (1990) and the Armed Forces Special Act.
- Measures to promote local security in the Valley: phasing military deployments out with community policing initiatives can contribute to demilitarization of society.
- Measures to broaden the peace process: community-level peace structures are essential; among the options are proliferating peace institutions in regional and local settings, institutionalizing the involvement of civil society, and involving international development and conflict-management specialists to work with Kashmiris to design comprehensive strategies for securing local communities.
- Measures to address militancy and extremist violence through vigorous but professional law enforcement, and continuing to develop cross-border collaboration between Indian and Pakistani intelligence and military officials.
- Measures to protect cultural and religious rights and sites through application of global norms and standards on tolerance of identity and belief and in resuscitation of the values of *Kashmiriat*.
- Measures to provide conflict-sensitive development aid, consistent with best practices for using development aid to address the root causes of

conflict; particularly, aid for developing and furthering democratic participation and inclusive decision-making in public policy decisions is critical.

- Measures to provide for international "credible commitment": despite the oft heard concern that "External mediation is not an option because the power asymmetry between India and Pakistan allows India to veto external intervention,"[25] it may be possible to explore with India and Pakistan the augmentation of UNMOGIP or the involvement of UN technical and observer personnel to provide credible commitment to agreements made in peace negotiations (as in neighboring Nepal).

A principal strategy in the peace process in Kashmir is reinforcing the fundamental impetus of interdependency in the subcontinent: the conflict cannot be solved unilaterally, through force, nor does violence contribute to the interests of any except the most extreme militants. In the immediate future the challenge remains to further demilitarize the Valley while providing for security and the careful addressing of spoiler violence from all sides; in the long run, and as a presumptive prerequisite to the end of violence, however, the key to peace in Kashmir is a comprehensive political settlement that addresses the thorny international (e.g. borders, "joint management" by India and Pakistan, cross-border) and internal (e.g. power sharing, elections, human security, and development) issues. Reinforcing the alternative of *failure* to progress in talks – thereby allowing extremist spoiler violence to "succeed" – is a strong reinforcing trend for the current peace process.

Likewise, calculating the present economic costs of conflict in Kashmir reinforces the sense of ripeness that presently prevails. Even in the absence of comprehensive settlement, the benefits of the peace process were being felt in Kashmir into 2008 as increased cross-border traffic and a diminution of violence prevailed. This sense of progress was felt even though there were ongoing clashes between Indian security forces and militants and terrorist bombings in India attributed to the Kashmiri factions or Pakistani sympathizers.[26]

The eruption of extensive protest and violence in August 2008 was driven by a land row concerning the Amarnath shrine, sacred to Hindus; the putatively religious dispute also had strong economic dimensions for the Valley's Muslim community given the shrine's strategic location along the main motorway from the Valley to the rest of India.

Finally, broadening multitrack diplomacy as the security situation improves will be essential over time, building on the progress in these efforts that has already been seen (Schaffer and Schaffer 2005: 313–314). As it is one of the world's most long-running, protracted conflicts, peace will not come easily to Kashmir; progress toward peace between Delhi and the moderate Kashmiri secessionists in the Valley will mean credibly committing to a security pact that links progress on self-government with increasing security on the ground (much like the long, phased process of political negotiation and demilitarization in Northern Ireland). Nonetheless, the peace process that began in 2003 offers an opportunity to gradually escape the trap of violence and despair that has gripped Kashmir for 15 years and bedeviled it for more than half a century.

9 Confronting bargaining with bullets

Powerful peacemaking

When do peace negotiations proceed despite of, and indeed because of, political violence, and under what conditions does international mediation contribute to progress? Progress in the peace processes of the 1990s and 2000s occurs as a consequence of choices by the protagonists – especially key political elites – in conflict when they are motivated by the enlightened awareness of the dire need to avoid a worse outcome: the further escalation of violence. Avoidance of further escalation by elites is central but only one of the factors that explains progress toward peace: these elites must also be able to envision a settlement that, if not mutually beneficial, contains sufficient personal and human security and rights guarantees, and they must be able to see a pathway – a peace process – to achieve a settlement and to prevent subsequent defection (cheating) in the period of implementation.

Thus, with these key elements, external peacemakers who can serve as proactive "custodians" of the peace process – often, and ideally, a Special Representative of the Secretary-General of the United Nations – play pivotal roles.[1] In the absence of such a role for the UN, successful peacemaking seems elusive: in the cases of Sri Lanka and Kashmir and in other instances where powerful states inhibit the UN's ability to play an active or direct peacemaking role (as in Chechnya or Colombia), progress is impeded. Where the UN's role is more active – as in South Africa with the deployment of an observer mission, and in Liberia and Burundi where the UN has played both peacemaking and peacekeeping roles – progress toward peace appears more likely.

Powerful peacemakers operating under the moral authority of the UN bring two fundamental ingredients to successful peace processes. The first is that they design and reinforce with incentives and sanctions a formula for settlement – the parameters of terms for agreement – and a definitive, legitimate process for talks. While the latter role is well understood in the literature and in practice, the roles powerful peacemakers play in articulating the terms of agreement are less appreciated: they must often be proactive and assertive in designing and leveraging the parties into a negotiating process and to persisting in it. Often, the basis of such formulas are to craft the parameters of agreement consistent with international norms (such as minority rights to balance majoritarian prerogatives through power-sharing pacts, as in South Africa in 1994–1996 or Burundi), or promoting democratic, integrative solutions for democratization (as in South Africa post-1996 and Liberia), or in articulating acceptable solutions to autonomy or territorial disputes (as in Kashmir and Sri Lanka).[2]

Whether through economic sanctions[3] to de-legitimize apartheid and demand non-racial democracy (as in South Africa), using indictment before the International Criminal Court to remove incorrigible spoilers (as in Liberia), or delivery of aid (as in Sri Lanka after the tsunami of December 2004) to bolster peace efforts, powerful peacemaking means the need to exercise strategic strength in leveraging the parties into peace precisely because civil wars are so globally injurious in an age of international interdependence. Establishing and reinforcing myriad incentives for parties to exchange bargaining with bullets for bargaining with words reinforces the internal, strategic motivations that lead the parties to begin the process of pursuing peace as an alternative to unwinnable war.

Second, international mediators must provide ways for parties to weather the turbulent, violent efforts to affect or disrupt a peace process. They do so by reinforcing the pressures to negotiate and penalizing acts of violence, by realizing that security will more likely follow peace agreements rather than precede them, and – most importantly – by providing assurances of credible commitment. While many situations do require actual or promised deployment of a Chapter VII authorized, tough UN force – as Liberia and Burundi have – it may be also possible in some instances (such as South Africa, in Nepal, and potentially in Kashmir) to provide credible commitment as reassurance through less militarized options such as a substantial international civilian observer mission. The most important elements for peacemaking are smart strategy, persistent determination, coherent mediator coalitions, and the willingness to employ a wide range of both facilitative *and* coercive measures to leverage the parties into peace and to guarantee negotiated settlements once they are reached.

Peace processes: expecting and confronting bargaining with bullets

Many peace processes in the post-Cold War era failed to progress as violent confrontations continued. Efforts to broker talks in protracted conflicts such as Chechnya, Colombia, Darfur (Sudan), or Sri Lanka have been a litany of frustration, failure, and disaster. Peace talks *are* vulnerable to return violence, especially those that yield partial agreements that do not resolve the truly underlying root causes of conflict, hoping to defer agreement on the principal dispute only after violence has ceased. The Oslo agreement of 1993, and later the Road Map to Peace, illustrate vividly how in the Israeli–Palestinian context violence escalated in part because there was intent – by spoilers on both sides of the great divisions there – to use murder, suicide bombing, and targeted assassinations as a way to affect the balance of power and ultimately the outcome of talks.

Violence while talks are ongoing normally undermines trust, impedes the willingness to talk further, constrains elites who might otherwise move to settlement, and perpetuates the entrapment of a society in insecurity, fear, and a phobia for the kinds of commitments to disarmament required in a peace settlement. From township faction-fighting in South Africa, the siege of Monrovia by the rebel forces of the LURD, to targeted assassination of moderates in Burundi, the bargaining with bullets that has been an insidious feature of talks in Sri Lanka, to fanatical *jihadist* violence in Kashmir, the most common effect of political violence is indeed to have a devastating and even debilitating effect on peace processes.

Yet more peace processes progress to settlement than fail, as the trend analysis in Chapter 1 reveals. If political violence always undermined, then there would be no reason to think they could ever progress to a settlement that yields sustainable peace; for this reason, some have argued to "give war a chance" (see Chapter 1). However, many deep-rooted wars of the 1990s (e.g. Cambodia, El Salvador, Mozambique, South Africa) and of the 2000s (e.g. Indonesia (Aceh), Burundi, Nepal and Liberia)[4] were in fact brought to an end by peace processes. Despite the vulnerabilities to new violence that peace processes create, it is important to keep in mind a simple fact highlighted in this book: progressing through to settlement in the face of persistent and even escalating violence, coupled with a subsequent process of concerted implementation, *has* yielded peace in societies that in years before were caught in the entanglement of civil war.

Re-evaluating escalation

The findings in this book reinforce the importance of thinking about the causes of civil war in "root cause" or structural terms; ethnic tension, elite predation, captured states, horizontal inequalities, and economic rent-seeking all resonate through these case studies. Underlying the slide into bloodletting are deep historical, social, political, and economic dimensions that produce grievances and give rise to the ability of desperately offended social forces to pursue violent challenges to the state (Fearon and Laitin 2003). But root cause analysis is insufficient: civil wars emerge not just from the social structural context and opportunities to contest, but also from the event-driven escalatory dynamics that initiates or propels violence and that often leads to entangling social traps.

Among the most pervasive structural causes are the mal-distribution of economic opportunity and political representation among social groups. In South Africa, patterns of hierarchal social relations under apartheid and a history of exclusion and discrimination were the ultimate root cause of violence as a long-oppressed black majority aggressively fought subordination and exploitation. In Liberia, patterned inequality dating back centuries set the stage for a volatile change of power and social relations, combined with elite predation of the very worst kind. Burundi, too, reinforces the finding that patterned inequality and historical narratives of subjugation are strong drivers of civil war. In Sri Lanka, changing social relationships of economic and political opportunity were accompanied by chauvinistic nationalism and religious fervor that has led to protracted conflict. Finally, Kashmir also represents a situation in which group grievance among the Muslim majority in the Valley, but minority in the country as a whole, has set the stage for a protracted struggle over territory and identity.

The inability to effect social change through purely political means – through dialogue, representation, and electoral power – justifies for many the turn to violence as a strategy for creating change; in these cases, violent challenge to the state is met with counter-vailing violence by the state, thus creating a cycle of revolt, rebellion, and repression. Such challenges, as these case studies show, often occur in the context of failed or disputed electoral processes. Mismanaged, fraudulent, stolen, or fair-but-ill-conceived elections (such as those that yield highly majoritarian outcomes) are *the* precipitant of violence in the cases analyzed. In South Africa, successive simple majority-rule elections among whites produced an increasingly ardent Afrikaner nationalist government that pursued apartheid, and a failed reform process in the early 1980s that led to racially restricted elections was the final straw that precipitated the unrest of the late 1980s and which set the scene for transitional violence in the 1990s. In Liberia, the now-infamous election of 1997 which confirmed Charles Taylor as warlord-president was the linchpin event in the escalation of the second civil war. In Burundi, the election of Ndadaye in 1993 and his subsequent assassination was the spark for a civil war that killed more than 100,000 in just a few months. In Sri Lanka, successive elections featuring chauvinist outbidding have constrained efforts to find moderates who can strike a bargain to end the war and to find a suitable autonomy arrangement as the basis for peace. In Kashmir, the faulty elections of 1987 gave rise to the Kashmiri *intifada*.

Once the slide into violence begins, its outcome is – more often than not – a military stalemate in which the state cannot succeed in quashing rebel challenges and the rebels are unable to definitively defeat the state. Stalemates are not stagnant and often the parties themselves realize that through violence alone they cannot prevail. In each of the conflict situations evaluated here, the stalemate was conditioned by an ebb and flow to violence that provided hope for victory-through-escalation to different sides at different times. Parties in such protracted conflicts may win battles, or achieve spectacular results in waging the fight, but rarely can they win the war.

Whether to continue fighting as a sole strategy, or to explore negotiation, is clearly a strategic decision: the presence or reinforcement of an ululating, mutually hurting stalemate can serve both to perpetuate a conflict and to open avenues for accommodation. As described in Chapter 3, the condition is defined by the inability of any given opponent to prevail and the presence of the perception of a rough symmetry of power, and by the condition of higher costs and benefits of armed conflict weighed against the costs and benefits of a negotiated settlement. This analysis of the risks and advantages of opening negotiation is consistently seen in the decisions of key elites to explore the escape of stalemate through a sustained process of negotiation. In each of the cases analyzed in this book, stalemate and indeed some perception of ripeness was indeed a precondition for elite decisions to enter into a sustained period of talks. Thus, among the most powerful motives for talks is the *perception* of a relative balance of power among disputants.[5] Conversely, profound asymmetries in balance of power relationships impede progress, leading parties to think that they can prevail through guns, bombs, or state repression.

Talking peace: endogenous factors

The notion of ripeness – that at times, the time is "ripe" for making progress in negotiation – is affirmed in this analysis; Zartman's theories (see Chapter 3) are borne out in these case studies, as are the findings of Licklider on the overall conditions required for negotiated settlement in civil wars.[6] Beyond Zartman, as well, there is good evidence from these case studies and in other research that the concept of ripeness need not be so intuitive: the concept is indeed amenable to being operationalized by empirical analysis.[7] However, ripeness involves more than just the structural condition of mutually injurious violence: there needs to be a direct and mind-focusing impetus to seek peace. One recurrent motivation for the exploration of talks is a violent, crisis-inducing event that reinforces the costs of violence, that creates mutual *expectations* for worsening and potentially more injurious violence, and that offers opportunity for escape. Ripe moments occur when levels of political violence remain stagnant for a prolonged period of time, yet the opportunities for dramatic escalation appear imminent. An impending crisis or precipitating event, in which violence is expected to surge, is on the immediate horizon. *Avoidance of a worse outcome* motivates the parties to take the peace process forward.

Ripeness is thus often linked to upsurges in violence that just occurred, and events on the immediate horizon that are expected to precipitate new violence. A ripe conflict requires a sense of urgency for progress toward settlement and its implementation. The incentives for violence in internal conflicts are directly related to the parties' perceptions of settlement opportunities. In South Africa, de Klerk's decision to seek a negotiated solution was motivated by the likelihood of continued escalation of violence on the ground and heightened sanctions from abroad. In Liberia, Taylor was compelled to negotiate by the bloody siege of Monrovia in

2003 which was a direct precipitant of the Accra talks that eventually led to settlement of the war. In Burundi, the international community's strong-arm approach to peacemaking was motivated by the need to avoid, again, genocide in the Great Lakes. In Kashmir, a line can be drawn from the Kargil crisis of 1999 to the cross-border India–Pakistan détente that has created some opportunity for negotiation between Kashmiris and Delhi to go forward.

The effects of political violence are usually dilatory to the negotiation process, but not always. Political violence does undermine the basis of negotiations by affecting public opinion about the viability of talks and the true intentions of opposing communities, by diminishing elite confidence and trust about the intent of their adversaries, or by demonstrating that elites at the table may not be able to deliver their constituencies. On the other hand, lack of progress in talks may lead certain parties to foment violence. This makes the violence–negotiation nexus theoretically and methodologically challenging to capture, which reinforces the need for humility in presenting the principal findings of this book.

When does violence lead away from, or toward, peace?

Sharp upsurges in overall levels of political violence, or critical events such as a high-profile terrorist bombing, can be critical turning points in negotiation processes *toward or away from peace.* That is, events such as these force those at the negotiation table to make critical choices – essentially whether to recoil and return to the fight, or hunker down, continue talking, and weather the political storm. Dramatic political violence can be *crisis-inducing*, in that the parties are required to make critical choices on whether and how the peace process should progress.

Following a crisis-inducing event, will the peace process be derailed? Sustainability or momentum in talks is a function of both the structural capacity of the parties in conflict to negotiate peace – especially their internal coherence – and the issues of sequencing, specificity of the formula for settlement, nature of spoilers, culpability in violence, and the timing of violence in the progression of the peace process; all these issues have strong effects on whether progress in negotiation occurs.

- *Internal party coherence.* Internal party coherence produces greater progress toward negotiated settlements, although in at least some instances where all sides to a conflict are fragmented or divided, parties produce progress when a moderate coalition is able to form that cross-cuts the long-standing lines of conflict (as in South Africa). However, the South Africa case may well be an exception; in the Israel–Palestine talks, or in Iraq's fractious post-2003 invasion environment, highly fragmented groups-in-conflict seem to be a consistent barrier to progress in peace talks.

- *Sequencing.* The sequencing of events significantly affects the incentives and disincentives for violence. When parties engage in negotiation prior to an armistice, their incentives for violence remain high – they may overtly engage in violence to affect the agenda, pace, and potential outcomes of talks. Successful sequencing requires agreement not only on the parameters of security and cease-fire, but on a formula for settlement that defines the strategic idea of peace; in South Africa, this is multiparty democracy, in Liberia, a departure from the *rentier* state, in Burundi, a disproportionate power-sharing pact, in Sri Lanka, autonomy and human rights, and in Kashmir delineation of the frontier and a Srinagar-Delhi pact.
- *The specificity of the formula.* The specificity of the formula that culminates the prenegotiation phase has a bearing on the subsequent incentive structure for violence. When agreements state the clear parameters of a conflict's outcome, incentives for violence are reduced because parties to the negotiation and those opposed to the negotiation cannot expect to significantly alter the outcome through violence. When the outcome parameters are broad and vague, incentives for violence are greater because parties expect to be able to affect the scope and nature of the outcome in the course of formal negotiation. Disputants engaged in negotiation, and those rejecting negotiation, may deliberately foment violence as a response to the uncertainty that the onset of structured talks unleashes. The more uncertain the situation, that is the less the specific outcomes of talks are identified and articulated, the greater the level of violence and the likelihood that violence will impede progress.
- *Spoilers: Forever rejectionists?* The onset of negotiations gives rise to rejectionist parties with a clear incentive for fomenting violence to derail talks. Not all spoiling is about bringing down the talks altogether, however. In multilateral negotiations, parties may have incentives to foment violence to ensure that the other parties do not reach agreements that are exclusive of the party. This pattern was seen poignantly in South Africa and Burundi, and may well be at play in Kashmir. Thus, as Höglund demonstrates, a critical strategy in the containment of violence is, when morally and practically possible, the further inclusion of perpetrators of violence into talks; she writes: "It has to be recognized that there will always be a core of hard-liners and extremists that are not willing to abandon the violence option nor are capable of sitting down with the enemy at the negotiating table. However, as more parties are drawn into the peace negotiation process and a peace settlement takes root on the ground, these groups will have less of a say" (Höglund 2004: 210).
- *Culpability in violence.* When a party to a negotiation process is perceived as culpable with regard to a specific violent incident, it has the effect of impeding progress in negotiation; certainly the attacks by the LTTE have signaled more on the battlefield their intent to fight than

the presence of their negotiators in talks. When parties not participating in the negotiations (i.e. outbidder or rejectionist parties or individuals) are considered culpable, or when parties to a negotiation are perceived (by international actors, for example) as *equally* culpable, incidents of political violence can reinforce pressures on negotiating parties to progress toward a settlement.

- *The timing of violence.* Violence at an early stage of talks (i.e. during prenegotiation or preliminary formal negotiation) disrupts and delays progress toward a settlement more than violence at later stages of talks. As Darby has found, "The further the process develops, the stronger its shock-absorbent facility is and the more capable it is to withstand the inevitable atrocities designed to undermine it" (Darby 2001: 117). Early on, moderate coalitions are fragile and violence undercuts their ability to moderate. Violence by rejectionists at a late stage of the process can, however, reinforce moderates' commitment to a negotiated settlement and accelerates progress, as the situations in South Africa and Burundi attest. Violence by rejectionists or negotiating parties alike may peak as the agreement on a settlement nears, as once a settlement is in place it becomes more difficult to affect its terms. Such violence may be a last-ditch effort to affect the terms of the pact or may be a desperate attempt to keep it from being consummated.

This last finding reinforces an insight of Stedman in evaluating the problem of violence's deleterious effects on peace processes. Dealing with total (i.e. not instrumental) spoilers will invariably involve the use of force, including by the international community. He writes:

> The presence of spoilers, spoils and hostile neighbors pose the gravest threat to fledgling peace processes. These threats tend to be more manageable by local parties when there is a high degree of economic interdependence, a local tradition of formal democratic politics and a lively civil society. When such factors are absent, the role of international actors in combating spoilers becomes paramount.
>
> (Stedman 2003: 104)

Getting to settlement does not ensure peace. While it is beyond the scope of this book, there are good reasons why so many pacts (roughly 23 percent according to a revised estimate as analyzed by Suhrke 2007) succumb to breakdown in the post-settlement period.[8] In no instance of a peace process can one say that peace is for evermore "consolidated"; in each of the settings of negotiated settlement, deep-rooted divisions and inequity, and new challenges such as coping with environmental and population issues and achieving sustainable development in an era of increasingly scarce resources, mean that violence could well erupt anew along prior lines of conflict.

Operationalizing "powerful peacemaking"

While the internal dynamics of the parties appears decisive, the idea that societies can endogenously develop out of protracted conflict is fanciful when compared with the evidence. Mediator interventions serve myriad functions: they increase communication and reduce uncertainty, build confidence and trust (in other words, they facilitate reciprocity), wield sanctions and incentives, and offer assurances or commitments in efforts to move the parties toward settlement (Rothchild 1997; Griffiths and Barnes 2008). Even if third-party preventive efforts are effective only at the margins, relative or marginal contributions can be the essential element in beginning talks or keeping them going through a difficult period of turbulent violence. Moreover, mediators need to be engaged throughout the process and for the long term; as Hampson finds,

> The negotiation and implementation phases of the peace process are overlapping, intertwined, and mutually dependent.... It is therefore more accurate to view ripeness as a cultivated condition that has to be sustained, even after a settlement is reached, to prevent the peace process from sliding back into violence.
>
> (Hampson 1996: 229)

Leveraging for peace

How does international peacemaking contribute to maintaining progress in negotiation? If the on-the-ground military conditions and perceptual requirements are in place for a turn to negotiation, the international community can indeed intervene strategically, and with innovation, can create and reinforce the incentives for peace processes. Mediators need smart strategy, and they need *power*: resources and the willingness to use them. In conducting international peacemaking, lead actors in the international coalition will be more effective if they articulate an overall *strategic idea* that drives the peace process and if they employ resources in a dogged pursuit of this strategy. This strategic concept links the immediate negotiation for a cessation of the war with a longer-term outcome of political reform (as embodied in a settlement pact), implementation, and reconciliation. The strategic idea should include an envisaged political process that defines the clear parameters of settlement and that outlines a set of sequential steps, to unfold over various phases, to create and encourage progress in negotiations to end the war and reconstruct state and society.[9]

The strategic idea of the "peace process" as a paramount political focal point can only emerge from sufficient consensus and coalescence among a coalition of international mediators, often known as a Contact Group. An essential part of leveraging peace is a clear political plan to engage the incumbent regime and the opposition parties in a well-defined process of power sharing, transition, and constitution-making. A clearly articulated political plan should inform the operational plan for managing the containment and eventual demobilization of the armed forces of both the regular and irregular government military and police forces and the insurgent militias. That is, it should define process and outcome linkages. International mediators should work diligently with the parties to arrive at, as a matter of first priority, the framework for settlement and then to seal the deal through incorporation of the principles in a UN Security Council resolution. For example, such a framework document was the key to success in Namibia, which through UN Security Council Resolution 435 of 1978 established the basis for its negotiated war-to-democracy transition to independence.[10]

As we know, once a protracted conflict takes hold, there are incentives for the government or insurgents to exchange the relative predictability of the military confrontation on the battlefield for an uncertain peace process but these incentives may be overcome by the parties' deepest fears: they face a security dilemma and thus require third-party guarantees (Walter and Snyder 1999). Peacemaking, then, is about resolving this dilemma in both the process and outcome dimensions. As Walter argues, "The more committed a third party appears to be in fulfilling its promise to verify or enforce, the more likely combatants are to sign and implement peace treaties" (Walter 2002: 166). Such commitment can be limited, however, not by the lack of enthusiasm or commitment by the mediators themselves, but from the multilevel game (see Chapter 2) that can generate powerful disruptions from below. As Crocker *et al.* argue, "the third party faces very strong internal domestic pressure – from groups that are allied, or see themselves as allied, to the parties in the conflict – which constricts its own negotiating options" (Crocker *et al.* 2005: 379). How can the international mediation be improved to provide such credible commitment?

A defined process backed by coordinated signals and action is the basis of an effective peacemaking strategy. International peacemakers should clearly articulate a defined plan for a peace process together with specific benchmarks for progress as it facilitates negotiations on a cease-fire. Prior consensus and coordination of policy and message by the international mediator coalition is a key: signals need to reflect that the coalition will behave in a consistent and predictable way. Acts of cooperation with the Group's calls for a cessation of hostilities should be met with tangible rewards for the parties that cooperate; those that do not comply should be targeted for gradually more serious and damaging coercive moves such as sanctions. This consistent, predictable, and unified action by the international community should continue through the clearly established process guidelines as the future unfolds. The extent to which Burundi has inchingly moved from the precipice of genocide toward peace is a function of the relative unity of action by the international community.

A *cooperate–reward, defect–punishment approach* conveys to the parties that the external parties are unanimous, determined, and possess the political will to insist on peace. It should also make clear that failure to cooperate will precipitate coercive intervention and peace enforcement, as in Sierra Leone or Afghanistan. The basis of such an approach is essentially coercive diplomacy with the possibility of overwhelming military intervention if the parties do not comply. Such an approach is not useful in every situation, and indeed should be calibrated to the severity of the situation; clearly in dire emergencies such as Darfur in Sudan, or other cases of genocidal acts, it is not only wise for the international community to pursue tough action, it is its moral and legal obligation.

Coercive diplomacy requires a credible threat of a peace enforcement operation. A determined international coalition that is prepared to intervene forcefully may lead to a situation where the international community can achieve peace *without* a costly peace enforcement operation. If the parties in conflict believe that the political will exists in the international community for military intervention to enforce peace, they may take the steps to end fighting and cooperate in a political process without the actual deployment of such a force. Less costly alternatives, such as a monitoring mission, are more likely to be successful if the armed factions believe that failure to comply will in fact precipitate a more extensive military deployment. For coercive diplomacy to work, the threat of force must be credible. For the threat of force to be credible, the international community must actually take the steps necessary for the deployment of a peace enforcement mission.

Tough measures first, soften if cooperation is forthcoming. The mix of sanctions and incentives targeted at the regime and opposition forces should initially involve more stick than carrot. A strategy that begins with a highly coercive approach and then moves toward conciliation over time is often most effective in securing the cooperation of an opponent.[11] The reasoning behind this recommendation is the establishment of a clear norm of reciprocity; consistently, cooperation will be rewarded with cooperation (including an easing of coercion) and defiance or resistance (defection) will be met with increased coercion. In sum, leverage should be employed to cajole the antagonists into a pattern of predictable tit-for-tat, demonstrating clearly and unambiguously over time the value of cooperation with the mediator's objectives.[12] This approach of tit-for-tat reinforces an essential finding that international intervention in civil wars is rarely, if ever, impartial (Betts 2001).

A multi-tiered approach. A comprehensive mediation strategy should blend sanctions and incentives targeted at the armed factions and political elite with a parallel approach to build conflict-management and recovery capacities among national grass-roots civic organizations. Additionally, a multi-tiered approach should feature carefully designed initiatives to address the usually forgotten players in peace processes that have the capacity to spoil. The strategy includes an *intensive focus on the armed mid-level elite* and insurgent forces that live by the gun, organize for violence as a way of life, and who harbor realistic fears about the implications of peace for their personal interests and survival. Specific initiatives should give mid-level militia leaders a clear choice: join a reconstituted military or police force or face criminal punishment and possible indictment in war crimes. For insurgent forces, the details of an amnesty program (perhaps in exchange for truth telling) should be clearly defined: in each of the case studies here, a focus on top elite incentives only is seen as an insufficient approach to peacemaking.

The problems of consensus-building and coordination among international players are well documented: national states have different national interests which infuse their peacemaking approaches and preferences; coordination of communication and of basics like on-the-ground projects is inefficient and cumbersome; and the plethora of organizations that become involved – indeed, the entire "network" of global and local actors – mixes apples and oranges from large bureaucracies such as the UN to the very smallest of NGOs.[13] NGOs have played critical roles in promoting conflict management in ways that international organizations and states cannot: in Burundi, for example, NGOs were at the forefront of sharing lessons for protagonists between peace processes. As Hara observes:

> A key element in the NGO contribution has been to introduce Burundians, by way of trips and training seminars, to political figures experienced in conflict resolution in South Africa and other countries in transition. Using similar techniques, some NGO programs have focused on the long term and have sought to change antagonism into cooperation by having Hutus and Tutsis work together on common projects and by building 'common ground'.... Through their partnership with civil society and communities, NGOs bring a unique element to international response, one that most state-led diplomatic initiatives ignore.
>
> (Hara 1999: 144–145)

Finally, mediators need staying power, even though it is widely recognized that such commitments are both politically and financially costly. As Crocker *et al.* observe:

> In almost every mediation, there are moments when it looks as if the wheels have flown off. A terrorist attack or a sudden escalation of violence destroys months of painstaking negotiations.... Confronted by calamity, the mediator faces some basic choices: identify some way to press on against the odds, back away from the engagement and hunker down, or pull out.
>
> (Crocker *et al.* 2004: 120)

Each of the choices posed in this quote relate to the strategies for mediators outlined above. To press on implies the capacity and willingness to press on through the crises induced by violence events; backing away and hunkering down implies negotiating, patiently and often in secret, with perpetrators of violence; and pulling out is about employing an exit option in which there is recognition that the mediation simply cannot be successful (as Norway apparently determined in Sri Lanka) or that the acceptability of an individual or organization as mediator has expired (as was the case with the Kissinger–Carrington mediation attempt in South Africa).

Sequencing for peace

For both humanitarian reasons, and for reasons of conflict de-escalation strategy, the international community pressures both governments and rebel factions to declare a cease-fire as an initial immediate step. Although everyone appreciates the humanitarian reasons for a cease-fire, the peace process strategy for a cease-fire has logic of its own. It begins the process of de-escalation and allows international mediators to sort out who is a redeemable ally of peace and who is likely to be a spoiler of a pact. For testing the intent of the parties and the durability of any initial containment and troop demobilization process, to allow for an extended period of political negotiations, to repatriate refugees, and to further stave off cross-border spillovers, the securing of a cease-fire should be seen as a crucial but highly limited interval for peace.

As the case of Sri Lanka shows, cease-fires without agreed-upon formulas for settlement can make matters worse if war recurs; the parties lose trust in the adversary rather than building trust. Cease-fires that leave the "final status" of the dispute open for subsequent negotiation, and that collapse in ruin when the parties fail to progress, may well be worse than no cease-fire in the first place. The failures of Oslo, the lack of progress over Nagorno-Karabagh, or the shaky cease-fire in Sri Lanka all point to the need to use leverage in peace negotiations to deal not just with cease-fires or transitional issues such as DDR, but to reach agreement in principle over the formula for resolving core issues in dispute. Whether in Aceh, Darfur, or Kosovo, recent peace negotiations have sought to define clearly future, final status or at least how the final status will be ultimately determined so as to limit the uncertainty that can lead to future violence.

The debate on sequencing often follows the simple but informative approaches of "security first, settlement will follow," and "settlement first, security will follow." Of the case studies in this research, as well as in other research (Höglund 2004; Newman and Richmond 2006; Darby 2006a), it is increasingly clear that to the extent to which there is any empirical support for one strategy over the other, it is the latter. When parties to conflict can agree on a formula for settlement, efforts to achieve security first should be prioritized through demobilization, collective responses to spoiler violence, and community-level conciliation.

Strategies for peacemaking

International mediators have significant opportunities to engage at various levels in a conflict setting to define and outline the parameters of a basic settlement and leverage the parties into an agreement on its basic parameters. These opportunities can be considered in terms of first-priority measures aimed at political elites, measures to address mid-level elites and their militias, and measures to build popular support for peacemaking.

In forging a more effective approach to peacemaking, the priority should be in analyzing the scope and strength of moderate, centrist elites committed to negotiations over violence *within* each of the contending parties, in addition to the more common focus on relations *between* the parties to the talks. That is, can a sustainable centrist coalition formed by moderates be struck and maintained? How vulnerable are moderate elites favoring talks when an act of street violence induces a crisis? The ability of political leaders, who are ostensibly committed to talks, to control their own *mid-level combatants* is the most critical problem; after all, it is many of these mid-level functionaries who have the most to lose from peace. It is simply not enough to hope for intra-group cohesion (in Kashmir, for example) without more carefully evaluating the incentive structure of mid-level elites.

Moreover, it is also important to analyze the relationships between elites and mid-level elites in each party to the talks, and the relationships between them and the broader groups they represent. Analyzing the relative strengths and weaknesses of the moderate coalition can also reveal the extent to which rejectionist violence will undermine moderates and exacerbate polarization to the point where talks are no longer sustainable. Thus, the focus of mediator intervention should be on the attitudes of these key elites, the stakes they perceive in terms of the relative costs and benefits of peace over violence, and the tactics that third parties might take to influence them. The focus of peacemaking efforts should be as much on the splits between hard-liners and moderates *within* each group or faction as on the differences between groups-in-conflict.

An accurate assessment of the parties' intentions is critical. In South Africa, peacemaking action was based on a correct assessment that the talks had only snagged, not derailed. Eminent persons mediation by a Special Representative of the Secretary-General and key states such as the United States made a critical difference at a key moment. In Sri Lanka, external parties were skeptical of the LTTE's commitment to peace; they doubted whether, given the latter's behavior, the peace process was really salvageable. There was no ability to generate sufficient political will to significantly intervene in Sri Lanka, especially when the parties were so resistant to a third-party role. Whether allowing Sri Lanka to slip back into civil war was a failure of peacemaking, or a justifiable unwillingness of the international community to become involved in a hopeless quagmire, depends on assessing the attitudes and intentions of tough characters in conflict such as the LTTE. The following policy-relevant findings flow from this research.

Elites

- *Offer credible commitment in some form to resolve the "security dilemma."* Both rebels and governments often object to any such deployment. If a force is deployed, it should be based on now-common principles in the deployment of peacekeepers, including an assertive mandate that includes the ability to enforce the peace and the dispatch of a force that has overwhelming military capacity. As above, a Chapter VI operation is too weak and places peacekeepers in jeopardy. In general, the August 2001 Brahimi report on UN peacekeeping provides a reasonable set of contemporary guidelines to inform the diplomatic and operational side of any military intervention. An international security stabilization force should also be equipped with an interim legal code and offer a considerable ability to conduct local law enforcement functions.

  The capacity of the international community to fully provide credible commitment is severely limited; peacekeeping and similar security missions such as civilian policing are hampered by donor and troop contributor fatigue, the unwillingness of powerful states (especially the United States) with the capacity to engage in peacekeeping to take on the task, and "overstretch" by the UN which has competing priorities and insufficient resources. United Nations peacekeeping operations remain woefully under-resourced relative to the demand.
- *Provide direct protection to political leaders,* especially those of the opposition and vulnerable members of the incumbent government. In Kosovo, Afghanistan, and Burundi, for example, international peacekeepers have played important new roles in providing basic personal security for political leaders through security details dedicated to their survival. This function is one of the most important roles to be played by any peacekeeping force.
- *Elections as exit, a salutary view.* Despite the fact that pushing electoral processes is not a sufficient situation for mediator "exit," promoting electoral processes as pathways from civil war and as the basis for a cease-fire can be a clever approach to peacemaking entry. The prospect of elections may provide both sides with the political "cover" they need to accept a cease-fire: for the government, a cease-fire commitment by the rebels would be a way to demonstrate that it is open to political competition from any group that does not pursue violence. For the rebel-allied political parties, the cease-fire may be a way to become involved in elections in such a way so as to defeat the government in the voting without further, costly military struggle. While it is difficult, mediators may be able to skillfully link a cease-fire to the prospect of elections in a way that gives both sides the opportunity to accept a truce

and agree to elections without losing face or backing down from long-held demands.

- *Continue to pursue arms embargoes as leverage for talks.* A smart approach suggests reinforcing and continuing to doggedly pursue the compliance mechanisms of the UN-mandated controls on exports and arms transfers and seek out specific methods to hold violators of the embargo accountable. International mediators should act collectively to pressure other states and business firms to systematically seek to dry up the sources of revenue which are used to buy arms. The UN Panel of Experts mechanism has proven a useful way to monitor compliance, which has played a useful role in highlighting and curbing cross-border support for rebel groups such as the murderous RUF in Sierra Leone.

Mid-level and militias

- *Establish an international Contact Group fact-finding mission to establish needs and priorities.* With the advent of cease-fire talks, it may be useful to immediately deploy an international fact-finding mission to determine the on-the-ground challenges of DDR and to begin the process of direct interaction with commanders, militia leaders, and rebel forces. Such a fact-finding mission could well precede the deployment of an intervention force with a clear assurance for their security from the various factions in talks; often, the international community has waited until much later to assess DDR needs.
- *Working committees.* Setting up working committees to address issues of programs for demobilizing soldiers, amnesty or prosecution, assuring the safe return of exiles, and protection for vulnerable individuals and communities has proven a useful approach. These committees were mostly internal in South Africa, while in Liberia and Burundi it made sense to have the mediators and technical advisors from the international mediation coalition countries manage these committees.

Addressing mass support

- *Address basic security needs.* This involves openly addressing the security concerns of armies, militias, local communities, and individuals through agreements on the permanency of the cease-fire and the methods of monitoring and verification. Child (1992) has shown that the roles of "peace verification" and "zones of peace" approaches, especially by the Organization of American States, were essential in ending the wars that afflicted Central America at the end of the Cold War.
- *Emphasize human security and the Responsibility to Protect.* Human rights components should be integrated into all levels of training for a reconstituted police, and effective disciplinary and other enforcement mechanisms should be put in place to respond to allegations of human rights abuse. International mediators must provide clear instructions to

combatants regarding international human rights and humanitarian law, to ensure that combatants respect the rights of civilians; governments must be held to account on the principle of Responsibility to Protect.[14]

- *A sustained public peace process.* A mechanism used successfully in other peace processes, notably South Africa, Tajikistan, and Northern Ireland, is a sustained meeting of a core group of representative but unofficial political and social leaders in an ongoing series of meetings to help design and oversee implementation of a peace process. A carefully selected group of influential second-tier elite with close ties to the official decision-makers – meeting regularly to build relationships among themselves – can provide an alternative forum for negotiating the difficult issues. These alternative tracks may be particularly useful in addressing issues such as amnesty, prosecution of war crimes, and compensation for the victims of violence. The essential purpose of such a process is to think ahead of the official negotiations, to probe assumptions that lie behind official positions, and to develop areas of potential consensus and obstacles to progress on the most difficult issues (Saunders 2001). This mechanism is different than simply having regular conferences of prominent exiles; instead, it is an ongoing working group, broadly representative, that provides an alternative internal channel for negotiation and that meets frequently (and often in secret) throughout the transitional period.

In war-torn societies, international organization and NGO observers have successfully established systematic relations with networks of local community conflict-management forums. An essential part of any international mediation strategy for peacebuilding should involve a systematic approach to local empowerment through an integrated, national dispute resolution system. The benefits of such an approach are threefold. First, it provides an arena for management of local problems that could escalate into violence that threatens the overall peace process (e.g. local ethnic tensions tied to political parties). Second, it provides a network for systematically linking the civilian and military dimensions of international intervention – both official and unofficial components – directly with local communities.[15] Finally, expanding or reinforcing the peace process at the level of civil society is part of an essential strategy of "reaching out and reaching down" as mediators seek to make settlements stick (Crocker *et al.* 2004: 165–184).

Passing the baton: from peacemaking to peacebuilding

The advent of the UN Peacebuilding Commission, created in late 2005 and launched in 2006, provides a unique moment to think strategically about how the international community can better respond to current and future armed conflicts. Peacebuilding is critical in the future to consolidate peace in those situations where armed conflict has been terminated by peace agreements but could recur, or where the conditions of war-torn societies lend themselves to the outbreak of new violence. New thinking on peacebuilding has emerged in a retrospective look at the lessons that peacemaking in the 1990s and early 2000s has left behind. Doyle and Sambanis argue that the task of peacebuilding is closely related to the extent of devastation that occurred in the war, writing that

> the greater the hostility, measured in terms of casualties, refugees, number of factions, type of war, and ethnic divisions, and the less the local capacity, the lower the probability of peacebuilding success and the greater must international capacities be increased to increase that probability.
>
> (Doyle and Sambanis 2006: 335)

Further evolution of post-settlement peacebuilding capacities is required if the proportion of sustainable peace settlements is to rise. First is onward evolution of the web of international organizations and institutions to address challenges of civil war. This global architecture has evolved considerably since 1990 – when the term peacebuilding wasn't even in the international peace and security lexicon – and it continues to evolve today, both at the global level of the UN and perhaps even more importantly in regional contexts such as the further development of peace operations where collective security organizations (such as NATO) and regional organizations (such as the AU) are working with regional organizations and the UN (e.g. Kosovo and potentially in Darfur).

Second, emphasis must be placed on the key unit of states. The focus in recent years on *peacebuilding-as-statebuilding* is informed by analysis that suggests that weak and failed states – where elite economic predation can flourish, and where group fears and insecurities are heightened – pose the most significant threats to peace. This perspective means that peacebuilding is long term, designed to develop state capacity, autonomy, and basic functions of rule of law, public order, and clean and fair service delivery provided without banal corruption, and focused first on security and economic stability and only later on "democracy," especially a narrow-minded emphasis on elections-as-exit strategy. As Paris observes,

> What is needed in the post-conflict period is not democratic ferment and economic upheaval, but political stability and the establishment of effective administration over territory. Only when a working governmental authority has been reestablished should peacebuilders initiate a series of gradual democratic and market-oriented reforms.
>
> (Paris 2004: 187–188)[16]

Third, states cannot be effective without strong societies. Without local ownership and local-level processes of security, reconciliation, and development, peacebuilding is not sustainable. Thus, in a more expansive definition of peacebuilding imagine that building peace is equally about the attainment of longer-term human security by emphasizing relationships among state capacity, socio-economic development, and the mitigation of "root causes" of conflict. This requires an on-the-ground strategy of civil society building that cross-cuts lines of conflict and promotes more conflict-mitigating inter-group relations by building integrated civil society, not sectarian organizations (Varshney 2001; see also Paris 2004: 194–196 and Belloni 2001). Such integrated civil society is also more likely to occur when post-war societies see sustained periods of economic growth that is distributed broadly across former lines of conflict.

Peacemaking with power: risks and rewards

A more expansive notion of peacemaking is required to improve capacities for facilitating exits to today's complex, internationalized but mostly internal wars. Recent innovative proposals include the creation of regional conflict-amelioration centers where comparative learning, trained mediators, and institutionalized forums for bargaining can directly address regional problems and offer immediate solutions; the regional approach is already well advanced in the Americas, Africa, and Europe, but is woefully underdeveloped in critical regions such as the Middle East and South Asia.[17] The regionalization of international responses to civil wars may also provide opportunities for quickly and effectively supplying the external military forces – through regional peacekeeping operations – necessary to provide credible commitments to negotiated settlements. Until the international community's ability to serve as a guarantor of peace agreements is bolstered, these opportunities will be inherently limited. Ongoing limitations emanate from the disjuncture of diplomatic and civilian responses to conflict through mediation and humanitarian aid, and the military imperatives of providing the all-important security elements of successful settlements.

Mediator efforts can help build a shelter to weather disputants through political violence-induced crises in negotiations. South Africa, Liberia, and Burundi managed to sustain a nascent peace process threatened by violence.[18] Clearly, in these three cases, sustained efforts by third parties to keep the process on track made a pivotal difference. Under other conditions, like in the Israeli–Palestinian case, Kashmir, and Sri Lanka, the talks break down, perhaps because one or all of the parties at the table wasn't really committed to reaching an agreement anyway. Whether a more sustained effort at third-party mediation – for example, if Norway had sought intervention by the UN Security Council when violence in Sri Lanka began to escalate anew in 2006 – could have prevented the recurrence of violence in that country is a counter-factual assessment that is difficult, if not impossible, to make.[19]

Recent experience reveals a confused international community on the necessity of quickly reinforcing peace through strong measures such as non-consensual external military intervention. In Kosovo, a strong, resolute, well-armed NATO force was envisioned to back up the failed Ramboulliet agreement, a force that was eventually deployed without the government of Yugoslavia's consent. A similarly strong military force was deployed in East Timor, although in that case the government of Indonesia had reluctantly agreed to its deployment. With these forces deployed, the process of peacemaking is moving forward with the clear understanding that external powers will in fact provide the military commitments required to help the warring protagonists overcome their deep-seated insecurities. Resolving security and credible commitment dilemmas remains *the* essential ingredient of effective peacemaking.

Unfortunately, the UN is not well placed to step up to the task anywhere, anytime it is needed. For mediators, long-term, credible guarantees of the security terms of settlement are the exception rather than the norm. This mixed record of recent responses to peacemaking in civil wars suggests that the international community must more quickly seize the opportunities and further develop institutions and normative principles for assisting peace processes – with global reach – and be willing to back them with strong, security-enhancing peacekeeping capabilities.

In addition to current coveys of special envoys and eminent persons, systematic international monitoring and observation through the deployment of UN missions such as observers, special rapporteurs, etc. should be enhanced. First, such missions provide an on-the-ground early warning system to determine when and to what extent violence is likely to occur and what can be done to defuse it. Second, observer missions, if sufficiently large, can actually deter violence if the parties know the "eyes and the ears" of the international community are upon them. Practical efforts to monitor human rights and diffuse community-level violence are prudent means of launching preventive action, in effect institutionalizing the intervention through a structure of ongoing engagement.

Those engaged in peacemaking have struggled with the appropriate means and ends of intervention. That is, resistance by the parties limits the extent of intervention, as does the cost of wielding influence to the mediators themselves; they may be directly costly, as in large aid packages, or they may be injurious to credulity if threats of intervention are not followed by action. Influencing the parties with tactics like wielding carrots and sticks, affecting the attitudes of elites and mass publics toward accommodation, and continuing the peacemaking intervention effort over time are all carried out with very little leverage over the parties (especially when the intervenor is an eminent person or a UN envoy). Success in these instances depends on persuasion: describing and manipulating the stakes, attempting to change attitudes, and determining the appropriate tactics – which instruments of diplomacy to employ and when to use them.

If the parties in civil wars *are* fundamentally motivated to avoid the abyss from which they are trying to escape, assertive peacemaking efforts may be *the* essential ingredient in the pursuit of peace. Peacemaking has a chance if the intervention is institutionalized in the form of an ongoing monitoring and observation mission, pursued by accepted, eminent, high-level envoys drawing their clout from close coordination with a coherent coalition of states, and if the intervention is aimed at reinforcing the basic compulsions of moderate elites that the risks of a negotiated settlement are preferable to the consequences of a return to war. Assertive and sustained peacemaking by the international community to end contemporary wars, backed up by a commitment to guarantee, then, seems an essential bridge for the turbulent and often violence-ridded path that is a peace process.

Notes

Introduction: pursuing war, negotiating peace

1 For an evaluation of what constitutes "victory" in modern wars, including the Afghanistan and Iraq imbroglios, see Martel (2006).
2 For regular updates, the Public International Law & Policy Group publishes a weekly round-up, *Peace Negotiations Watch,* available at www.publicinternationallaw.org.
3 In this book, I use the terms "international peacemaking" and "international mediation" interchangeably.
4 For an analysis of the collapse of the Arusha Accord as a result of insufficient credible commitment guarantees by the international community, see the account in Walter (2002: 143–159) and the comprehensive analysis by Jones (2001).
5 For a fuller treatment of political violence in the post-settlement period, see Darby (2006a).
6 See Iklé (1971).
7 For an insider account of the Oslo peacemaking process, see Egeland (1999); for analysis, see Aggestam (2002).
8 For an analysis of the effects of political violence on the peace process in the Israeli–Palestinian conflict during the immediate post-Oslo period, see Wallach (2001), Hermann and Newman (2000), and Telhami (2005). For a brief comparison of the South Africa, Israel–Palestine, and Northern Ireland talks, see Miall *et al.* (1999: 168–184). For an earlier comparison of these three conflicts, see Giliomee and Gagiano (1990).
9 For an account of spoilers in the Israeli–Palestinian peace process, see Ranstorp (2006), who argues that the parties used the process for "devious objectives," or disingenuous motives, and Kurtzer and Lasensky (2008), who analyze the critical role of the United States.
10 The term "coercive peacemaking" draws on the broader notion of coercive diplomacy, developed most extensively by George (1993, 1994).
11 See Global Humanitarian Assistance 2007, Development Initiatives, at www.globalhumanitarianassistance.org/pdfdownloads/GHA%202007.pdf.
12 Statement by UN Secretary-General Kofi Annan to the North Atlantic Council, NATO Headquarters, January 28, 1999, at www.nato.int/docu/speech/1999/s990128a.htm.
13 For the role of the UN in humanitarian intervention to stem civil wars, see the statement of the Chairman of the Norwegian Nobel Committee, Gunnar Berge, on the presentation of the prize to Annan and the UN on December 10, 2001, at http://nobelprize.org/nobel_prizes/peace/laureates/2001/presentation-speech.html.

14 On the NATO intervention as it relates to peacemaking initiatives in Kosovo, see Covey *et al.* (2004).
15 For a systematic evaluation of the costs of conflict as a stimulus for international intervention to prevent or ameliorate them, see Brown and Rosecrance (1999).
16 The author thanks an anonymous reviewer for this argument.
17 In terms of the structured, focused comparison approach, the cases feature variance on the dependent variable, "progress" in conflict de-escalation through negotiation (George 1979; Lijphart 1971).
18 Azar defined protracted conflicts as "prolonged and often violent struggle by communal groups for such basic needs as security, recognition and acceptance, fair access to political institutions, and economic participation" (Azar 1991: 93). For an analysis of the literature on the factors that affect the duration of wars, see Licklider (2005).

1 Untold sorrow: civil wars and war termination, 1990–2007

1 The idea that major war is "obsolete" is developed in Mueller (1989).
2 See Chesterman (2001: 2), who reports that in the 1990s 90 percent of all casualties were civilian, compared with 50 percent during World War II and 5 percent in World War I; see also Kaldor (1999).
3 The term "human security" was coined to capture threats to civilians emanating at times from the very states that presumably have the responsibility to protect their citizens from harm; see Hampson *et al.* (2002).
4 Charter of the United Nations (www.un.org/charter). The "scourge of war" is a term coined by Andrew Carnegie.
5 The Uppsala Conflict Database (www.pcr.uu.se/database) definitions of these categories are as follows:

- *War:* More than 1,000 battle-related deaths during a single year.
- *Intermediate conflicts:* More than 1,000 battle-related deaths during the course of a conflict, and at least 25, but less than 1,000, deaths in a single year.
- *Minor armed conflicts*: Total battle-related deaths are less than 1,000, but more than 25 in a single year.

6 The number of deaths in the violence was a point of contention in public debate; the 60,000 figure is from an unofficial, best-guess source, www.iraqbodycount.org.
7 Others, such as Stein and Lebow (1994), demurred, arguing that the era of "mutually assured destruction" between the superpowers was a highly dangerous period whose passing should by no means be mourned. They argue that the strategies of deterrence and "compellence" that characterized Cold War policy-making led to unnecessary international crises that threatened mutually assured destruction.
8 Rosenau had seen internal conflicts as international problems since the 1960s; see Rosenau (1964).
9 Horowitz, in the final chapter of his book *The Deadly Ethnic Riot*, provides the most cogent and clear analysis of alternative theories of violence, emphasizing at the end of the day its essentially orchestrated nature as "calculated passion" (Horowitz 2001: 523–525). For earlier, seminal works on social and political violence see Tilly (2003), Michael Taylor (1988), Rule (1988), Maxwell Taylor (1991), and Hewitt (1993).
10 Despite estimates that reached some 100,000 in the war, demographic research by scholars at the International Criminal Tribunal for the Former Yugoslavia at the Hague used pre- and post-war census data to determine the number of war-related fatalities (compared with what would have been expected in terms of

demographic change without the war); Tabeau and Bijak argued that a minimum estimate of fatalities to mid-2003 was 67,530, of which 45,980 were Muslim, 12,642 were Serbs, 5,629 were Croats, and some 3,279 were "other" (Tabeau and Bijak 2005: 204). See also Trudy Huskamp Peterson, "Temporary Courts, Permanent Records," a United States Institute of Peace Special Report No. 170, August 2006, for an analysis of how ultimately how post-facto analysis of war in transitional justice processes creates a more accurate and durable understanding of the conduct and intensity of the war itself.

11 On terrorism and internal war, see Crenshaw (1983) and Sederberg (1989, 1994).

12 See the website of the United Nations High Commissioner for Refugees (www.unhcr.org) for updated data; the organization presents an annual report "Refugees by Numbers."

13 Indeed, the spillover of internal violence into the international arena was appreciated by some analysts for many years. For a mid-post Cold War analysis, see Brown (1996). For further on contemporary linkages, see "Civil wars: the elusive search for causation," on the political economy of contemporary armed conflict.

14 Walker and Stern (1993: 7), summarizing a US National Research Council workshop on "Balancing and Sharing Political Power in Multiethnic Societies," offer a useful typology of the types of ethnic conflicts in the former Soviet Union: interstate conflicts, indigenous minorities, settler communities, forcible relocation, formerly autonomous regions, and communal violence.

15 For an evaluation of whether globalization and trade linkages have an exacerbating effect on internal conflict, see Schneider *et al.* (2003).

16 For a concise review of the "causes of conflict" debate, see Rubin (2002) and Large and Sisk (2006: 27–35).

17 The classic work on this theory is Horowitz (1985); for a more recent analysis of structured inequalities and the implications for peacebuilding strategies, see Stewart (2001, 2005). For a "primordial" analysis of grievance, see Geertz (1963). For an overview of ethnic conflicts worldwide, see Gurr's reporting on the findings of the Minorities at Risk project (Gurr 2000, 1993).

18 The literature on ethnic conflict has burgeoned since the end of the Cold War. A useful, recent evaluation of this literature by leading authors is found in Wimmer *et al.* (2004).

19 Structured inequality is what Galtung (1969) refers to as the "violence of the status quo." See also Gurr (1970) on the salience of relative deprivation and its role in generating frustration.

20 Richard Goldstone, the international special prosecutor investigating genocide in the former Yugoslavia and Rwanda and who conducted inquiries into political violence in his native South Africa, finds patterns of social discrimination set the stage for ethnic violence, allowing normally peaceful and tolerant people to forego social norms against violence and justify attacks on subordinate groups (Goldstone 2004).

21 The problem of ethnic outbidding is not only one of errant or manipulative political leadership, but also a more general one of collective action. If appeals to ethnic solidarity do not resonate among the populace, political leaders would have very little incentive to resort to them. For a formal theory treatment of the problem of outbidding, see Rabushka and Shepsle (1972).

22 See Duffy and Frensley (1989) for an earlier evaluation of mid-level elites as pivotal agents in conflict mobilization and demobilization.

23 Esman (1994: 2–3), in a useful typology drawn from evaluation of ethnic conflict, identifies three sources of multiethnic pluralism in contemporary states: conquest, decolonization, and migration. He also identifies an important and

critical distinction between homeland societies, that is, groups that claim a historical right to specific territory, and diasporas that have migrated to places other than their traditional homeland either voluntarily or involuntarily (Esman 1994: 6–9).

24 As Brass writes:

> Every state ... tends to support particular groups, to distribute privileges unequally, and to differentiate among various categories in the population.... The state itself is the greatest prize and resource over which groups engage in a continuing struggle in societies that have not developed stable relationships among the main institutions and centrally organized social forces.
>
> (Brass 1985: 9, 29)

25 Zartman defines state failure in these terms:

> Collapse means that the basic functions of the state are no longer performed. As the decision-making center of government, the state is paralyzed and inoperative: laws are not made, order is not preserved, and societal cohesion is not enhanced. As a symbol of identity, it has lost its power of conferring a name on its people and a meaning to their social action. As a territory, it is no longer assured security and provisionment by a central sovereign organization. As the authoritative political institution, it has lost its legitimacy, which is therefore up for grabs, and so has lost the right to command and conduct public affairs.
>
> (Zartman 1995a: 5)

See also Rotberg (2003) on the state failure theme.

26 For an evaluation, see the report by Amnesty International at www.amnestyusa.org/diamonds/index.do.

27 Examples include Angola during its protracted civil war. State elites siphoned off wealth from oil revenues and built security forces, and the rebel UNITA faction (*União Nacional para a Independência Total de Angola*, National Union for the Total Independence of Angola) accessed the diamond wealth in the territory it controlled to maintain a well-equipped army. For further, see Collier and Hoeffler (1998); for a systematic analysis of the Collier–Hoeffler model in relation to case studies in Africa and Europe, Central Asia and other regions, see Collier and Sambanis (2005).

28 If political violence is strategic and responsive to incentives, how is suicide bombing explained? Isn't suicide the ultimate act of irrationality? Pape argues that suicide terrorism is merely a coercive tool used by organizations for a "secular and strategic goal": to achieve self-determination by coercing an occupying military force from a democratic country to leave the terrorists' homeland (Pape 2005). The attackers receive "eternal rewards," they are celebrated as martyrs, their families are compensated, and most rationally, they are effective in achieving the group's political goals (Pape 2005). Bloom's acclaimed analysis of suicide bombing focuses on the social and political context rather than individual motives per se (Bloom 2005). While those such as Pape and Bloom have insights by emphasizing the contextual incentives for suicide bombers, it is clear that in some situations the perpetrators are true believers, seeing their acts essentially as altruistic in pursuit of some higher good (such as faith or nationalism).

29 See also Mason (1984) for an evaluation of rational peasant arguments.

30 For a good definition of violence that affirms this point, see Taylor (1991: 3–18).

31 On the ladder metaphor for conflict escalation, see Kahn (1965). See Smoke (1977) for an analysis of the concept of limited war.

32 See also Hironaka (2006) for an extensive analysis of war duration. She argues that the principal explanation for longer civil wars in the contemporary era is their internationalization; she concludes that

> civil wars of the late twentieth century are, to a certain extent, creatures of the international system. Although the principal triggers of civil wars are local in origin, the magnitude and duration of these are the product of international processes and resources.
>
> (Hironaka 2006: 149)

33 See Stedman (1991) and Fortna (2004a; see also 2004b: 87).
34 Wallensteen and Sollenberg (2000: 640).
35 Military victories are arguably more unstable than negotiated settlements because they leave grievances among the vanquished unresolved, only to re-erupt at the first opportunity when strength has been re-gathered. For the argument that military victories are more durable than peace agreements, see Wagner (1993).
36 See Touval and Zartman (1989: 11).
37 A good example is the suspension of Russian voting rights in the Council of Europe in April 2000 over its prosecution of the war in Chechnya. The EU countries pressured Russia to suspend its military campaign in the war-torn region and negotiate with the Chechen insurgents. Russia rebuffed the EU entreaties. On the origins of the Chechnya war, see Tishkov (1997).
38 For an evaluation of the humanitarian intervention question in the UN Security Council see Weiss (2004). The impetus for intervention and the UN's performance in such missions are evaluated in Holzgrefe and Keohane (2003), Berdal and Economides (2007), and Doyle and Sambanis (2006: 6–10).
39 For evaluation of peace processes in the Americas during this period, see Child (1992); for evaluation of peace processes in the Americas during the latter period of the 1990s, see Arnson (1998).
40 For analysis on the human costs of civil war, see Ghobarath *et al.* (2002). On the relationship between war and food insecurity in the 1990s, see the article "Armed Conflict and Hunger: Calculating the Costs of Conflict," at www.worldhunger.org/articles/fall2000/messer7.htm.
41 Boutros Boutros-Ghali, "An Agenda for Peace: Preventive Diplomacy, Peacemaking, and Peacekeeping," June 17, 1992, Report of the Secretary-General pursuant to the statement adopted by the Summit Meeting of the Security Council on January 31, 1992, at www.un.org/docs/SG/agpeace.html. Arguably, the Agenda codified and rationalized practices that had already emerged in the first years of the 1990s.
42 See Peck (1998).
43 "Supplement to the Agenda for Peace: Position Paper of the Secretary-General on the Occasion of the Fiftieth Anniversary of the United Nations," A/50/60, S/1995/a, January 3, 1995, p. 5.
44 Carnegie Commission on Preventing Deadly Conflict, *Final Report*, 1998, p. 21. See also Cranna (1994).
45 See William Schabas, "The Genocide Convention at Fifty," a United States Institute of Peace Special Report, January 7, 1999.
46 For analysis, see Dobbins (2005).
47 See Diamond (2005), Phillips (2005), and Ricks (2006).
48 Zalmay Khalilizad, "Why the United Nations Belongs in Iraq," *New York Times*, July 20, 2007.
49 Report of the United Nations Secretary-General Kofi A. Annan, "In Larger Freedom: Towards Development, Security, and Human Rights for All," May 26, 2006 (paragraph 114).

50 See Thomas Friedman, "The Bus is Waiting," *New York Times*, October 11, 2006.
51 For an argument that improved policy instruments and practice lie at the heart of the decline in armed conflicts into the twenty-first century, see Gareth Evans, "Ending Deadly Conflict: Dream or Delusion," Second Sir Zelman Cowan Oration, Australian Institute of International Affairs, August 22, 2007, available at www.crisisweb.org.
52 For an analysis of the dilemmas inherent in war-to-democracy transitions, see Jarstad and Sisk (2008).
53 For analysis of the referendum as consultative mechanism that had the effect of reinforcing the peace process, see MacGinty (2003).

2 Peace processes as a bargaining problem

1 On the role of rule structures in conflict termination, see Blalock (1989: 231–248) and Sisk (1995).
2 Stephen Brams, in a *Theory of Moves* (1993), refers to the use of "threat moves" as a part of integrated bargaining strategies.
3 In conventional international conflicts, this phenomenon has also been witnessed. For example, prior to the convening of the Paris peace talks to end the Vietnam War, military engagements (including aerial bombings by the United States) escalated sharply (Pillar 1983).
4 Schelling defines the *strategy* of conflict as the "interdependence of the adversaries' decisions and on the expectation of each others' behavior" (Schelling 1966: 17). In essence, they adopt rational strategies to advance their aims, and the choice to talk or to fight is one such decision. According to Schelling, "The best course of action for each participant depends on what he expects the other participants to do" with the knowledge that the other participants are making similar calculations with similar information (Schelling 1966: 9–10).
5 This focus on intra-group differences builds on our understanding of the role of ethnic "outbidders" in exacerbating conflicts. See Rabushka and Shepsle (1972) and Horowitz (1985).
6 The phases approach to negotiation in international and internal conflicts has also been extensively developed by Bloomfield and Leiss (1969), Lockhart (1979), Pillar (1983), Kriesberg (1987), Kriesberg and Thorson (1991), Zartman and Faure (2005), and Zartman (1985, 1991a, 1991b, 2000).
7 See Saunders (1985).
8 Analyzing peace processes in terms of phases does not mean that, for any given conflict situation, a phase cannot be skipped, or that phases cannot overlap, or that the issues normally entertained at a very early stage of the process in one case may be those found at a later stage in another. See Zartman (1989).
9 Analysis of the relations among escalation and negotiation – together with mediator interventions – is found comprehensively in Zartman and Faure (2005); in the volume, the editors provide a list of those factors that "serve to dampen, interrupt, or reverse (brake or break) escalation and so allow negotiation and settlement of the dispute to take place" (Zartman and Faure 2005: 11–13). Of the list provided, this research highlights the importance of several, but not all, of these variables as most powerfully explanatory in terms of progress in negotiation: fear (of further escalation) and fatigue, mutually hurting stalemate, changes in parties, changes in attitudes, and learning processes. Less emphasized here are approaches that involve cultural factors or emotive issues such as vengeance.
10 Carlson has evaluated the relationship between escalation patterns, the type of crisis, and decisions to negotiate in her analysis of how the use of violence

to respond to a crisis further entraps the parties in an escalation dynamic (Carlson 2005).

11 Bacharach and Lawler (1981: 105) argue that "punitive tactics essentially attempt to force the opponent to make additional concessions beyond those that can be exacted by [ordinary] tactical concessions."

12 On threats, see Lauren (1979).

13 Concerning the rationality assumption, Schelling (1966: 16) observes:

> Threats and responses to threats, reprisals and counter-reprisals, limited war, arms races, brinksmanship, surprise attack, and trusting and cheating can be viewed as hot-headed or cool-headed activities. In suggesting that they can be viewed as cool-headed activities, it is not asserted that they are in fact entirely cool-headed. Rather it is asserted that the assumption of rational behaviors is a productive one in the generation of systematic theory.

14 On formal theories of strategic choice, see Ordeshook (1989).

15 For general and readable reviews of the application of game theory to negotiation in conflict situations, see Rabow (1990), Brams (1990), and Raiffa (1982).

16 A game-theoretic model for application to contemporary peace processes would have the following properties or assumptions: iterated, open-ended interaction with a determinate point of agreement on common rule structures; multiple players (two or more principal players, but *N* possible players with the possibility of special patron/client relationships among players); incomplete information; a variable-sum payoff structure; and recursive influences. Clearly, such a game would be a challenge to map.

17 See Tsebelis (1991) for an analysis of legislative behavior from a multiple-level game perspective.

18 For further analysis of the importance of within-party relationships, see Snyder and Diesing (1977) and Lockhart (1979).

19 For works on mediation in international conflict settings, see Princen (1992), Bercovitch and Rubin (1992), and the several articles and books by Bercovitch (1992, 1989, 1984, 2002).

20 For interviews with several SRSGs on their approach to peacemaking, see Martin (2006); for an earlier analysis, see Otunnu and Doyle (1998).

21 On the "group of friends" approach, see Krasno (2003).

22 The efforts of the UN permanent Security Council members to redefine Chinese-Vietnamese relations in the context of mediating the civil war in Cambodia is cited as an example of how the five countries, together with regional players such as Australia and ASEAN (Association of Southeast Asian Nations), fundamentally changed relationships in the region that fueled the conflict. Changing the regional dynamic eventually allowed for a negotiated settlement in Cambodia (Solomon 1999).

23 For a perspective on this decision, see Holbrooke (1999). See also "The Military Balance in Bosnia and its Effect on the Prospects for Peace," United States Institute of Peace Special Report, 1995, and the analysis of the relationship between NATO bombing and war-ending settlement in Mockaitis (1999: 115–116).

24 This typology draws upon the work of Rothchild (1997).

25 For an analysis of the Mozambique peace process and the role of the Catholic lay organization Sant'Egidio in working with the UN and other multiparty mediators, see Hume (1994) and Bartoli (1999); see also Rothchild (1997: 251–253).

26 NATO intervention in Bosnia, however, provided a form of insurance to the signatories of the Dayton Peace Accords.

27 For details on the Sudan situation and the range of US congressional and executive branch pressures, which include further legitimation of the SPLM's John Garang with an early 2002 White House visit, see Ted Dagne, "Sudan: Humanitarian Crisis, Peace Talks, Terrorism, and U.S. Foreign Policy," CRS *Issue Brief* to Congress (Congressional Research Service, Library of Congress), March 2002.

28 Although the Congo Crisis of 1960–1964 was arguably the first peace enforcement mission in a civil war.

3 Peace through negotiation: escaping untold sorrow

1 See Druckman and Green (1986) for an attempt to quantify the concept (through indices) in the Philippines.

2 On the concept of ripeness, see Zartman (1985: 232–235, 2000), Haass (1989), Pillar (1983: 50–51), and the essays in Kriesberg and Thorson (1991).

3 For an analysis of reciprocity, see Kriesberg (2003: 196–197).

4 See Fisher (1989).

5 This point is substantiated by experimental research, notably Axelrod's now-famous games in which it is demonstrated that a tit-for-tat strategy is the most successful one for inducing cooperation (Axelrod 1984).

6 For an account, see Stedman (1991).

7 On the opening of formal negotiations in war termination, see Pillar (1983: 44–64).

8 On conciliation as a counter-terrorist strategy in internal wars, see Sederberg (1995).

9 See Pillar (1983: 221–235) on sequencing as it relates to multiple issue "packaging" in preliminary formal negotiation.

10 See Sisk (1995: 38–55).

11 The author thanks an anonymous reviewer for this insight and formulation.

12 For a variety of perspectives on the peace process, see also Elliott (2002).

13 See Darby and MacGinty (2000a), especially pp. 78–79.

14 For a thorough overview of power-sharing options, see Harris and Reilly (1998).

15 See also Lapidoth (1997), Hannum (1990), and Hannum and Babbitt (2006).

16 In multiethnic Fiji, for example, a four-year expert review of the country's political system produced a set of recommendations for a recently adopted constitution that combines measures to guarantee a minimum level of traditional Fijian (as opposed to Indo-Fijian) representation in parliament (a group building-block option) with measures to promote the formation of political alliances across group lines (an integrative option). The Fiji experience points to how a well-conceived process, featuring a balanced panel of experts with firm political support, can arrive at creative solutions specifically tailored to a unique set of problems. See the report of the Constitutional Review Commission, "The Fiji Islands: Toward a United Future," Suva, 1996. The Fiji case is instructive precisely because the efforts of spoilers to disrupt integration along ethnic lines were only temporarily successful; as Fiji recovers from the attempted coup d'état of 2000, it has returned to an integrationist formula for resolving its ethnic tensions.

17 For some works in this genre, see Cooper and Berdal (1993), Stedman (1995), Paris (2004), Doyle and Sambanis (2006), and Jarstad and Sisk (2008).

18 UN Secretary-General Kofi Annan, "Why Democracy is an International Issue," Cyril Foster Lecture, Oxford University (UK), June 19, 2001, available at www.escwa.org.lb/information/press/un/2001/word-pdf/19june.pdf.

19 On this method, see also George and McKeown (1985).

4 South Africa: negotiating democracy after apartheid

1 On the South African process as a "miracle," see *Financial Times* reporter Patti Waldmeir's account of the transition, *Anatomy of a Miracle* (1997).

2 The phrase "adapt or die" was coined by South African president P.W. Botha; see his obituary in *New York Times*, "P.W. Botha, Defender of Apartheid, is Dead at 90," November 1, 2006. See Schrire (1992).

3 Quoted in Sisk (1995: 243).

4 See Thompson (1990) for an engaging and insightful narrative of South Africa's "internal colonialism."

5 On the Afrikaners, see Giliomee (2003).

6 Thompson (1985) persuasively presents apartheid as a re-imagined nationalist ideology by Afrikaner nationalist politicians and highlights how capture of the state in 1948 was then used to reinforce the historical myths on which the ideology was based.

7 For a definitive account of the evolution of the ANC's Charterist or non-racial ideology, see Lodge (1983).

8 The regionalization of the conflict and its implications for influencing ripeness within South Africa are well described in Jaster *et al.* (1992).

9 See Friedman (1987) for an authoritative account of this period.

10 See Amnesty International (1992) for detailed personal accounts of many of these types of violent incidents.

11 For further on this interpretation of the KwaZulu fighting, and the levels, nature, and intensity of the fighting, see Indicator South Africa, *Capturing the Event: Conflict Trends in the Natal Region*, 1986–1992.

12 See the *South African Journal of Human Rights*, Human Rights Index, Vol. 8, Part 2, 1992, pp. 277–278.

13 The text of the early agreements (Groote Schuur and Pretoria) can be found in Race Relations Survey 1991/1992, South African Institute of Race Relations, Johannesburg, 1992, pp. 512–515).

14 See Sisk (1995: 88–115, 200–223) for an evaluation of these pacts as interim steps on the path to a comprehensive settlement; for a skeptic's view of these preliminary talks, and of the South African transition as a whole, see Ottaway (1993: 174–175, 204), who described the talks as "cheating" and "treachery" by the government, pronouncing the peace process (prematurely, in retrospect) as doomed to failure by arguing that "In practice, the goals of the various parties, and their vested interests, were too divergent for [a permanent political system to emerge] as a harmonious outcome."

15 For analysis of the political violence in 1990 and later in 1991, see Simpson *et al.* (1991) and Simpson and Rauch (1992).

16 See Human Rights Watch (1991), which reported that:

> there is abundant evidence that the state is implicated in the past six years of so-called "black-on-black violence." The bias of the state security forces, who have either intervened or failed to intervene on a selective basis, has fueled the conflict.... That the members of the government and the security forces opposed to negotiations with the black majority would have an interest in promoting such violence is easy to imagine: certainly a divided African population is less threatening than a united one.
>
> (Human Rights Watch 1991: vi)

17 Detailed monitoring of violence during the transition can be found in several sources, for example in the monitoring by the South African Institute of Race Relations (Race Relations Survey), the work of Mary de Haas (e.g. de Haas 1994), and the reporting of the *South African Journal of Human Rights*, which

published a detailed "index" of key events in the peace process from 1990 to 1994 (especially Vols. 7–9) covering unrest areas, detentions, train violence, police abuses, assassinations, and alleged "third force" atrocities. The Survey also includes monthly fatality totals in political violence; however, more corrected and updated data may be found in Guelke (2000) (see Figure 4.1).

18 Allegations of de Klerk's complicity in the violence carried on well into the post-apartheid era; in July 2007, former policeman Eugene de Kock claimed the president's hands were "soaked in blood"; de Klerk responded, "my conscience is clear." BBC News, "Jailed Policeman Accuses de Klerk," July 7, 2003.

19 See Peter Waddington and Richard Goldstone, "Report of the Inquiry into Police Response to, and Investigation of, Events in Boipatong on June 17, 1992" (mimeo). Allegations of police orchestration of the attacks are found in *The Sowetan*, "Background to the Boipatong Massacre," June 29, 1992, p. 12.

20 While the onus of culpability in this instance actually lies with the Ciskei's Defense and Police forces, ANC leaders – especially Ronnie Kasrils – had attempted to stage a dramatic (non-violent) seizure of Bisho's streets by exiting the soccer stadium where the demonstration was to have taken place through a curious gap in razor wire designed to keep the protesters in. See the Goldstone Commission Report, "Commission of Inquiry Regarding the Prevention of Public Violence and Intimidation, Report on the Bisho Incident, September 7, 1992" (mimeo). Also see "Hardline Communists Hijacked the March on Bisho in a Classic East European-style Attempt at Takeover," *The Sunday Star*, September 13, 1992, p. 28.

21 Some, such as analyst John Kane-Berman, believe Hani was assassinated because, as an ANC hard-liner, he had endorsed the peace process. See Kane-Berman (1993: 80–84).

22 The full text of the Mandela speech is found at www.anc.org.za/ancdocs/history/mandela/1993/sp930410.html.

23 For an overview, see "Shell House: How it Went Wrong," *Mail and Guardian* (electronic version), July 8, 1994.

24 See Sisk (1995: 221).

25 The original text of the amnesty plea and decision is found at www.doj.gov.za/trc/decisions/1998/980611_makoma%20mkhumbuzi%20mlambisi.htm.

26 Among the other types of politicized social violence during the period were individual attacks on racial and ethnic lines, conflicts between shack dwellers and hostel dwellers, vigilante and "people's courts" violence, sabotage bombings, power struggles in traditional Zulu areas, burning of witches, and train violence. For overviews, see the annual publications Race Relations Survey (especially 1992/1993, 1993/1994, and 1994/1995) from the South African Institute of Race Relations.

27 For an evaluation of the white right's roles in violence, see the Truth and Reconciliation Commission Final Report (2000), Vol. 2, pp. 632–662.

28 For an account, see Waldmeir (1997: 238–240, 246–247).

29 The organization was supported by the United States and other external donors as part of a broader pattern of international support for internal conflict resolution organizations; see Lyman (2000: 77–125) for a detailed account of the wide range of measures undertaken to support the peace process through direct aid, the gradual elimination of the sanctions regime, and targeted interventions to share comparative knowledge on negotiations and constitutional options.

30 Remarks at the June 5, 1995 symposium, "Elections and Conflict Management," United States Institute of Peace, 1996.

31 Signals of good intent continued to be important in this stage of the process as well. For example, Mandela's personal rapport with Afrikaner hard-liner Con-

stand Viljoen and his brief but enormously important meeting with H.F. Verwoerd's widow in Orania (Verwoerd, a former NP prime minister, is known as the "architect" of apartheid and Orania is a remote town that claims to be the heartland of the proposed Afrikaner state) have gone a long way to reassure Afrikaners of a dignified place in a new order. (At the same time, the ANC stood firm against the territorialization of ethnicity in terms of an Afrikaner *volksstaat.*) Similarly, just when IFP leader Mangosuthu Buthelezi was making noises about withdrawing from the cabinet in the post-election period, Mandela designated him as interim president while Mandela and deputy president Mbeki traveled abroad.

32 As South African constitutional scholar Heinz Klug observed:

> Deals done in smoke-filled rooms, conversations conducted at a high level of constitutional abstraction were really not likely to produce a populous which would adhere and be obedient and support the constitution. The point was made that when the constitution is threatened from within or without, it is the people who defend it.
>
> (Remarks made at the United States Institute of Peace Constitution-making Working Group, September 28, 2001)

33 These negotiations are covered by ANC insider Hassen Ebrahim (2000).

34 The final weeks of constitutional negotiations are captured in an entertaining and endearing documentary produced by the *Weekly Mail and Guardian*, simply titled "The Deadline."

35 On religious perspectives of reconciliation in South Africa, see van Vugt and Cloete (2000).

36 Mandela's and de Klerk's acceptance speeches in Oslo are found in Abrams (1999); the Mandela quotation is from p. 68.

37 For further analysis of post-apartheid politics in South Africa, see Lodge (2003).

38 To be fair, scholars such as Arend Lijphart (1985) and Donald Horowitz (1991) predicted severe ethnic strife if the cluster of political institutions they advocated for South Africa (consociational versus integrative institutions, respectively) were not adopted. Horowitz predicted "Zulu-Xhosa" polarity as the greatest threat to post-apartheid South Africa (Horowitz 1991). Ottaway predicted ethnic nationalism increasing and threatening any political settlement that might emerge (Ottaway 1993: 183).

39 As Friedman writes:

> The post-1948 legacy of violence and racial polarization seems likely to ensure that a South African democracy will be partial, at least for the next decade. South Africa remains a divided society in which pluralism and compromise presented themselves to political leaders as an unavoidable necessity, not a preferred option.
>
> (Friedman 1996: 167; see also Friedman 1999)

5 Liberia: leveraging peace by pursuing justice

1 The regional dimension of Liberia's conflict is documented well in the International Crisis Group report "Tackling Liberia: The Eye of the Regional Storm," Africa Report No. 62, April 30, 2003.

2 For details on Taylor's plundering, see Global Witness (2005).

3 "The Coming Anarchy" view of the conflict in Liberia is reflected in the views expressed by Robert Kaplan in his original article in *The Atlantic Monthly* (February 1994); a more thorough description of the argument appears in Kaplan (1996).

4 Remarks by Ellen Johnson-Sirleaf, USIP Current Issues Briefing, December 9, 2002.
5 See Howe (2001) for evidence on the allegations against ECOMOG.
6 See Joseph (1996). For a more positive view of the 1990s ECOMOG intervention in Liberia and the 1996 agreement as a "warlords' peace," see Adebajo (2002a, 2002b).
7 Some analysts argue that the Abuja agreement was the least bad option available in 1996 and that, given Taylor's strength, Nigeria's intent to withdraw from ECOMOG, and the realities of Taylor's power, the peace process that led to Taylor's emergence as president was the only alternative to continuing war; see Lyons (1999).
8 Others, such as Lyons, believe the elections were appropriate for the time. He argues that given the conditions of fear and violence, the most powerful faction leader (Taylor) won votes as the public tried to appease him (Lyons 1999). See also Lyons (2005: 157–158).
9 Like in Angola in 1992, presidential elections in immediate post-war conditions set up zero-sum, winner-take-all scenarios; for this reason, other post-war elections in Bosnia, South Africa, East Timor, and Kosovo have astutely avoided strong-president systems.
10 Fadiru B. Koromo, "War in Liberia Threatens to Destabilize Region," August 14, 2002, at www.worldpress.org (reproduced from the Freetown, Sierra Leone *Standard Times*).
11 Special Court for Sierra Leone *Indictment*. Case No. SCSL 03-I, The Prosecutor against Charles Ghankay Taylor, March 3, 2003.
12 "Face Justice, Critics Tell Taylor," CNN August 11, 2003.
13 For a detailed accounting of the war and the peace process, see Max Ahmadu Sesay, "Bringing Peace to Liberia," *ACCORD: The Review of Peace Initiatives* (Conciliation Resources, London), 1997. For analysis of the war, see Uband (1998), Ellis (1999), and Berkeley (2001).
14 Human Rights Watch World Report 2002; Letter from Human Rights Watch to the United Nations Security Council Regarding the Mano River Union; United States Department of State Religious Freedom Report 2002; United States Department of State Human Rights Report 2001 (released March 2002).
15 Global Witness, "Logging Off: How the Liberian Timber Industry Fuels Liberia's Humanitarian Disaster and Threatens Sierra Leone," September 2002, and Human Rights Watch, "No Questions Asked: The Eastern Europe Arms Pipeline to Liberia," November 2001.
16 "Liberia: Fighting Resumes in Lofa County," IRIN News October 29, 2002.
17 International Crisis Group, "Liberia: Unravelling," August 19, 2002.
18 Yusuf Bangura, United Nations Research Institute for Social Development (UNRISD), Geneva, April 1996.
19 Quoted in "Liberian Head Under Pressure as UN Court Official Makes Murder Allegations," *Agence France Presse*, May 15, 2003.
20 Security Council presidential statement S/PRST/2002/36, "Security Council Condemns the Government of Liberia, Other Parties for Failure to Comply with Arms Embargo, Continuation of Weapons Imports," December 13, 2002.
21 "Liberia: Taylor urges ECOWAS to arrange talks with LURD," IRIN News November 27, 2002.
22 Other meetings include the Abuja, Nigeria gathering of March 14–15, 2002 and the Bethesda, Maryland meeting of June 28–29, 2002. The Monrovia conference was convened in October 2002, but it is widely seen as lacking essential participation by opposition parties and opposition civil society figures.
23 Based on the IRI "Observations" of the July civil society/political party conference.

24 Associated Press, June 26, 2003.
25 Quoted in "Monrovia Braces for Fresh Rebel Attack as Bush Meets Annan," IRIN July 14, 2003.
26 The full text of the Comprehensive Peace Agreement is found at the United States Institute of Peace digital peace agreements library at www.usip.org/library/pa/liberia/liberia_08182003_toc.html.
27 "Government and Rebels Sign Peace Agreement," IRIN August 18, 2003.
28 "Monrovia Businessman to head Transitional Government," IRIN August 21, 2003.
29 "Thousands Displaced by Renewed Fighting Near Airport," IRIN August 24, 2003.
30 Quoted in the International Crisis Group report "Liberia and Sierra Leone: Rebuilding Failed States," Crisis Group Africa Report No. 87, December 8, 2004, p. 1.
31 Quoted in "UN Fury over New Liberia Clashes," BBC News November 4, 2003.
32 National Commission on Disarmament, Demobilization, Rehabilitation, and Reintegration, "DDRR Consolidated Report Phases 1, 2 and 3," 2005, p. 1.
33 Struggles over land, property, and power have been heightened by the wartime migration in Liberia and the post-war return of refugees; see "Liberia: Refugee Returns Creating Ethnic 'Time Bomb'," IRIN News February 12, 2007.

6 Burundi: empowering the fragile center

1 The Twa are the remaining 1 percent of the Burundi population. These categories, however, are dangerous as consistent lenses of analysis into the Burundian problem, as like elsewhere intra-group cleavages are as important in understanding violence and peace processes as between-group differences. As Lemarchand and Martin have observed with regard to Burundi,

> However satisfying to most European observers, such [ethnic proportionality] simplicities can only convey a highly distorted view of Burundi's traditional social system. Not only do they conceal the existence of major differences within each group, but they also tend to exaggerate the depth of cultural discontinuities among them. These distortions are closely connected. Neglect of intra-ethnic cleavages is liable to obscure the basis for cross ethnic links among each group at the same time that it reduces their respective physical and cultural characteristics to a parody of reality.
> (Lemarchand and Martin 1974: 6)

2 Quoted in Daniel L. Kalinaki, "Burundi Rebels Finally Agree to Ceasefire Deal," *The East African*, January 29, 2007.
3 For details on the 1992 Constitution and its consociational characteristics, see Reyntjens (1993: 566ff.).
4 See also Reyntjens (1993: 581) for an account of Ndadaye's assassination.
5 Ould-Abdallah's memoirs on the period are found in his book *Burundi on the Brink, 1993–95: A UN Special Envoy Reflects on Preventive Diplomacy* (2000).
6 For an account of mediation during this period and the subsequent mediation by Nyerere, see Maundi *et al.* (2006: 57–84).
7 In August 2006, he was arrested in an alleged coup plot; he was acquitted in January 2007.
8 For an insider's account of the Great Lakes mediation efforts, see Kiplagat (1997).
9 For an account of interviews with negotiators in the early talks, held first in Mwanza and later in Arusha, see *Track Two* (Centre for Conflict Resolution, Cape Town), Vol. 11.

10 Van Eck's situation report of November 1999 is archived at the Center for Conflict Resolution (Cape Town) website: http://ccrweb.ccr.uct.ac.za/archive/burundi_reports/burrep-nov99.html.

11 The BBC report on the South African's arrival as the vanguard of the African Force is found at http://news.bbc.co.uk/2/hi/africa/1624979.stm. See also "South Africa's Peacekeeping Role in Burundi: Challenges and Opportunities for Future Peace Missions," ACCORD (African Center for the Constructive Resolution of Disputes) Occasional Paper series Vol. 2, No. 2, 2007.

12 As quoted by the BBC, "Calm in Bujumbura Greets New Era" November 2, 2001.

13 As quoted in IRIN, "Rebels Urged to Join Peace Process," November 25–December 1, 2001.

14 "Burundi Army 'Kills 500 Rebels'," BBC News December 25, 2005.

15 The Security Council statement is at www.un.org/News/Press/docs/2003/sc7966.doc.htm.

16 Betniko Kayaya, "Burundi Inches Closer to Peace," *Times of Zambia* July 5, 2006.

17 The Peacebuilding Commission's Strategic Framework, which carefully balances the internal needs of the protagonists, international priorities and resources, and gives specific benchmarks for progress; see "Strategic Framework for Peacebuilding in Burundi," United Nations Peacebuilding Commission, at www.un.org/News/Press/docs/2007/pbc15.doc.htm.

18 See "Burundi: Democracy and Peace at Risk," International Crisis Group Africa Report No. 120, November 30, 2006.

7 Sri Lanka: mediating without power

1 Within the Tamil community, there is the distinction between indigenous Sri Lankan Tamils (about 12 percent of the total population) and the so-called Plantation Tamils, immigrants who arrived during British rule.

2 With regard to the arguments regarding prior harmony, Little notes that the "colonial education system had produced an inter-communal elite with a shared language and common values and ... the elite had learned the art of political adjustment and compromise" (Little 1994: 4; see also 30–33).

3 For an analysis of the role of language policy in exacerbating ethnic grievance, see Brown and Ganguly (2003); for an analysis of the Sri Lanka case in this context, see DeVotta (2003) in the same volume.

4 As described by Rajasingham (2006, chapter 17).

5 Little demonstrates that religion itself has not directly been evoked to justify killing, but instead has been used instrumentally by both Sinhalese and Tamil political elite. He writes:

> True enough, Tamils and Sinhala may not have been targeted for intolerant treatment because of their religious beliefs. Nevertheless, specific religious texts, symbols, and legends, whether Buddhist or Hindu (or Christian, for that matter), served, under certain conditions, as the justification and inspiration for intolerance and discrimination.
>
> (Little 1994: 104)

6 For analysis of the role of suicide bombings in the strategy of the Tigers, see Bloom (2003).

7 For details on the riots and the slide into conflict in Sri Lanka, see the classic work of Tambiah (1986: on the 1983 riots, see 13–22).

8 For analysis of the IPKF, see Crenshaw (2000).

9 For detailed analysis of the intra-community dimensions of the conflict, see Bush (2003).

10 Over time, however, the JVP has reinvented itself as a more moderate political party representing the rural poor and with considerable support in the Sri Lankan Armed Forces; in the violent run-up to the 2001 elections, the JVP was commended for condemning election-related violence.
11 For an in-depth assessment of the peace process during the period 1994–1997, see the ACCORD publication *Demanding Sacrifice: War and Negotiation in Sri Lanka* (Conciliation Resources, London), 1998.
12 *International Herald Tribune*, August 8, 1995, p. 4.
13 Tiruchelvam represented the Tamil United Liberation Front and had drafted a devolution plan that was to be introduced by the Kumaratunga government in the coming days following his death. See Cecilia W. Dugger, "A Leading Sri Lankan Moderate is Killed," *New York Times*, July 30, 1999, p. A10.
14 They apparently also tried to kill Wickramasinghe; at a rally for him, an explosion near simultaneous to the one injuring Kumaratunga killed a dozen. See also Seth Mydans, "As Sri Lankans Choose a President, Ethnic War Rages On," *New York Times*, December 22, 1999.
15 "Sri Lankan President Partially Blinded," BBC World News December 30, 1999.
16 Details on Norway's entry as a mediator are recounted by Martin (2006). For additional evaluation of the Norwegian role, see Bullion (2001).
17 Quoted in Martin (2006: 104).
18 Quoted in Simon Montlake, "Exhausted by War, Sri Lanka Ponders Peace," *Christian Science Monitor*, September 16, 2002, p. 7.
19 Quoted by BBC World News, "Senior Sri Lankan Minister Killed," July 13, 2005; http://news.bbc.co.uk/2/hi/south_asia/4147196.stm.
20 For an evaluation of the economic dimensions of civil war in Sri Lanka, see Kelegama (1999); she estimates the cost of the war (in terms of direct, primary, and secondary costs) at $16 billion by 1994 (Kelegama 1999: 77).
21 For an analysis of the renewed war and the motivations of the parties, see "Sri Lanka: A War Stranger than Fiction," *The Economist*, June 8, 2007. The use of violence by both sides in a "dirty war" is detailed in the International Crisis Group report "Sri Lanka's Human Rights Crisis," ICG Asia Report No. 135, June 14, 2007.
22 "Sri Lanka: No 'Military Solution,' Departing Peace Monitors Warn," IRIN January 24, 2008.
23 See "Sri Lanka: Donor Threats Unlikely to Stop War Machine," InterPress News Service, February 5, 2007.
24 "Sri Lanka: The Failure of the Peace Process," International Crisis Group Asia Report No. 124, November 24, 2006.
25 All sides in the conflict are deeply culpable in human rights abuses in the conduct of the war that approach the level of crimes against humanity. See the Human Rights Watch report, "Return to War: Human Rights Under Siege," August 2007, available at http://hrw.org/reports/2007/srilanka0807/. States in the UN agreed, and voted against the participation of Sri Lanka on the United Nations Human Rights Council in May 2008.

8 Kashmir: the power of imagination

1 For an account, see Collins and Pierre (1975: 356–366). Of course, the history of the creation of Jammu and Kashmir (J&K) has antecedents into the colonial era and in particular the signing of the Treaty of Amritsar in 1846 which created the J&K territory in its 1947 manifestation as a princely state within the British colonial context. Muslim demands within the society also emerged prior to post-colonial independence as in the 1931 protests and killings which have led to the designation today of July 13 as "Martyr's Day," an annual event that continues to

serve to mobilize Muslim grievances. By 1932, the first Muslim political party was founded, the All Jammu and Kashmir Muslim Conference.

2 The effects on the global climate of a nuclear exchange between India and Pakistan have been simulated by atmospheric scientists, who report that from such a nuclear exchange

> We find significant cooling and reductions of precipitation lasting years, which would impact the global food supply. The climate changes are large and long-lasting because the fuel loadings in modern cities are quite high and the subtropical solar insolation heats the resulting smoke cloud and lofts it into the high stratosphere, where removal mechanisms are slow.
>
> (Robock *et al.* 2006: abstract)

3 See the summary of various estimates provided by Sidhu (2006: 8, note 5).

4 "Rally Opposes Kashmir Peace Deal," BBC News January 19, 2007.

5 On the 1962 war, see Ganguly (1994).

6 These events are analyzed in detail in Desmond (1995).

7 For detailed analysis, see Ganguly (1997).

8 In 1992 and 1993, for example, the United States Institute of Peace in Washington held a number of informal dialogues among unofficial Kashmiri, Pakistani, and Indian political leaders in venues in the United States. These talks underscored the difficulty of finding Kashmiri voices that could faithfully represent the disparate views of the Kashmiris themselves as organizations such as the JKLF were deemed unlawful and Kashmiri political elites found themselves as the "grass on which two fighting elephants trample." The author served as facilitator in these talks with former US diplomats Harold Saunders, Samuel Lewis, and Robert B. Oakley. See also *Peace Initiatives* 1(3) (1995) *Special Issue* "Political Leaders and Track Two Diplomacy in South Asia."

9 See Barry Bearak, "A Kashmiri Mystery," *New York Times Magazine*, December 31, 2002, pp. 26–46.

10 The complexity of the *jihadi* insurgency in Kashmir, and an articulation of the linkages to broader Islamist networks, is found in Zeb (2006).

11 For analysis of the intra-party factional politics of the APHC, see Kaur (2006: 22–25).

12 "Who are the Kashmir Militants?" BBC News April 6, 2005.

13 Scott Baldauf, "Heroin Money Could Fund Kashmir's Militants," *Christian Science Monitor*, October 20, 2003.

14 Quoted in Suhjaat Bukhari, "PM Extends 'Hand of Friendship' to Pakistan," *The Hindu*, April 19, 2003.

15 "Pakistan Makes Kashmir Concession," BBC News December 18, 2003.

16 These talks are detailed in the International Crisis Group report "India/Pakistan Relations and Kashmir: Steps toward Peace," ICG Asia Report No. 79, June 24, 2004.

17 Among the organizations most extensively involved in facilitating the building of confidence between India and Pakistan is the Washington, D.C.-based Henry L. Stimson Center. Stimson's ongoing programs of facilitation and research are reported in a number of studies that detail, evaluate, and recommend further development of the Indo-Pak CBM regime. For updated analysis, see the site "Documents and Resources on Confidence-Building Measures in South Asia," at www.stimson.org/southasia/?sn=sa2001112048.

18 The Pugwash reports from the Kashmir dialogue sessions reveal considerable common ground on broad principles in the conflict (among their participants) and outline specific process recommendations and outcome options. For the March 10–12, 2006 workshop report from which the quotation is drawn (p. 4)

and the reports of the other Pugwash track-two initiatives on Kashmir (including lists of participants for some workshops), see www.pugwash.org/reports/rc/sa.

19 See Sakia (2006: 306–315) for analysis of spoilers in Kashmir; the quotation is from p. 315.

20 Indian Police Chief claimed that nine of the 11 plotters came from Pakistan, and that "The entire episode was done on behalf of the ISI." CNN News October 1, 2006.

21 "Pakistan Strongly Condemns 'Terrorist' Blasts in India," *Agence France Presse*, July 11, 2006.

22 See "Kashmir Militants Feel the Squeeze," BBC News February 7, 2007.

23 Reasonable consensus proposals that may be in the zone of agreement are found in Swami (2005).

24 The BBC News dedicated site for the Kashmir conflict features interactive maps that illustrate seven scenarios for final status of Kashmir. See http://news.bbc.co.uk/2/hi/in_depth/south_asia/2002/kashmir_flashpoint/.

25 A. Heather Coyne, "Building Blocks, Stumbling Blocks: Prospects for Peace in Kashmir," United States Institute of Peace *USIPeace Briefing*, January 2007, p. 1.

26 See Jason Motlagh, "After Brutal Years, Kashmiris Embrace New Calm," *Christian Science Monitor*, March 20, 2008.

9 Confronting bargaining with bullets: powerful peacemaking

1 As Bercovitch (2002: 261) observes:

> Regional organizations and the UN have credible claims as mediators because of their moral authority, the fact that they embody some generally agreed upon norms, and, above all, their legitimacy. Such organizations have neither power, nor 'teeth,' they give concrete expression to the legitimate voices of a regional or the global community, and use this legitimacy to intervene effectively.

See Chernick (1996: 305) for a similar argument that UN stewardship of peace processes in the Americas in the early 1990s was preferable because "the United Nations, which was seen as more impartial, was in a better position to move the negotiations forward." Also see Covey, who writes that "Success in achieving a viable peace will be determined, in part, by how adroitly the custodian guides the transformation of conflict among rivals in the postwar period" (Covey 2004: 77).

2 Opportunities for addressing such conflicts consistent with interpretations of the principle of self-determination are articulated in Chesterman *et al.* (2001).

3 For an analysis of the use of economic sanctions to bring about resolution of internal conflicts, see Rogers (1996).

4 For a comprehensive list, see Hartzell and Hodie (2007: 6) and Mack (2006).

5 See Bacharach and Lawler (1981: 179–203) for a fuller treatment of this theme in a generalized bargaining framework.

6 Licklider (1993) identified four clusters of variables: (1) the nature of the underlying issues (e.g. ethnic or non-ethnic); (2) the military balance in the field; (3) the internal politics of each side; (4) the role of third-party mediators. In an earlier study, Bloomfield and Leiss (1969) suggested the following variables: degree of commitment of parties; their autonomy of action; environmental contexts; information available to disputants; time pressures; disputants' military relationships; the nature of the conflict (the role of ethnicity); the role of ideology; the parties' internal cohesion; past relationships; and the actions of external parties, especially international organizations and great powers. This

analysis takes these findings further by specifying more clearly how these variables affect progress in the actual conduct of negotiations.

7 For example, see Wilkenfeld *et al.* (2002: 143–146) who use a "zones of agreement" approach.

8 For some time in the early 2000s, UN officials used a figure of 50 percent of war recurrence following negotiated settlements; this common "factoid" was based on an analysis by Paul Collier of the World Bank. Suhrke (2007) shows not only that the figure was grossly inflated due to the fact that Collier included both cease-fires and comprehensive settlements in the analysis, but also how the figure made its way into being the commonly accepted wisdom at the UN.

9 There is an ongoing debate about whether the long-term goal of settlements and their implementation should be democratization or the building of states, and in what sequence. For evaluation of the dilemmas that face societies and international mediators in pursuing democratization and statebuilding, see Paris (2004), Jarstad and Sisk (2008), and Paris and Sisk (2008).

10 It served as the basis of the 1988 Tripartite Agreement (Angola, Cuba, South Africa) that strategically linked Namibian independence to Cuban withdrawal from Angola. Also based on Resolution 435, the Western Contact Group established a set of constitutional principles in 1982 that eventually served as the basis for the settlement ultimately reached by the parties in Namibia in a constitution-making forum after the 1990 elections.

11 See Rothchild (1997: 107).

12 For an analysis of the opportunities, and challenges, in using leverage in internal conflicts, see also Coleman and Grene (2003).

13 On coordination problems in international mediation, see Crocker *et al.* (1999), Jones (2002), and Paris (2004: 227–233).

14 See further and specific recommendations in Chesterman (2001). On the Responsibility norm, see Gareth Evans, "The Limits of Sovereignty: The Responsibility to Protect in the 21st Century," Eighth Neelam Tiruchelvam Memorial Lecture, International Center for Ethnic Studies, Colombo, July 29, 2007, available at www.crisisgroup.org/home/index.cfm?id=4967.

15 In South Africa, for example, the UN observer mission there linked up with a National Peace Committee run by civil society, together with a plethora of regional and local committees. With representatives of local churches, political parties, security forces (police and army), and the various militia or other armed groups (e.g. local self-defense militias), these committees managed to handle any number of disputes that may have eventually become significant enough to threaten the national peace process. Additionally, when national crises did emerge – for example, when Communist Party leader Chris Hani was assassinated in April 1993 – the local committees were activated to monitor protests, demonstrations, and marches. See also Risley and Sisk (2005).

16 See also Barnett (2006) on the statebuilding theme.

17 For an elaboration of these proposals, see Peck (1998).

18 As did the parties in Northern Ireland; see Darby (2001: 15–27) for an authoritative analysis.

19 See Jentleson (1996: 8) for an assessment of the methodological issues in assessing preventive diplomacy, including the inherent difficulties of counterfactual analysis.

References

Abrams, Irwin, ed. 1999. *Nobel Lectures: Peace, 1991–1995*. Singapore: World Scientific and the Nobel Foundation.

Adebajo, Adekeye. 2002a. *Building Peace in West Africa: Liberia, Sierra Leone, and Guinea-Bissau*. New York and Boulder, Colorado: International Peace Academy and Lynne Rienner.

Adebajo, Adekeye. 2002b. "Liberia: A Warlords' Peace," in Stephen Stedman, Donald Rothchild, and Elizabeth Cousens, eds. *Ending Civil Wars: The Implementation of Peace Agreements*. Boulder, Colorado: Lynne Rienner.

Aggestam, Karin. 2002b. "Quasi-informal Mediation in the Oslo Channel: Larsen and Holst as Individual Mediators," in Jacob Bercovitch, ed. *Studies in International Mediation: Essays in Honor of Jeffrey Z. Rubin*. London: Palgrave Macmillan.

Amnesty International. 1992. *South Africa: State of Fear*. New York: Amnesty International.

Arnson, Cynthia, ed. 1998. *Comparative Peace Processes in Latin America*. Stanford, California: Stanford University Press.

Arnson, Cynthia and I. William Zartman, eds. 2005. *Rethinking the Economics of War: The Intersection of Need, Creed, and Greed*. Washington, D.C.: The Woodrow Wilson Center Press.

Asia Watch. 1993. *The Human Rights Crisis in Kashmir: A Pattern of Impunity*. New York: Asia Watch and Physicians for Human Rights.

Axelrod, Robert. 1984. *The Evolution of Cooperation*. New York: Basic Books.

Azar, Edward. 1991. "The Analysis and Management of Protracted Conflicts," in Vamik Volkan, Joseph Montville, and Demetrios Julius, eds. *The Psychodynamics of International Relationships*. Lexington, Massachusetts: Lexington Books.

Bacharach, Samuel B. and Edward J. Lawler. 1981. *Bargaining: Power, Tactics and Outcomes*. San Francisco, California: Jossey-Bass.

Bajpai, Kanti. 1997. "Diversity, Democracy, and Devolution in India," in Michael E. Brown, ed. *Government Policies and Ethnic Relations in Asia and the Pacific*. Cambridge, Massachusetts: MIT Press.

Baker, Pauline. 1996. "Conflict Resolution versus Democratic Governance," in Chester A. Crocker, Fen Osler Hampson, with Pamela Aall, eds. *Managing Global Chaos: Sources of and Responses to International Conflict*. Washington, D.C.: United States Institute of Peace Press.

Ballentine, Karen and Jake Sherman. 2003. *The Political Economy of Armed Conflict: Beyond Greed and Grievance*. Boulder, Colorado: Lynne Rienner.

Barnett, Michael. 2006. "Building a Republican Peace: Stabilizing States after War," *International Security* 30(4): 87–112.

Bartoli, Andrea. 1999. "Mediating Peace in Mozambique: The Role of the Community of Sant'Egidio," in Chester Crocker, Fen Osler Hampson, and Pamela Aall, eds. *Herding Cats: Multiparty Mediation in a Complex World.* Washington, D.C.: United States Institute of Peace Press.

Belloni, Roberto. 2001. "Civil Society and Peacebuilding in Bosnia and Herzegovina," *Journal of Peace Research* 38: 163–180.

Belloni, Roberto. 2008. *Statebuilding and International Intervention in Bosnia.* London: Routledge.

Bentley, Kristina A. and Roger Southall. 2005. *An African Peace Process: Mandela, South Africa, and Burundi.* Cape Town: Human Sciences Research Council Press.

Bercovitch, Jacob. 1984. *Social Conflicts and Third Parties.* Boulder, Colorado: Westview Press.

Bercovitch, Jacob. 1989. "International Dispute Mediation: A Comparative Empirical Analysis," in Kenneth Kressel, ed. *Mediation Research.* San Francisco, California: Jossey-Bass.

Bercovitch, Jacob. 1992. "Mediators and Mediation Strategies in International Relations," *Negotiation Journal* 8(2): 99–112.

Bercovitch, Jacob. 2002. "Conclusion: Some Thoughts on the Process and Potential of Mediation," in Jacob Bercovitch, ed. *Studies in International Mediation: Essays in Honor of Jeffrey Z. Rubin.* London: Palgrave Macmillan.

Bercovitch, Jacob and Jeffrey Z. Rubin. 1992. *Mediation in International Relations: Approaches to Conflict Management.* New York: St. Martin's Press.

Berkeley, Bill. 2001. *The Graves are Not Yet Full: Race, Tribe and Power in the Heart of Africa.* New York: Basic Books.

Berdal, Mats and Sypros Economides, eds. 2007. *United Nations Interventionism 1991–2004.* Cambridge: Cambridge University Press.

Betts, Richard. 2001. "The Delusion of Impartial Intervention," in Chester Crocker, Fen Osler Hampson, and Pamela Aall, eds. *Turbulent Peace: The Challenges of Managing International Conflict.* Washington, D.C.: United States Institute of Peace Press.

Blalock, Hubert M. 1989. *Power and Conflict: Toward a General Theory.* Newbury Park, California: Sage Publications.

Bloom, Mia M. 2003. "Ethnic Conflict, State Terror, and Suicide Bombing in Sri Lanka," *Civil Wars* 6(1): 54–85.

Bloom, Mia. 2005. *Dying to Kill: The Allure of Suicide Terror.* New York: Columbia University Press.

Bloomfield, David. 1997. *Peacemaking Strategies in Northern Ireland: Building Complementarity in Conflict Management Theory.* London: Macmillan.

Bloomfield, David, Teresa Barnes, and Luc Huyse, eds. 2003. *Reconciliation after Violent Conflict: A Handbook.* Stockholm: International IDEA.

Bloomfield, Lincoln and Amelia C. Leiss. 1969. *Controlling Small Wars: Strategies for the 1970s.* New York: Alfred Knopf.

Boutros-Ghali, Boutros. 1992. *An Agenda for Peace.* New York: United Nations.

Brams, Steven J. 1990. *Negotiation Games.* New York: Routledge.

Brams, Steven J. 1993. *Theory of Moves.* Cambridge: Cambridge University Press.

Brass, Paul R. 1985. "Ethnic Groups and the State," in Paul Brass, ed. *Ethnic Groups and the State.* London: Croom Helm.

Brockner, Joel and Jeffrey Z. Rubin. 1985. *Entrapment in Escalating Conflicts.* New York: Springer Verlag.
Brown, Michael, ed. 1993. *Ethnic Conflict and International Security.* Princeton, New Jersey: Princeton University Press.
Brown, Michael, ed. 1996. *The International Dimensions of Internal Conflict.* Cambridge, Massachusetts: MIT Press.
Brown, Michael and Sumit Ganguly, eds. 2003. *Fighting Words: Language Policy and Ethnic Relations in Asia.* Cambridge, Massachusetts: MIT Press.
Brown, Michael and Richard Rosecrance. 1999. *The Costs of Conflict: Prevention and Cure in the Global Arena.* Lanham, Maryland: Rowman and Littlefield.
Bullion, Alan. 2001. "Norway and the Peace Process in Sri Lanka," *Civil Wars* 4(3): 70–92.
Burg, Steven. 1995. "The International Community and the Yugoslav Crisis," in Milton Esman and Shibley Telhami, eds. *International Organizations and Ethnic Conflict.* Ithaca, New York: Cornell University Press.
Bush, Kenneth. 2003. *The Intra-Group Dimensions of Ethnic Conflict in Sri Lanka: Learning to Read between the Lines.* London: Palgrave.
Byrne, Sean and Michael J. Ayulo. 1998. "External Economic Aid and Ethno-political Conflict: A View from Northern Ireland," *Security Dialogue* 29(4): 421–434.
Carlson, Lisa. 2005. "Escalation, Negotiation, and Crisis Type," in I. William Zartman and Guy Faure, eds. *Escalation and Negotiation in International Conflicts.* Cambridge: Cambridge University Press.
Chadda, Maya. 2004. "Between Consociationalism and Control: Sri Lanka," in Ulrich Schneckener and Stefan Wolff, eds. *Managing and Settling Ethnic Conflicts.* London: C. Hurst & Co.
Chandler, David. 2002. *From Kosovo to Kabul: Human Rights and International Intervention.* London: Pluto Press.
Chandra, Suba D. 2005. "Manmohan Singh-Hurriyat Meeting: Beginning of an Internal Peace Process?" *Peace & Conflict* (Delhi) 8(10): 8–9.
Chernick, Marc W. 1996. "Violence and Peacemaking in Latin America," in Michael Brown, ed. *The International Dimension of Internal Conflicts.* Cambridge, Massachusetts: MIT Press.
Chesterman, Simon, ed. 2001. *Civilians in War.* Boulder, Colorado: Lynne Rienner.
Chesterman, Simon, Tom Farer and Timothy D. Sisk. 2001. "Competing Claims: Self Determination and Security in the United Nations," an *International Peace Academy Policy Brief,* April 2001.
Child, Jack. 1992. *The Central American Peace Process, 1983–1991: Sheathing Swords, Building Confidence.* Boulder, Colorado: Lynne Rienner.
Coakley, John, ed. 1993. *The Territorial Management of Ethnic Conflict.* London: Frank Cass.
Coleman, Christopher and Andrew Grene. 2003. "Challenges in the Exercise of Leverage in Peacekeeping," in Jean Krasno, Bradd C. Hayes, and Donald C.F. Daniel, eds. *Leveraging for Success in United Nations Peace Operations.* Westport, Connecticut: Praeger.
Collier, Paul and Anke Hoeffler. 1998. "Greed and Grievance in Civil Wars," *Oxford Economic Papers* 50(4): 563–595.
Collier, Paul and Nicholas Sambanis. 2005. *Understanding Civil War: Evidence and Analysis* (Vol. 1, Africa; Vol. 2, Europe, Central Asia, and Other Regions). Washington, D.C.: The World Bank.

Collin Marks, Susan. 2000. *Watching the Wind: Conflict Resolution in South Africa's Transition.* Washington, D.C.: United States Institute of Peace Press.
Collins, Larry and Dominique Pierre. 1975. *Freedom at Midnight.* New York: Simon and Schuster.
Commonwealth Secretariat. 1986. *Mission to South Africa, The Commonwealth Report; The Findings of the Commonwealth Eminent Persons Group on Southern Africa.* London: Penguin Books for the Commonwealth Secretariat.
Cooper, Robert and Mats Berdal. 1993. "Outside Intervention in Ethnic Conflict," in Michael Brown, ed. *Ethnic Conflict and International Security.* Princeton, New Jersey: Princeton University Press.
Cousens, Elizabeth M. 2001a. "Building Peace in Bosnia," in Elizabeth M. Cousens and Chetan Kumar, eds. *Peacebuilding as Politics: Cultivating Peace in Fragile Societies.* Boulder, Colorado and London: Lynne Rienner.
Cousens, Elizabeth M. 2001b. "Introduction," in Elizabeth M. Cousens and Chetan Kumar, eds. *Peacebuilding as Politics: Cultivating Peace in Fragile Societies.* Boulder, Colorado and London: Lynne Rienner.
Covey, Jack. 2004. "The Custodian of the Peace Process" and "Making a Viable Peace: Moderating Political Conflict," in Jack Covey, Michael J. Dziedzic, and Leonard B. Hawley, eds. *The Quest for Viable Peace: International Intervention Strategies for Conflict Management.* Washington, D.C.: United States Institute of Peace Press.
Covey, Jack, Michael J. Dziedzic, and Leonard B. Hawley, eds. 2004. *The Quest for Viable Peace: International Intervention Strategies for Conflict Management.* Washington, D.C.: United States Institute of Peace Press.
Cranna, Michael, ed. 1994. *The True Cost of Conflict.* New York: New Press.
Crenshaw, Martha, ed. 1983. *Terrorism, Legitimacy, and Power: The Consequences of Political Violence.* Middletown, Connecticut: Wesleyan University Press.
Crenshaw, Martha. 2000. "Democracy, Commitment Problems, and Managing Ethnic Violence," *Terrorism and Political Violence* 12(3/4): 135–160.
Crocker, Chester A. 1999. "Peacemaking in Southern Africa: The Namibian-Angola Settlement of 1988," in Chester Crocker, Fen Osler Hampson, and Pamela Aall, eds. *Herding Cats: Multiparty Mediation in a Complex World.* Washington, D.C.: United States Institute of Peace Press.
Crocker, Chester, Fen Osler Hampson, and Pamela Aall, eds. 1999. *Herding Cats: Multiparty Mediation in a Complex World.* Washington, D.C.: United States Institute of Peace Press.
Crocker, Chester, Fen Osler Hampson, and Pamela Aall. 2004. *Taming Intractable Conflict: Mediation in the Hardest Cases.* Washington, D.C.: United States Institute of Peace Press.
Crocker, Chester, Fen Osler Hampson, and Pamela Aall, eds. 2005. *Grasping the Nettle: Analyzing Cases of Intractable Conflict.* Washington, D.C.: United States Institute of Peace Press.
Daley, Patricia. 2006. Book Review, "An African Peace Process: Mandela, South Africa and Burundi," *African Affairs* 105: 153–154.
Darby, John. 2001. *The Effects of Political Violence on Peace Processes.* Washington, D.C.: United States Institute of Peace Press.
Darby, John, ed. 2006a. *Violence and Reconstruction.* Notre Dame, Indiana: Notre Dame University Press.
Darby, John. 2006b. "Post-Accord Violence in a Changing World," in John Darby, ed. *Violence and Reconstruction.* Notre Dame, Indiana: Notre Dame University Press.

Darby, John. 2006c. "The Post-Accord Context," in John Darby, ed. *Violence and Reconstruction.* Notre Dame, Indiana: Notre Dame University Press.
Darby, John and Roger MacGinty, eds. 2000a. *The Management of Peace Processes.* New York: St. Martin's Press.
Darby, John and Roger MacGinty. 2000b. "Northern Ireland: Long, Cold Peace" and "Conclusion: The Management of Peace," in John Darby and Roger MacGinty, eds. *The Management of Peace Processes.* New York: St. Martin's Press.
Darby, John and Roger MacGinty, eds. 2003. *Contemporary Peacemaking: Conflict, Violence and Peace Processes.* London: Palgrave Macmillan.
De Haas, Mary. 1994. "Political Violence," *South African Yearbook of Human Rights* (5): 222–246.
Denardo, James. 1985. *Power in Numbers: The Political Strategy of Protest and Rebellion.* Princeton, New Jersey: Princeton University Press.
Desmond, Edward. 1995. "The Insurgency in Kashmir (1989–1991)," *Contemporary South Asia* 4(1): 5–16.
DeVotta, Neil. 2003. "Ethnolinguistic Nationalism and Ethnic Conflict in Sri Lanka," in Michael E. Brown and Sumit Ganguly, eds. *Fighting Words: Language Policy and Ethnic Relations in Asia.* Cambridge, Massachusetts: MIT Press.
DeVotta, Neil. 2004. *Blowback: Linguistic Nationalism, Institutional Decay, and Ethnic Conflict in Sri Lanka.* Stanford, California: Stanford University Press.
DeVotta, Neil. 2005. "From Ethnic Outbidding to Ethnic Conflict: The Institutional Basis for Sri Lanka's Separatist War," *Nations and Nationalism* 11(1): 141–159.
Diamond, Larry. 2005. *Squandered Victory: The American Occupation and the Bungled Effort to Bring Democracy to Iraq.* New York: Times Books.
Dobbins, James. 2005. "Nation-Building: UN Surpasses U.S. on Learning Curve," *Rand Review* 29(1): 24–29.
Doyle, Michael W. 2004. "Liberal Internationalism: Peace, War, and Democracy." Oslo: Nobel Peace Center, available at http://nobelprize.org/nobel_prizes/peace/articles/doyle/index.html.
Doyle, Michael W. and Nicholas Sambanis. 2006. *Making War and Building Peace.* Princeton, New Jersey: Princeton University Press.
Druckman, Daniel. 1986. "Stages, Turning Points, and Crises," *Journal of Conflict Resolution* 30: 327–360.
Druckman, Daniel. 2001. "Turning Points in International Negotiation: A Comparative Analysis," *Journal of Conflict Resolution* 45(4): 519–544.
Druckman, Daniel and Justin Green. 1986. *Political Stability in the Philippines: Framework and Analysis.* Monograph Series in World Affairs, Vol. 22, No. 3. Denver, Colorado: University of Denver.
Du Toit, Pierre. 2001. *South Africa's Brittle Peace: The Problem of Post-Settlement Violence.* London: Palgrave.
Du Toit, Pierre. 2003. "Why Post-Settlement Settlements?" *Journal of Democracy* 14(3): 104–118.
Duffy, Gavin and Natalie Frensley. 1989. "Community Conflict Processes: Mobilization and Demobilization in Northern Ireland." Program on the Analysis and Resolution of Conflicts, Maxwell School of Citizenship and Public Affairs, Syracuse University (Working Paper No. 13).
Ebrahim, Hassen. 2000. *The Soul of a Nation: Constitution-Making in South Africa.* Oxford: Oxford University Press.

Egeland, Jan. 1999. "The Oslo Accord: Multiparty Facilitation through the Norwegian Channel," in Chester Crocker, Fen Osler Hampson, and Pamela Aall, eds. *Herding Cats: Multiparty Mediation in a Complex World.* Washington, D.C.: United States Institute of Peace Press.

Elliott, Marianne, ed. 2002. *The Long Road to Peace in Northern Ireland.* Liverpool: Liverpool University Press.

Ellis, Stephen. 1999. *The Mask of Anarchy: The Destruction of Liberia and the Religious Dimension of an African War.* New York: New York University Press.

Esman, Milton J. 1994. *Ethnic Politics.* Ithaca, New York: Cornell University Press.

Fearon, James D. 2006. Testimony to the U.S. House of Representatives, Committee on Government Reform, "Iraq: Democracy or Civil War," September 15, 2006. At www.stanford.edu/group/ir_workshop/fearon%20testimony.pdf.

Fearon, James D. and David D. Laitin. 2003. "Ethnicity, Insurgency, and Civil War," *American Political Science Review* 97(1): 75–90.

Fisher, Ronald. 1989. "Pre-Negotiation Problem-Solving Discussions: Enhancing the Potential for Successful Negotiation," in Janice Gross Stein, ed. *Getting to the Table: The Processes of International Prenegotiation.* Baltimore, Maryland: The Johns Hopkins University Press.

Fixdal, Mona and Dan Smith. 1998. "Humanitarian Intervention and Just War," *Mershon International Studies Review* 42: 283–312.

Fortna, Virginia Page. 2003. "Scraps of Paper? Agreements and the Durability of Peace," *International Organization* 57(2): 337–372.

Fortna, Virginia Page. 2004a. "Does Peacekeeping Keep Peace? International Intervention and the Duration of Peace after Civil War," *International Studies Quarterly* 48(2): 269–292.

Fornta, Virginia Page. 2004b. *Peace Time: Cease-Fire Agreements and the Durability of Peace.* Princeton, New Jersey: Princeton University Press.

Friedman, Steven. 1987. *Building Tomorrow Today: African Workers in the Trade Unions, 1970–1985.* Johannesburg: Raven Press.

Friedman, Steven. 1996. "No Easy Stroll to Dominance," *Towards Democracy* (Institute for Democracy in South Africa) [Fourth Quarter]: 4–13.

Friedman, Steven. 1999. "No Easy Stroll to Dominance: Party Dominance, Opposition and Civil Society in South Africa," in Hermann Giliomee and Charles Simkins, eds. *The Awkward Embrace: One-Party Domination and Democracy.* Cape Town: Tafelberg.

Galtung, Johann. 1969. "Violence, Peace, and Peace Research," *Journal of Peace Research* 6(3): 167–191.

Ganguly, Sumit. 1994. "The Evolution of Sino-Indian Relations since 1962." Washington, D.C.: Woodrow Wilson Center for Scholars, Occasional Paper No. 60.

Ganguly, Sumit. 1997. *The Crisis in Kashmir: Portents of War, Hopes for Peace.* Cambridge: Cambridge University Press.

Gastrow, Peter. 1995. *Bargaining for Peace: South Africa and the National Peace Accord.* Washington, D.C.: United States Institute of Peace Press.

Geertz, Clifford. 1963. "The Integrative Revolution: Primordial Sentiments and Civil Politics in the New States," in Clifford Geertz, ed. *Old Societies and New States: The Quest for Modernity in Asia and Africa.* New York: The Free Press.

George, Alexander L. 1979. "Case Studies and Theory Development: The Method of Structured, Focused Comparison," in Paul Gordon Lauren, ed. *Diplomacy: New Approaches in History, Theory, and Policy.* New York: The Free Press.

George, Alexander L. 1993. *Forceful Persuasion: Coercive Diplomacy as an Alternative to War.* Washington, D.C.: United States Institute of Peace Press.
George, Alexander L. 1994. "Theory and Practice," in George E. Williams, ed. *The Limits of Coercive Diplomacy.* Boulder, Colorado: Westview Press.
George, Alexander and Timothy J. McKeown. 1985. "Case Studies and Theories of Organizational Decision-Making," *Advances in Information Processing in Organizations* 2: 21–58.
Ghai, Yash. 2000. "Autonomy as a Strategy for Diffusing Conflict," in Paul Stern and Daniel Druckman, eds. *International Conflict Resolution after the Cold War.* Washington, D.C.: National Research Council.
Ghobarath, Hazem, Paul Huth, and Bruce Russett. 2002. "Civil Wars Kill and Maim People – Long after the Shooting Stops." Leitner Program in International and Comparative Political Economy, Yale University, Working Paper 2002-10.
Gibson, James. 2004. *Overcoming Apartheid: Can Truth Reconcile a Divided Nation?* New York: Russell Sage Foundation.
Gibson, Kevin, Leigh Thompson, and Max Bazerman. 1996. "Shortcomings of Neutrality in Mediation," *Negotiation Journal* 12(1): 69–80.
Giliomee, Hermann. 2003. *The Afrikaners: Biography of a People.* Cape Town: Tafelberg.
Giliomee, Hermann and Jannie Gagiano, eds. 1990. *The Elusive Search for Peace: South Africa, Israel, Northern Ireland.* Cape Town: Oxford University Press.
Global Witness. 2005. "Timber, Taylor, Soldier, Spy." Report submitted by Global Witness to the United Nations Security Council, June 15, 2005.
Goldstone, Richard. 2004. "Justice and Reconciliation in Fragmented Societies," in Andreas Wimmer *et al.*, eds. *Facing Ethnic Conflicts: Toward a New Realism.* Lanham, Maryland: Rowman and Littlefield.
Griffiths, Aaron and Catherine Barnes. 2008. "Powers of Persuasion: Incentives, Sanctions, and Conditionality in Peacemaking." *Accord* 19. London: Conciliation Resources.
Guelke, Adrian. 2000. "Interpretations of Political Violence during South Africa's Transition," *Politikon* (South African Journal of Political Studies) 27(2): 239–254.
Gunaratna, Rohan. 2003. "Feeding the Tamil Tigers," in Karen Ballentine and Jakes Sherman, eds. *The Political Economy of Armed Conflict: Beyond Greed and Grievance.* Boulder, Colorado: Lynne Rienner.
Gurr, Ted Robert. 1970. *Why Men Rebel.* Princeton, New Jersey: Princeton University Press.
Gurr, Ted Robert. 1993. *Minorities at Risk: A Global View of Ethnopolitical Conflicts.* Washington, D.C.: United States Institute of Peace Press.
Gurr, Ted Robert. 2000. *Peoples versus States: Minorities at Risk in the New Century.* Washington, D.C.: United States Institute of Peace Press.
Haass, Richard. 1989. *Conflicts Without End.* New Haven, Connecticut: Yale University Press.
Habibullah, Wajahat. 2004. *The Political Economy of the Kashmir Conflict: Opportunities for Peacebuilding and for US Policy.* Washington, D.C.: United States Institute of Peace.
Hampson, Fen Osler. 1996. *Nurturing Peace: Why Peace Agreements Succeed or Fail.* Washington, D.C.: United States Institute of Peace Press.
Hampson, Fen *et al.* 2002. *Madness in the Multitude: Human Security and World Disorder.* Oxford: Oxford University Press.

Hannum, Hurst. 1990. *Autonomy, Sovereignty and Self-Determination: The Accommodation of Conflicting Rights.* Philadelphia, Pennsylvania: University of Pennsylvania Press.

Hannum, Hurst and Eileen F. Babbitt, eds. 2006. *Negotiating Self-Determination.* Lanham, Maryland: Lexington Books.

Hara, Fabienne. 1999. "Burundi: A Case of Parallel Diplomacy," in Chester Crocker, Fen Osler Hampson, and Pamela Aall, eds. 1999. *Herding Cats: Multiparty Mediation in a Complex World.* Washington, D.C.: United States Institute of Peace Press.

Harbom, Lotta, Stina Högbladh and Peter Wallensteen. 2006. "Armed Conflict and Peace Agreements," *Journal of Peace Research* 43(5): 617–631.

Harris, Peter and Ben Reilly, eds. 1998. *Democracy and Deep-Rooted Conflict: Options for Negotiators.* Stockholm: International IDEA.

Hartlyn, Jonathan. 1993. "Civil Violence and Conflict Resolution: The Case of Colombia," in Roy Licklider, ed. *Stopping the Killing: How Civil Wars End.* New York: New York University Press.

Hartzell, Caroline A. and Matthew Hodie. 2007. *Crafting Peace: Power-Sharing Institutions and the Negotiated Settlement of Civil Wars.* University Park, Pennsylvania: Pennsylvania University Press.

Hermann, Tamar and David Newman. 2000. "A Path Strewn with Thorns: Along the Difficult Road of Israeli and Palestinian Peacemaking," in John Darby and Roger MacGinty, eds. *The Management of Peace Processes.* New York: St. Martin's Press.

Hewitt, Christopher. 1993. *Consequences of Political Violence.* Aldershot, Hants, England: Dartmouth Publishing Co.

Hironaka, Ann. 2006. *Neverending Wars: The International Community, Weak States, and the Perpetuation of War.* Cambridge, Massachusetts: Harvard University Press.

Hoeffler, Anke and Mara Reynal-Querol. 2003. *Measuring the Costs of Conflict.* Oxford: Centre for the Study of African Economies, University of Oxford.

Höglund, Kristine. 2004. *Violence in the Midst of Peace Negotiations: Cases from Guatemala, Northern Ireland, South Africa, and Sri Lanka.* Uppsala, Sweden: Uppsala University Department of Peace and Conflict Research Report No. 69.

Höglund, Kristine and I. William Zartman. 2006. "Violence by the State: Official Spoilers and their Allies," in John Darby, ed. *Violence and Reconstruction.* Notre Dame, Indiana: Notre Dame University Press.

Holbrooke, Richard. 1999. *To End a War.* New York: Modern Library.

Holl, Jane. 1993. "When War Doesn't Work," in Roy Licklider, ed. *Stopping the Killing: How Civil Wars End.* New York: New York University Press.

Holzgrefe, J.L. and Robert Keohane, eds. 2003. *Humanitarian Intervention: Ethical, Legal, and Political Dimensions.* Cambridge: Cambridge University Press.

Homer-Dixon, Thomas. 1991. "On the Threshold: Environmental Changes as Causes of Acute Conflict," *International Security* 16(2): 76–116.

Homer-Dixon, Thomas. 1994. "Environmental Scarcities and Violent Conflict: Evidence from Cases," *International Security* 11(1): 5–40.

Horowitz, Donald. 1985. *Ethnic Groups in Conflict.* Berkeley and Los Angeles, California: University of California Press.

Horowitz, Donald. 1991. *A Democratic South Africa? Constitutional Engineering in a Divided Society.* Berkeley and Los Angeles, California: University of California Press.

Horowitz, Donald. 2001. *The Deadly Ethnic Riot.* Berkeley and Los Angeles, California: University of California Press.
Howe, Herbert. 2001. *Ambiguous Order: Military Forces in African States.* Boulder, Colorado: Lynne Rienner.
Human Rights Watch. 1991. *The Killings in South Africa: The Role of the Security Forces and the Responses of the State.* New York: Human Rights Watch.
Human Rights Watch. 1995. *Playing the Communal Card: Communal Violence and Human Rights.* New York: Human Rights Watch.
Hume, Cameron R. 1994. *Ending Mozambique's War.* Washington, D.C.: United States Institute of Peace Press.
Huntington, Samuel P. 1981. "Reform and Stability in a Modernizing, Multi-Ethnic Society," *Politikon* 8(2): 8–26.
Idris, Iffat. 2006. "Settling the Kashmir Conflict: The Internal Dimension," in Waheguru Pal Singh Sidhu, Bushra Asif, and Cyrus Samii, eds. *Kashmir: New Voices, New Approaches.* Boulder, Colorado: Lynne Rienner.
Iklé, Fred C. 1971. *Every War Must End.* New York: Columbia University Press.
Jarstad, Anna and Timothy D. Sisk, eds. 2008. *War to Democracy Transitions: Dilemmas of Peacebuilding.* Cambridge: Cambridge University Press.
Jaster, Robert S., Meoletsi Mbeki, Morley Nkosi, and Michael Clough. 1992. *Changing Fortunes: War, Diplomacy, and Economics in Southern Africa.* New York: The Ford Foundation.
Jentleson, Bruce. 1996. *Preventive Diplomacy and Ethnic Conflict: Possible, Difficult, Necessary.* IGCC Policy Paper No. 27. San Diego, California: University of California Institute on Global Cooperation and Conflict.
Jones, Bruce D. 2001. *Peacemaking in Rwanda: The Dynamics of Failure.* Boulder, Colorado: Lynne Rienner.
Jones, Bruce D. 2002. "The Challenges of Strategic Coordination," in Stephen Stedman, Donald Rothchild, and Elizabeth Cousens, eds. *Ending Civil Wars: The Implementation of Peace Agreements.* Boulder, Colorado: Lynne Rienner.
Joseph, Richard. 1996. "Negotiating for Peace in Liberia: Conclusions and Recommendations," in Timothy D. Sisk, ed. *New Approaches to International Negotiation and Mediation.* Washington, D.C.: United States Institute of Peace Press.
Kahn, Herman. 1965. *On Escalation: Metaphors and Scenarios.* New York: Praeger.
Kaldor, Mary, 1999. *New and Old Wars: Organized Violence in a Global Era.* Stanford, California: Stanford University Press.
Kalyvas, Stathis N. 2003. *The Logic of Violence in Civil War.* Cambridge: Cambridge University Press.
Kane-Berman, John. 1993. *Political Violence in South Africa.* Johannesburg: South African Institute of Race Relations.
Kaplan, Robert. 1993 (reprinted 2005). *Balkan Ghosts: A Journey through History.* New York: St. Martin's Press.
Kaplan, Robert. 1996. *The Ends of the Earth: A Journey to the Frontiers of Anarchy.* New York: Random House.
Kaufman, Chaim. 1996. "Possible and Impossible Solutions to Ethnic Civil Wars," *International Security* 20(4): 136–175.
Kaur, Inpreet. 2006. "Warring over Peace in Kashmir," in Waheguru Pal Singh Sidhu, Bushra Asif, and Cyrus Samii, eds. *Kashmir: New Voices, New Approaches.* Boulder, Colorado: Lynne Rienner.

Kelegama, Saman. 1999. "Economic Costs of Conflict in Sri Lanka," in Robert I. Rotberg, ed. *Creating Peace in Sri Lanka: Civil War and Reconciliation.* Washington, D.C.: Brookings Institution.

King, Charles. 1997. *How Civil Wars End.* London: International Institute for Strategic Studies (Adelphi Paper No. 308).

Kiplagat, Betheul A. 1997. "African Governments, African Conflicts," in Gunnar Sørbø and Peter Vale, eds. *Out of Conflict: From War to Peace in Africa.* Uppsala: Nordiska Afrikainstitutet.

Krasno, Jean. 2003. "The Group of Friends of the Secretary-General: A Useful Leveraging Tool," in Jean Krasno, Bradd C. Hayes, and Donald C.F. Daniel, eds. *Leveraging for Success in United Nations Peace Operations.* Westport, Connecticut: Praeger.

Kriesberg, Louis. 1987. "Timing and the Initiation of De-Escalation Moves," *Negotiation Journal* 3: 375–384.

Kriesberg, Louis. 2003. *Constructive Conflicts: From Escalation to Resolution.* Lanham, Maryland: Rowman and Littlefield.

Kriesberg, Louis and Paul Thorson, eds. 1991. *Timing and the De-Escalation of International Conflict.* Syracuse, New York: Syracuse University Press.

Kumar, Krishna, ed. 1999. *Post-Conflict Elections, Democratization, and International Assistance.* Boulder, Colorado: Lynne Rienner.

Kurtzer, Daniel C. and Scott B. Lasensky. 2008. *Negotiating Arab-Israeli Peace: American Leadership in the Middle East.* Washington, D.C.: United States Institute of Peace Press.

Lake, David and Donald Rothchild, eds. 1998. *The International Spread of Ethnic Conflict: Fear, Diffusion, and Escalation.* Princeton, New Jersey: Princeton University Press.

Lapidoth, Ruth. 1997. *Autonomy: Flexible Solutions to Ethnic Conflicts.* Washington, D.C.: United States Institute of Peace Press.

Large, Judith and Timothy D. Sisk. 2006. *Democracy, Conflict and Human Security: Pursuing Peace in the 21st Century.* Stockholm: International IDEA.

Lauren, Paul Gordon. 1979. "Theories of Bargaining with Threats of Force: Deterrence and Coercive Diplomacy," in Paul Gordon Lauren, ed. *Diplomacy: New Approaches in Theory, History, and Policy.* New York: The Free Press.

Lemarchand, René. 2006. "Consociationalism and Power Sharing in Africa: Rwanda, Burundi, and the Democratic Republic of Congo," *African Affairs* 106/422: 1–20.

Lemarchand, René and David Martin. 1974. *Selective Genocide in Burundi.* London: Minority Rights Group.

Levitt, Jeremy I. 2005. *The Evolution of Deadly Conflict in Liberia.* Durham, North Carolina: Carolina Academic Press.

Licklider, Roy, ed. 1993. *Stopping the Killing: How Civil Wars End.* New York: New York University Press.

Licklider, Roy. 1995. "The Consequences of Negotiated Settlements in Civil Wars, 1945–1993," *American Political Science Review* 89(3): 681–690.

Licklider, Roy. 2005. "Comparative Studies of Long Wars," in Chester Crocker, Fen Osler Hampson, and Pamela Aall, eds. *Grasping the Nettle: Analyzing Cases of Intractable Conflict.* Washington, D.C.: United States Institute of Peace Press.

Lijphart, Arend. 1971. "Comparative Politics and the Comparative Method," *American Political Science Review* 65(3): 682–693.

Lijphart, Arend. 1977. *Democracy in Plural Societies.* New Haven, Connecticut: Yale University Press.

Lijphart, Arend. 1985. *Power-Sharing in South Africa.* Policy Papers in International Affairs No. 24. Berkeley, California: University of California, Berkeley, Institute of International Studies.
Lijphart, Arend. 2004. "Constitutional Design for Divided Societies," *Journal of Democracy* 15(2): 96–109.
Little, David. 1994. *Sri Lanka: The Invention of Enmity.* Washington, D.C.: United States Institute of Peace Press.
Lockhart, Charles. 1979. *Bargaining in International Conflicts.* New York: Columbia University Press.
Lodge, Tom. 1983. *Black Politics in South Africa since 1945.* London: Longman.
Lodge, Tom. 2003. *Politics in South Africa from Mandela to Mbeki.* Oxford: James Currey.
Lund, Michael S. 1996. *Preventing Violent Conflicts: A Strategy for Preventive Diplomacy.* Washington, D.C.: United States Institute of Peace Press.
Lundestad, Geir. 1993. "Beyond the Cold War: New and Old Dimensions in International Relations," in Geir Lundestad and Odd Arne Westad, eds. *Beyond the Cold War: New Dimensions in International Relations.* Oslo: Scandinavian University Press.
Luttwak, Edward N. 1999. "Give War a Chance," *Foreign Affairs* 78(4): 36–44.
Lyman, Princeton. 2000. *Partner to History: The U.S. Role in South Africa's Transition to Democracy.* Washington, D.C.: United States Institute of Peace Press.
Lyons, Terrence. 1999. *Voting for Peace: Post-conflict Elections in Liberia.* Washington, D.C.: Brookings Institution.
Lyons, Terrence. 2005. *Demilitarizing Politics: Elections on the Uncertain Road to Peace.* Boulder, Colorado: Lynne Rienner.
MacGinty, Roger. 2003. "Constitutional Referendums and Ethnopolitical Conflict: The Case of Northern Ireland," *Nationalism and Ethnic Politics* 9(2): 1–22.
MacGinty, Roger. 2006. *No War, No Peace: The Rejuvenation of Stalled Peace Processes and Peace Accords.* London: Palgrave Macmillan.
MacGinty, Roger. 2008. "Indigenous Peace-Making versus the Liberal Peace," *Cooperation and Conflict* 43(2): 139–163.
MacGinty, Roger and Pierre du Toit. 2007. "A Disparity of Esteem: Relative Group Status in Northern Ireland after the Belfast Agreement," *Political Psychology* 28(1): 13–30.
Mack, Andrew. 2005. *Human Security Report 2005: War and Peace in the 21st Century.* New York and Oxford: Oxford University Press.
Mack, Andrew. 2006. *Human Security Brief 2006.* Vancouver: University of British Columbia Liu Centre for Human Security. At www.humansecuritycentre.org.
Mack, Andrew. 2008. *Human Security Brief 2007.* British Columbia: Simon Fraser University, Human Security Project Report.
Mani, Rama. 2002. *Beyond Retribution: Seeking Justice in the Shadows of War.* Cambridge, UK: Polity Press.
Marshall, Monty G. 2002. "Measuring the Societal Impact of War," in Fen Osler Hampson and David Malone, eds. *From Reaction to Conflict Prevention: Opportunities for the UN System.* Boulder, Colorado: Lynne Rienner.
Martel, William C. 2006. *Victory in War: Foundations of Modern Military Policy.* Cambridge: Cambridge University Press.
Martin, Harriet. 2006. *Kings of Peace, Pawns of War: The Untold Story of Peacemaking.* Geneva: The Centre for Humanitarian Dialogue.

Mason, T. David. 1984. "Individual Participation in Collective Racial Violence and Terror: A Rational Choice Synthesis," *American Political Science Review* 78: 1040–1052.

Mason, T. David. 2004. *Caught in the Crossfire: Revolutions, Repression and the Rational Peasant.* Lanham, Maryland: Rowman and Littlefield.

Mason, T. David, Joseph P. Weingarten, and Patrick J. Fett. 1999. "Win, Lose, or Draw: Predicting the Outcomes of Civil Wars," *Political Research Quarterly* 52(2): 239–268.

Maundi, Mohammed O., I. William Zartman, Gilbert M. Khadiagala, and Kwaku Nuamah. 2006. *Getting In: Mediator's Entry into the Settlement of African Conflicts.* Washington, D.C.: United States Institute of Peace Press.

Mearsheimer, John. 1990. "Why We Will Soon Miss the Cold War," *Atlantic Monthly* 226: 35–50.

Miall, Hugh, Oliver Ramsbotham, and Tom Woodhouse. 1999. *Contemporary Conflict Resolution.* Oxford: Blackwell Publishing.

Mockaitis, Thomas R. 1999. *Peace Operations and Intrastate Conflict: The Sword or the Olive Branch?* Westport, Connecticut: Praeger.

Mueller, John. 1989. *Retreat from Doomsday: The Obsolescence of Major War.* New York: Basic Books.

Neuheiser, Jorg and Stefan Wolff. 2002. *Peace at Last: The Impact of the Good Friday Agreement on Northern Ireland.* London: Berghahn.

Newman, Edward and Oliver Richmond. 2006. *Challenges to Peacebuilding: Managing Spoilers during Conflict Resolution.* Tokyo: United Nations University Press.

O'Donnell, Guillermo, Phillippe C. Schmitter, and Laurence Whitehead. 1986. *Transitions from Authoritarian Rule: Prospects for Democracy.* Baltimore, Maryland and London: The Johns Hopkins University Press.

Ordeshook, Peter C. 1989. *Models of Strategic Choice in Politics.* Ann Arbor, Michigan: University of Michigan Press.

Ostrom, Elinor. 1991. "Rational Choice Theory and Institutional Analysis: Toward Complementarity," *American Political Science Review* 85(1): 237–243.

Ottaway, Marina. 1993. *South Africa: The Struggle for a New Order.* Washington, D.C.: The Brookings Institution.

Otunnu, Olara and Michael Doyle, eds. 1998. *Peacemaking and Peacekeeping for a New Century.* Lanham, Maryland: Rowman and Littlefield.

Ould-Abdallah, Ahmedou. 2000. *Burundi on the Brink, 1993–95: A UN Special Envoy Reflects on Preventive Diplomacy.* Washington, D.C.: United States Institute of Peace Press.

Pape, Robert. 2005. *Dying to Win: The Strategic Logic of Suicide Terrorism.* New York: Random House.

Paris, Roland. 2004. *At War's End: Building Peace after Civil Conflict.* Cambridge: Cambridge University Press.

Paris, Roland and Timothy Sisk, eds. 2008. *The Dilemmas of Statebuilding: Confronting the Contradictions of Post-War Peacebuilding.* London: Routledge.

Peck, Connie. 1998. *Sustainable Peace: The Role of the UN and Regional Organizations in Preventing Conflict.* Lanham, Maryland: Rowman and Littlefield (Carnegie Commission on Preventing Deadly Conflict).

Phillips, David L. 2005. *Losing Iraq: Inside the Postwar Reconstruction Fiasco.* Boulder, Colorado: Westview Press.

Pillar, Paul R. 1983. *Negotiating Peace: War Termination as a Bargaining Process.* Princeton, New Jersey: Princeton University Press.

Popkin, Samuel. 1979. *The Rational Peasant*. Los Angeles, California: University of California Press.
Popkin, Samuel. 1988. "Political Entrepreneurs and Peasant Movements in Vietnam," in Michael Taylor ed. *Rationality and Revolution*. Cambridge: Cambridge University Press.
Price, Robert M. 1991. *The Apartheid State in Crisis: Political Transformation in South Africa, 1975–1990*. Oxford: Oxford University Press.
Princen, Thomas. 1992. *Intermediaries in International Conflict*. Princeton, New Jersey: Princeton University Press.
Putnam, Robert D. 1988. "Diplomacy and Domestic Politics: The Logic of Two-Level Games," *International Organization* 42(3): 427–460.
Rabow, Gerald. 1990. *Peace Through Agreement: Replacing War with Non-Violent Dispute Resolution Methods*. New York: Praeger.
Rabushka, Alvin and Kenneth A. Shepsle. 1972. *Politics in Plural Societies: A Theory of Democratic Instability*. Columbus, Ohio: Charles E. Merrill.
Raiffa, Howard. 1982. *The Art and Science of Negotiation*. Cambridge, Massachusetts: Harvard University Press.
Rajasingham, K.T. 2006. *Sri Lanka: The Untold Story*. Hong Kong: Asia Online, (www.atimes.com).
Ranstorp, Magnus. 2006. "The Israeli–Palestinian Peace Process: The Strategic Art of Deception," in Edward Newman and Oliver Richmond, eds. *Challenges to Peacebuilding: Managing Spoilers during Conflict Resolution*. Tokyo: United Nations University Press.
Regan, Patrick M. 2000. *Civil Wars and Foreign Powers: Outside Intervention in Intrastate Conflicts*. Ann Arbor, Michigan: University of Michigan Press.
Reilly, Benjamin. 2003. "Democratic Validation," in John Darby and Roger MacGinty, eds. *Contemporary Peacemaking: Conflict, Violence and Peace Processes*. London: Palgrave Macmillan.
Reyntjens, Filip. 1993. "The Proof of the Pudding is in the Eating: The June 1993 Elections in Burundi," *Journal of Modern African Studies* 31(4): 563–583.
Reyntjens, Filip. 2005. "Briefing: Burundi. A Peaceful Transition after a Decade of War?" *African Affairs* (105/418): 117–135.
Richmond, Oliver. 2002. *Maintaining Order, Making Peace*. London: Palgrave.
Richmond, Oliver. 2006. "Devious Objectives and Spoiling Behavior," in Edward Newman and Oliver Richmond, eds. *Challenges of Peacebuilding: Managing Spoilers during Conflict Resolution*. Tokyo: United Nations University Press.
Ricks, Thomas. 2006. *Fiasco: The American Military Adventure in Iraq*. New York: Penguin Books.
Risley, Paul and Timothy Sisk. 2005. *Democracy and United Nations Peacebuilding at the Local Level: Lessons Learned*. Stockholm: International IDEA. Available at www.idea.int/publications/democracy_un/index.cfm.
Robock, Alan, Luke. Oman, Georgiy L. Stenchikov, Owen B. Toon, Charles Bardeen, and Richard P. Turco. 2006. "Climatic Consequences of Regional Nuclear Conflicts," *Atmospheric Chemistry and Physics Discussions* 6: 11,817–11,843.
Roeder, Philip and Donald Rothchild, eds. 2005. *Sustainable Peace: Power and Democracy after Civil War*. Ithaca, New York: Cornell University Press.
Rogers, Elizabeth S. 1996. "Economic Sanctions and Internal Conflict," in Michael E. Brown, ed. *The International Dimensions of Internal Conflict*. Cambridge, Massachusetts: MIT Press.

Rosenau, James N. 1964. "Internal War as an International Event," in James N. Rosenau, ed. *International Aspects of Civil Strife*. Princeton, New Jersey: Princeton University Press.

Rosenau, James N. 1990. *Turbulence in World Politics: A Theory of Change and Continuity*. London: Harvester Wheatsheaf.

Ross, Michael. 2004. "How Does Natural Resource Wealth Influence Civil Wars?" *International Organization* 58(1): 35–67.

Rotberg, Robert. 1999. "Sri Lanka's Civil War: From Mayhem toward Diplomatic Resolution," in Robert I. Rotberg, ed. *Creating Peace in Sri Lanka: Civil War and Reconciliation*. Washington, D.C.: Brookings Institution Press.

Rotberg, Robert, ed. 2003. *State Failure and State Weakness in a Time of Terror*. Washington, D.C.: Brookings Institution Press.

Rothchild, Donald. 1997. *Managing Ethnic Conflict in Africa: Pressures and Incentives for Cooperation*. Washington, D.C.: Brookings Institution Press.

Rothchild, Donald. 2002. "Settlement Terms and Post-Agreement Stability," in Stephen Stedman, Donald Rothchild, and Elizabeth Cousens, eds. *Ending Civil Wars: The Implementation of Peace Agreements*. Boulder, Colorado: Lynne Rienner.

Rothchild, Donald and Alexander L. Groth. 1995. "Pathological Dimensions of Domestic and International Ethnicity," *Political Science Quarterly* 110(1): 69–82.

Rubin, Barnett R. 2002. *Blood on the Doorstep: The Politics of Preventive Action*. New York: The Century Foundation Press.

Rule, James. 1988. *Theories of Civil Violence*. Berkeley and Los Angeles, California: University of California Press.

Sakia, Jaideep. 2006. "Spoilers and Devious Objectives in Kashmir," in Edward Newman and Oliver Richmond, eds. *Challenges to Peacebuilding: Managing Spoilers during Conflict Resolution*. Tokyo: United Nations University Press.

Samii, Cyrus. 2006. "Kashmir: From Persistence to Progress," in Waheguru Pal Singh Sidhu, Bushra Asif, and Cyrus Samii, eds. *Kashmir: New Voices, New Approaches*. Boulder, Colorado: Lynne Rienner.

Saravanamuttu, Paikiasothy. 2000a. "Sri Lanka: The Intractability of Ethnic Conflict," in John Darby and Roger MacGinty, eds. *The Management of Peace Processes*. New York: St. Martin's Press.

Saravanamuttu, Paikiasothy. 2000b. "Sri Lanka in 1999: The Challenges of Peace, Governance, and Development," *Asian Survey* 40(1): 219–225.

Saunders, Harold. 1985. "We Need a Larger Theory of Negotiation: The Importance of Pre-negotiating Phases," *Journal of Conflict Resolution* 1(3): 249–262.

Saunders, Harold. 2001. "Prenegotiation and Circum-negotiation: Arenas of the Multilevel Peace Process," in Chester Crocker, Fen Osler Hampson, and Pamela Aall, eds. *Turbulent Peace*. Washington, D.C.: United States Institute of Peace Press.

Sawyer, Amos. 2005. *Beyond Plunder: Toward Democratic Governance in Liberia*. Boulder, Colorado: Lynne Rienner.

Schaffer, Howard B. and Teresita C. Schaffer. 2005. "Kashmir: Fifty Years of Running in Place," in Chester Crocker, Fen Osler Hampson, and Pamela Aall, eds. *Grasping the Nettle: Analyzing Cases of Intractable Conflict*. Washington, D.C.: United States Institute of Peace Press.

Schelling, Thomas. 1966. *Arms and Influence*. New Haven, Connecticut: Yale University Press.

Schneider, Gerald, Katherine Barbieri, and Nils Petter Gleditch, eds. 2003. *Globalization and Armed Conflict*. Lanham, Maryland: Rowman & Littlefield.

Schrire, Robert. 1992. *Adapt or Die: The End of White Politics in South Africa*. London: Hurst & Co.

Sederberg, Peter C. 1989. *Terrorist Myths: Illusion, Rhetoric, and Reality*. Englewood Cliffs, New Jersey: Prentice Hall.

Sederberg, Peter C. 1994. *Fires Within: Political Violence and Revolutionary Change*. New York: HarperCollins.

Sederberg, Peter C. 1995. "Conciliation as a Counter-Terrorist Strategy," *Journal of Peace Research* 32(3): 295–312.

Shastri, Amita. 1997. "Government Policy and the Ethnic Crisis in Sri Lanka," in Michael E. Brown, ed. *Government Policies and Ethnic Relations in Asia and the Pacific*. Cambridge, Massachusetts: MIT Press.

Sidhu, Waheguru Pal Singh. 2006. "Introduction," in Waheguru Pal Singh Sidhu, Bushra Asif, and Cyrus Samii, eds. *Kashmir: New Voices, New Approaches*. Boulder, Colorado: Lynne Rienner.

Simpson, Graeme and Janine Rauch. 1992. "Political Violence: 1991," in M. Robertson and A. Rycroft, *Human Rights and Labour Law Yearbook 1992* (Vol. 2). Cape Town: Oxford University Press.

Simpson, Graeme, Steve Mokwena, and Lauren Segal. 1991. "Political Violence: 1990," in M. Robertson and A. Rycroft, *Human Rights and Labour Law Yearbook 1991* (Vol. 2). Cape Town: Oxford University Press.

Sisk, Timothy D. 1995. *Democratization in South Africa: The Elusive Social Contract*. Princeton, New Jersey: Princeton University Press.

Sisk, Timothy D. 1996. *Power Sharing and International Mediation in Ethnic Conflicts*. New York: Carnegie Commission on Preventing Deadly Conflict, Carnegie Corporation of New York.

Sisk, Timothy D. 2001. "Intrastate Violence," in P.J. Simmons and Chantal de Jonge Oudraat, eds. *Managing Global Issues: Lessons Learned*. Washington, D.C.: Carnegie Endowment for International Peace.

Smith, Chris. 1999. "South Asia's Enduring War," in Robert I. Rotberg, ed. *Creating Peace in Sri Lanka: Civil War and Reconciliation*. Washington, D.C.: Brookings Institution Press.

Smith, James D.D. 1995. *Stopping Wars: Defining Obstacles to Cease-fires*. Boulder, Colorado: Westview Press.

Smoke, Richard. 1977. *War: Controlling Escalation*. Cambridge, Massachusetts: Harvard University Press.

Smoke, Richard. 1979. "Theories of Escalation," in Paul Gordon Lauren, ed. *Diplomacy: New Approaches in History, Theory, and Policy*. New York: The Free Press.

Snyder, Glenn H. and Paul Diesing. 1977. *Conflict among Nations: Bargaining, Decision Making, and System Structure in International Crises*. Princeton, New Jersey: Princeton University Press.

Solomon, Richard. 1999. "Bringing Peace to Cambodia," in Chester Crocker, Fen Osler Hampson, and Pamela Aall, eds. *Herding Cats: Multiparty Mediation in a Complex World*. Washington, D.C.: United States Institute of Peace Press.

Stedman, Stephen John. 1991. *Peacemaking in Civil War: International Mediation in Zimbabwe, 1974–1980*. Boulder, Colorado: Lynne Rienner.

Stedman, Stephen John. 1995. "United Nations Intervention in Civil Wars: Imperatives of Choice and Strategy," in Donald C. Daniel and Bradd C. Hayes, eds. *Beyond Traditional Peacekeeping*. London: Macmillan.

Stedman, Stephen John. 1997. "Spoiler Problems in Peace Processes," *International Security* 22(2): 5–53.
Stedman, Stephen John. 2003. "Peace Processes and the Challenges of Violence," in John Darby and Roger MacGinty, eds. *Contemporary Peacemaking: Conflict, Violence and Peace Processes*. London: Palgrave Macmillan.
Stedman, Stephen, Donald Rothchild, and Elizabeth Cousens, eds. 2002. *Ending Civil Wars: The Implementation of Peace Agreements*. Boulder, Colorado: Lynne Rienner.
Stein, Janice Gross. 1989. "Getting to the Table: The Triggers, Stages, Functions and Consequences of Prenegotiation," in Janice Gross Stein, ed. *Getting to the Table: The Processes of International Prenegotiation*. Baltimore, Maryland: The Johns Hopkins University Press.
Stein, Janice Gross and Richard Ned Lebow. 1994. *We All Lost the Cold War*. Princeton, New Jersey: Princeton University Press.
Stewart, Frances. 2001. "Horizontal Inequalities: A Neglected Dimension of Development." Working Paper No. 1, Centre for Research on Inequality, Human Security and Ethnicity. London: Queen Elizabeth House.
Stewart, Frances. 2005. "Policies toward Horizontal Inequalities in Post-War Reconstruction." CRISE Working Paper No. 7, Centre for Research on Inequality, Human Security and Ethnicity. London: Queen Elizabeth House, University of Oxford.
Stremlau, John and Helen Zille. 1997. *A House No Longer Divided: Progress and Prospects for Democratic Peace in South Africa*. Washington, D.C.: Carnegie Commission on Preventing Deadly Conflict.
Suhrke, Astri. 2007. "What's in a Figure? Estimating the Recurrence of Civil War," *International Peacekeeping* 14(2): 195–203.
Swami, Praveen. 2005. "Quickstep or Kadam Taal? The Elusive Search for Peace in Jammu and Kashmir." United States Institute of Peace *Special Report* 133. Washington, D.C.: United States Institute of Peace.
Tabeau, Ewa and Jakub Bijak. 2005. "War-Related Deaths in 1992–1995: Armed Conflicts in Bosnia and Herzogovina: A Critique of Previous Estimates and Recent Results," *European Journal of Population* 21(2–3): 187–215.
Tambiah, Stanley. 1986. *Sri Lanka: Ethnic Fratricide and the Dismantling of Democracy*. Chicago, Illinois: University of Chicago Press.
Taylor, Maxwell. 1991. *The Fanatics: A Behavioral Approach to Political Violence*. London: Brassey's.
Taylor, Michael, ed. 1988. *Rationality and Revolution*. New York: Cambridge University Press.
Telhami, Shibley. 2005. "Beyond Resolution? The Palestine-Israeli Conflict," in Chester Crocker, Fen Osler Hampson, and Pamela Aall, eds. *Grasping the Nettle: Analyzing Cases of Intractable Conflict*. Washington, D.C.: United States Institute of Peace Press.
Thompson, Leonard. 1985. *The Political Mythology of Apartheid*. New Haven, Connecticut: Yale University Press.
Thompson, Leonard. 1990. *A History of South Africa*. New Haven, Connecticut: Yale University Press.
Tilly, Charles. 2003. *The Politics of Collective Violence*. Cambridge: Cambridge University Press.
Tishkov, Valery. 1997. *Ethnicity, Nationalism and Conflict In and After the Soviet Union: The Mind Aflame*. Oslo: Peace Research Institute Oslo.

Touval, Saadia. 1996. "Mediator's Leverage." Discussion paper prepared for the Committee on International Conflict Resolution, National Research Council, Washington, D.C.
Touval, Saadia and I. William Zartman. 1989. "Mediation in International Conflicts," in Kenneth Kressel, ed. *Mediation Research.* San Francisco, California: Jossey-Bass.
Truth and Reconciliation Commission. 1998. *Truth and Reconciliation Commission of South Africa: Final Report.* Available at www.info.gov.za/otherdocs/2003/trc/rep.pdf.
Tsebelis, George. 1991. *Nested Games: Rational Choice in Comparative Politics.* Berkeley, California: University of California Press.
Uband, Mark. 1998. *The Liberian Civil War.* London: Frank Cass.
Van Vugt, William E. and G. Daan Cloete, eds. 2000. *Race and Reconciliation in South Africa: A Multicultural Dialogue in Comparative Perspective.* New York: Lexington Books.
Varshney, Ashutosh. 2001. "Ethnic Conflict and Civil Society," *World Politics* 53: 362–398.
Väyrynen, Raimo. 1993. "The Nature of Conflicts in Future International Relations," in Geir Lundestad and Odd Arne Westad, eds. *Beyond the Cold War: New Dimensions in International Relations.* Oslo: Scandinavian University Press.
Wagner, R. Harrison. 1993. "The Causes of Peace," in Roy Licklider, ed. *Stopping the Killing: How Civil Wars End.* New York: New York University Press.
Wagner, R. Harrison. 2000. "Bargaining and War," *American Journal of Political Science* 44(3): 469–484.
Waldmeir, Patti. 1997. *Anatomy of a Miracle: The End of Apartheid and the Birth of the New South Africa.* New York: W.W. Norton.
Walker, Lee and Paul Stern. 1993. *Balancing and Sharing Power in Multiethnic Societies.* Washington, D.C.: National Research Council, National Academy Press.
Wallach, John. 2001. "The Israeli–Palestinian Conflict," in John Darby, ed. *The Effects of Violence on Peace Processes.* Washington, D.C.: United States Institute of Peace Press.
Wallensteen, Peter and Margareta Sollenberg. 1998. "Armed Conflict and Regional Conflict Complexes, 1989–97," *Journal of Peace Research* 35(5): 621–634.
Wallensteen, Peter and Margareta Sollenberg. 2000. "Armed Conflict, 1989–99," *Journal of Peace Research* 37(5): 635–649.
Walter, Barbara F. 1997. "The Critical Barrier to Civil War Settlement," *International Organization* 51(3): 335–364.
Walter, Barbara F. 2002. *Committing to Peace: The Successful Settlement of Civil Wars.* Princeton, New Jersey: Princeton University Press.
Walter, Barbara F. and Jack Snyder. 1999. *Civil War, Insecurity, and Intervention.* New York: Columbia University Press.
Wardlaw, Grant. 1990. *Political Terrorism: Theory, Tactics, and Countermeasures.* Cambridge: Cambridge University Press.
Waterman, Harvey. 1993. "Political Order and the 'Settlement' of Civil Wars," in Roy Licklider, ed. *Stopping the Killing: How Civil Wars End.* New York: New York University Press.
Weiss, Thomas J. 2004. "The Humanitarian Impulse," in David M. Malone, ed. *The UN Security Council: From the Cold War to the 21st Century.* Boulder, Colorado: Lynne Rienner.

Wennmann, Achim. 2008. *Money Matters: Economic Dimensions of Peace Mediation.* Geneva: Program for Strategic and International Security Studies, Graduate Institute of International Studies, University of Geneva.

Wilkenfeld, Jonathan, Kathleen J. Young, David M. Quinn, and Victor Asal. 2002. *Mediating International Crises.* London: Routledge.

Wilson, A. Jeyaratnam. 2000. *Sri Lankan Tamil Nationalism: Its Origins and Development in the Nineteenth and Twentieth Centuries.* Vancouver: University of British Columbia Press.

Wimmer, Andreas *et al.*, eds. 2004. *Facing Ethnic Conflict: Toward a New Realism.* Baltimore, Maryland: Rowman and Littlefield.

Wolff, Stefan. 2003. *The Transnational Dynamics of Ethnic Conflict Settlement.* London: Berghahn Books.

Zahar, Marie-Joëlle. 2003. "Reframing the Spoiler Debate in Peace Processes," in John Darby and Roger MacGinty, eds. *Contemporary Peacemaking: Conflict, Violence and Peace Processes.* London: Palgrave Macmillan.

Zahar, Marie-Joëlle. 2006a. "Understanding the Violence of Insiders: Loyalty, Custodians of Peace, and the Sustainability of Conflict Settlement," in Edward Newman and Oliver Richmond, eds. *Challenges to Peacebuilding: Managing Spoilers during Conflict Resolution.* Tokyo: United Nations University Press.

Zahar, Marie-Joëlle. 2006b. "Political Violence in Peace Processes: Voice, Exit, and Loyalty in the Post-Accord Period," in John Darby, ed. *Violence and Reconstruction.* Notre Dame, Indiana: Notre Dame University Press.

Zartman, I. William. 1985. *Ripe for Resolution: Conflict and Intervention in Africa.* New York: Oxford University Press.

Zartman, I. William. 1989. "Prenegotiation: Phases and Functions," in Janice Gross Stein, ed. *Getting to the Table: The Processes of International Prenegotiation.* Baltimore, Maryland: The Johns Hopkins University Press.

Zartman, I. William. 1991a. "Common Elements in the Analysis of a Negotiation Process," in J. William Breslin and Jeffrey Z. Rubin, eds. *Negotiation Theory and Practice.* Cambridge, Massachusetts: Program on Negotiation, Harvard Law School.

Zartman, I. William. 1991b. "Conflict and Resolution: Contest, Cost and Change," *The Annals of the American Society of Political and Social Science* 518: 11–22.

Zartman, I. William. 1993. "The Unfinished Agenda: Negotiating Internal Conflicts," in Roy Licklider, ed. *Stopping the Killing: How Civil Wars End.* New York: New York University Press.

Zartman, I. William. 1995a. "Introduction: Posing the Problem of State Collapse," in I. William Zartman, ed. *Collapsed States: The Disintegration and Restoration of Legitimate Authority.* Boulder, Colorado: Lynne Rienner.

Zartman, I. William, ed. 1995b. *Elusive Peace: Negotiating an End to Civil Wars.* Washington, D.C.: The Brookings Institution.

Zartman, I. William. 2000. "Ripeness: The Hurting Stalemate and Beyond," in Paul C. Stern and Daniel Druckman, eds. *International Conflict Resolution after the Cold War.* Washington, D.C.: National Academy Press.

Zartman, I. William. 2005. "Need, Creed, and Greed in Intrastate Conflicts," in Cynthia Arnson and I. William Zartman, eds. *Rethinking the Economics of War: The Intersection of Need, Creed, and Greed.* Washington, D.C.: The Woodrow Wilson Center Press.

Zartman, I. William. 2008. "The Timing of Peace Initiatives: Hurting Stalemates

and Ripe Moments," in John Darby and Roger MacGinty, eds. *Contemporary Peacemaking*, 2nd edition. London: Palgrave Macmillan.
Zartman, I. William and Maureen Berman. 1982. *The Practical Negotiator*. New Haven, Connecticut: Yale University Press.
Zartman, I. William and Guy Olivier Faure, eds. 2005. *Escalation and Negotiation in International Conflicts*. Cambridge: Cambridge University Press.
Zartman, I. William and Jeffrey Z. Rubin, eds. 2000a. *Power and Negotiation*. Ann Arbor, Michigan: University of Michigan Press.
Zartman, I. William and Jeffrey Z. Rubin. 2000b. "Symmetry and Asymmetry in Negotiation," in William I. Zartman and Jeffrey Z. Rubin, eds. *Power and Negotiation*. Ann Arbor, Michigan: University of Michigan Press.
Zeb, Rizwan. 2006. "Pakistan and Jihadi Groups in the Kashmir Conflict," in Waheguru Pal Singh Sidhu, Bushra Asif, and Cyrus Samii, eds. *Kashmir: New Voices, New Approaches*. Boulder, Colorado: Lynne Rienner.

Index

#0058 - 070918 - C0 - 234/156/15 - PB - 9780415609401